The English Parish Clergy
on the Eve of the Reformation

STUDIES IN SOCIAL HISTORY

edited by

HAROLD PERKIN

Senior Lecturer in Social History, University of Lancaster

◇◇

The English Parish Clergy
on the Eve of the Reformation

by

PETER HEATH

Lecturer in History at the University of Hull

38213
LONDON: Routledge & Kegan Paul
TORONTO: University of Toronto Press
1969

First published 1969
by Routledge & Kegan Paul Limited
Broadway House, 68–74 Carter Lane, London, E.C.4

Printed in Great Britain by
W & J Mackay & Co Ltd, Chatham, Kent

© *Peter Heath 1969*

R.K.P. SBN 7100 6216 8

U.T.P. SBN 8020 1574 3

Contents

CONTENTS

Acknowledgements

My first and greatest debt is to my wife, without whose un-flagging patience, timely encouragement and endless typing this book would not have been completed.

Of my many academic helpers none has given more generously of his time than Professor A. G. Dickens, to whose advice, inspiring example and stimulating criticism I owe so much. Professor C. H. Williams, who supervised the thesis from which this book grew, has exerted a benign influence upon it and upon the author over many years. Professors F. R. H. Du Boulay and E. F. Jacob, the examiners of my thesis, have also left their much appreciated mark. More recently I have profited from the help of several colleagues: Dr. D. L. Douie who read the whole in draft; Mr. John Lawson who searchingly criticised some of the draft chapters; Dr. J. J. N. Palmer who kindly laboured through the proofs; Professor A. F. Norman who allowed me to quote from his unpublished translation of Melton's sermon; and Miss Brenda Moon who enlightened me on the mysteries of early printing. Outside Hull, for assistance on particular points I wish to thank Dr. D. B. Dobson, Mr. G. A. J. Hodgett, and Mrs. D. M. Owen.

In pursuit of this study a necessarily large debt to numerous archivists has been incurred, and to Mrs. N. K. Gurney of York and Mrs. J. Varley of Lincoln I owe particular thanks for especial help. My obligation to the Borthwick Institute, York, is all the greater for permission to reproduce part of an earlier work of mine in Chapter VIII below. I was fortunate on the eve of going to press to see the proofs of Mrs. Bowker's excellent book, and I am grateful for her kindness in this matter. Until that time our studies had been wholly independent and it was a reassuring experience to find so much agreement emerging from such different approaches.

The errors and weakness which remain after all this expert assistance are, of course, entirely the author's responsibility.

1968   PETER HEATH

Abbreviations

A.A.S.R.	*Associated Architectural Societies' Reports*
A.H.R.	*American Historical Review*
B.I.H.R.	*Bulletin of the Institute of Historical Research*
B.M.	British Museum
C 1/	Early Chancery Proceedings
C.C.R.	*Calendar of Close Rolls*
C.P.L.	*Calendar of Papal Letters*
C.P.R.	*Calendar of Patent Rolls*
D.N.B.	*Dictionary of National Biography*
E.E.T.S.	*Early English Text Society*
Econ. H.R.	*Economic History Review*
E.H.R.	*English Historical Review*
Emden, *Cambridge*	*A Biographical Register of the University of Cambridge to 1500* (Cambridge, 1963)
Emden, *Oxford*	*A Biographical Register of the University of Oxford to A.D. 1500*, 3 vols (Oxford, 1957–9)
G.L.C.	Greater London Council Record Office
H.M.C.	*Historical Manuscripts Commission*
J.E.H.	*Journal of Ecclesiastical History*
L. & P.	*Letters and Papers of Henry VIII's Reign*
Lyndwood	W. Lyndwood, *Provinciale seu Constitutiones Angliae* (Oxford, 1679)
M.C.A.	*Medieval Clerical Accounts*, ed. P. Heath (St. Anthony's Hall Publications No. 26)
N.C.C.D.	*Norwich Consistory Court Depositions*, ed. E. D. Stone and E. Cozens-Hardy (Norfolk Record Society No. 10)
P.C.C.	Prerogative Court of Canterbury
P.R.O.	Public Record Office MS.
R.	York Diocesan Archives MS.
Reg(s).	Episcopal Register(s)
T.R.H.S.	*Transactions of the Royal Historical Society*
V.C.H.	*Victoria County History*

ix

Wilkins	D. Wilkins, *Concilia Magnae Brittaniae et Hiberniae* . . . *446–1718* (London 1737)
Y.A.J.	*Yorkshire Archaeological Journal*
York Visitations	York Dean and Chapter MS. L.2(3)c (Visitation Book 1472–1550)

NOTE

The county locations of all places are given in the General Index.

Introduction

We are also nowe a dayes greved of heretykes, men mad with
marveylous folysshenes. But the heresies of them are nat so pesti-
lent and pernicious unto us and the people, as the evyle and wicked
lyfe of pristes; the whiche, if we beleve Saynt Barnard, is a certeyn
kynde of heresye, and chiefe of all and most perillous.

(John Colet to Canterbury Convocation 1512)

T H E average man's link with the Church was most familiar,
continuous and intense, and consequently most sensitive, in the
parish and in his relations with the parish clergy. It is obvious
that the Reformers in sixteenth-century England would tap all
too readily any disillusion and indignation which a lax and venal
clergy might induce in laymen, but what the dimensions of this
heresy 'chiefe of all and most perillous' were and who or what
was responsible for them have yet to be carefully assessed.

If the clergy were far from suitable, diligent or competent,
how far was this due to indiscriminate ordination, or how far to
irresponsible appointments by patrons, lay and ecclesiastical?
Or was it because of economic factors: poverty which impelled
them to avarice, pluralism and neglect; or wealth which seduced
them into arrogance and greed? Or did it result from timid
and capricious enforcement of discipline? Was it due to defective
administrative machinery or to defaulting administrators? Or
was it merely the consequence of original sin working in men
endowed with power and privilege? What could and did the
Church do, and where and why was it inactive or ineffective?
The answers to these questions will have implications far beyond
the parish clergy; the present study is, as it were, a 'blood test'
of the pre-Reformation Church in England.

A variety of terms denote the parish clergy, and of these
'rector' and 'vicar' scarcely need interpretation. There are others,
however, which are not so free from ambiguity: *cantarista*,

curatus, capellanus, and *stipendarius.* The first refers to a chantry priest, whose principal task was to sing for the soul of the founder of the chantry, but who shared to a varying degree in the service of the parish, and on occasions kept a school; he was often regarded as having a benefice, but his income was from rents and he had no claim upon tithes or oblations. Parochially he was an auxiliary, and a fugitive one who has left few records of active participation in the cure of souls; in addition to this, the excellent studies of Miss Wood-Legh have rendered unnecessary any lengthy treatment of him here. The *curatus, capellanus* and *stipendarius* present more difficulties. The first term implies the *regimen animarum* (the rule of souls) and indicates either the incumbent or the parish priest, that is the principal deputy of the rector or vicar, or else a chaplain in charge of part of the parish, for example an isolated hamlet with a chapel of ease. *Capellanus* denotes a man who assisted the *curatus,* perhaps by serving a daughter chapel, and *stipendarius* a clerk or priest who had no permanent charge, but was hired and employed when and so long as he was wanted. Yet to put such a narrow interpretation on these terms may be to strain at unwarranted precision; for in medieval records they often appear to have been interchangeable. Collectively they witness that alongside the rector or vicar there were men with little or no security of tenure, sharing to different degrees responsibility for the cure of souls and for the maintenance of services within the parish.

Any attempt to analyse the lives which these men led and the part which they played in the alienation of England from the international Church is confronted by some very real difficulties of methodology. There were some practices, such as simony, which it was in the interest of the agents to conceal, and their extent must, therefore, remain uncertain. Even on more innocent matters a statistical approach is often thwarted by the discontinuous or inconsistent nature of the sources as with wills, or—as with non-residence—by a total lack of a specific and comprehensive survey. It might have been easier to evaluate the rhetoric of literary and homiletic sources if the documentary evidence had been less equivocal, but on such a crucial question as clerical education we shall see below that record material is extremely fragmentary and that contradictions abound between and within categories of evidence. When a more personal and intimate approach is tried, we find that few letters written by the clergy—and those mainly on behalf of some layman's business—survive, and only one item—a brief memorandum roll—approaching a clerical diary is known to be extant; private, domestic accounts are non-existent, and barely half a dozen records of 'beneficial' income and expenditure are known. The nearest one gets to biography or memoirs is in the sworn evidence offered in litigation, whether in the royal or in episcopal courts, but this is rare and not infrequently contradicted by the sworn testimony of others. There are further difficulties: in no one diocese and at no one time are all these types of records to be found, nor is even one type, for example the bishop's register, equally informative on the same matters even within one diocese.

It is for these reasons that the decision has been taken rather to conduct strategic raids on key material than to concentrate the attack on the sources of one diocese; this survey has consequently been extended geographically to cover the nation and chronologically to include the later fifteenth century from *c.* 1450.

For manuscripts this study relies largely on the records of Canterbury, Lichfield, London, Norwich, and York dioceses, and for printed sources on those of Bath and Wells, Durham, Hereford, and Lincoln. The evidence has been selected, as in the chapter on discipline, where it has been most informative or manageable, but the author is well aware that there are whole archives virtually unexplored—at Chichester, Winchester, and Worcester for example—which may yet illuminate points still obscure or qualify conclusions reached here.

I

The Priestly Life

I: *The Vocation*

A PRIEST in England at the end of the Middle Ages who wanted to know more about his vocation was not without guidance, provided he was tolerably literate and within reach of books. In response to the Fourth Lateran Council's insistence on annual confession and the consequent need for adequate instruction of the clergy as well as of the parishioners, there began to appear shrewd and learned tracts dispensing the law, theology and practical advice necessary for the parochial cure of souls.[1] The *Oculus Sacerdotis* by William of Pagula, probably the best known now, was among the most comprehensive, providing a manual for confessors in its first part and a guide to the sacraments in its third; in the second part it expatiated on the duties of the layman in baptism, mass, confession and tithe paying, and then outlined the doctrinal instruction required. There were several variations on this during the fourteenth century: the anonymous *Cilium Oculi*, which supplemented Pagula's work on several matters, in particular on tithes and preaching; the *Regimen Animarum*, which enlarges on the duties of parish priests, the instruction of the laity, and the seven sacraments, all in 140 chapters; and the *Pupilla Oculi*, probably by John de Burgh, a methodical and personal rewriting of Pagula's work, so popular that it was printed at Rouen in 1510.[2] For those with less stamina and less

---

[1] For what follows, except where otherwise indicated, see W. A. Pantin, *The English Church in the Fourteenth Century*, pp. 195–205, 213–14.

[2] L. E. Boyle, 'The Oculus Sacerdotis and some other works of William of Pagula', *T.R.H.S.* (5th series) v, 81–110.

1

Latin, however, another volume had appeared in the early fifteenth century, the *Manuale Sacerdotis*, written by an Austin canon of Lilleshall, John Myrc, and running to some 320 pages of clear and convenient script.[1]

Myrc addressed this work to a certain John C[2] and deliberately eschewed eloquence, 'the language of the flatterer', and cleaved to rustic speech, preferring to be called unsophisticated rather than unbelieving.[3] This modesty scarcely conceals his condescension: he was addressing his work to no doctor or graduate, but to the average literate priest. He goes on to urge that the contents should be communicated to others,[4] and that when the book is read, it should not be tossed into a corner and allowed to moulder among the rubbish, but should be constantly consulted and never leave the priest's hands, so that it might appropriately be called *Manuale Sacerdotis*.[5]

This work, more one of exhortation than of detailed guidance, and more about the life of the priest rather than his office and duties, is divided into five books, and these into a total of seventy-nine chapters. What the duties of the priest were Myrc comprehensively outlined in nearly 2,000 lines of vernacular verse entitled *Instructions for Parish Priests*, explicitly translated from the fourteenth-century canonist text *Pars Oculi*, and aimed at the humble, not the 'grete', clerk.[6] These two approaches, of exhortation and practical information, which Myrc separated into two books, in other texts are frequently combined, most clearly in the items in that theological 'rag-bag', Burney MS. 356.[7] Among its contents are a tract of some dozen pages entitled *Qualiter sacerdotes qui alios regere praesumunt se ipsos primo regere debent ad exemplum subditorum*; another called the *De Officio Sacerdotis* whose five chapters treat successively preaching, prayer, the sacraments, scripture and perfection; and

[1] I have consulted the copy in the York Dean and Chapter Library (MS. XVI.0.11) which differs in some minor details, such as the address, from that used by Pantin, op. cit., pp. 215–17.
[2] Manuale Sacerdotis, fo. 6r.
[3] Ibid., fo. 6r.
[4] Ibid., fo. 6v.
[5] Ibid., fos. 7v–8r.
[6] *Instructions for Parish Priests by John Myrc*, ed. E. Peacock (E.E.T.S. o.s. 31), pp. 1, 59, 60.
[7] Pantin, op. cit., pp. 277–9 briefly describes its contents.

thirdly the *Speculum Sacerdotis*.[1] Innumerable other tracts survive, often barely distinguishable from sermons, on the Lord's Prayer, the Ten Commandments, the deadly sins, the cardinal virtues, and the Mass, but they differ in arrangement and address rather than in content.

The ideal which emerged from these works was exalted and arduous. Christ had ordained all his priests at the Last Supper and they should, therefore, be doubly honoured by the people over whom God had exalted them; but they had to comport themselves before laymen in a way deserving double respect.[2] This entailed the expected abstinence from lust and fornication, from hunting and trade, from ostentatious dress and violence, from taverns (*capella diaboli*) and other fleshpots (*loca gulosa*).[3] Indeed, when to eat, how to eat, and what subjects—gossip and trade—to avoid at table were carefully prescribed; the priest was to be content with a brief and light supper, or none at all, seeing that nothing so excites the sexual desires as rich, indigestible food;[4] and when he did eat, he was to do so not *bestialiter* but *tardius*, and to cease before his belly swelled and his eyes became glazed like a madman's and his face as red as blood or as grey as ashes, for such men are the priests of the Devil.[5] Avoiding excesses of this kind only constituted a part of the ideal: vain and worldly thoughts were to be eschewed; charity, piety and mercy evinced.[6] Mortal sin, which could also be achieved by omissions, and the innumerable perils which awaited the celebrant of a Mass had to be eluded; the nocturnal approaches of the Devil resisted or averted.[7] A careful regulation of conscience and the frequent confession of sins, since many venial ones—in St. Augustine's view—amounted to a mortal one, were therefore vital.[8] The priest was daily to offer his heart to God and assiduously to read and pray, for by prayer man talks with God and by reading God talks to man.[9] His study should be the ascent

---

[1] B. M. Burney MS. 356, fos. 29v–35r, 105v–107r, 107v–117r, respectively. Only two of the three parts of the 'Speculum Sacerdotis' are included in this manuscript.

[2] Manuale Sacerdotis, fos. 15r, 18v–20v.

[3] B. M. Burney MS. 356, fo. 110r.

[4] Manuale Sacerdotis, fos. 132r–134r, 148v–149r.

[5] B. M. Burney MS. 356, fo. 110r.

[6] Ibid., fo. 109r; Manuale Sacerdotis, fos. 63v–64v.

[7] Manuale Sacerdotis, fos. 56r–58r, 63v–69r.

[8] Ibid., fos. 66v–68r, 75r–76v; B. M. Burney MS. 356, fo. 109r.

[9] Manuale Sacerdotis, fos. 54v–55r; B. M. Burney MS. 356, fo. 129r.

to sanctity, his *regula*—the equivalent of the monk's rule—should be Holy Scripture, and his life, if righteous, a cross and a martyrdom.[1] Some relief was prescribed for his leisure in the tranquil pursuits of reading, writing, walking and gardening,[2] but clearly the man who was excited by this sort of challenge was more likely to enter a Charterhouse where at least one had the advantages of a sympathetic environment and seclusion from the anxieties of economics and public relations. For the good parish priest, indeed, life in early Tudor England must have been a martyrdom.

II : *The Duties*

'Seven times a day I shall give you praise' said the Psalmist and the parish priests were expected to do likewise and keep the canonical hours in their churches with music and devotion.[3] Not only the curate, but all the chaplains in the parish, even those serving chantries, were obliged to attend in the chancel for the canonical hours, the antiphons of the Virgin, and for processions; they were to sing the hymns, responses and antiphons, and—at the will of the curate—to read the lessons, epistles and gospels; while services were going on in the parish church they were forbidden to celebrate elsewhere.[4] The hours to be said began with Matins at day-break, though it was permissible to say them the evening before if some legitimate occupation obstructed morning celebration, but never in order to extend sleep.[5] Prime, less precisely fixed, followed and in England only after these two could the Mass of the day be celebrated.[6] Terce may have coincided with the Mass, which should have been said at the third hour of daylight on days other than Christmas.[7] The remaining hours followed throughout the day and while explicit times are lacking in the legal texts, some rough guide may be attained by combining

[1] Manuale Sacerdotis, fos. 2r–v, 22v, 51r–54r.
[2] Ibid., fos. 138r–v.
[3] *Councils & Synods*, ed. F. M. Powicke and C. R. Cheney, ii, 641, 1018—statutes of London diocese 1245–59, and of Exeter diocese 1287.
[4] Lyndwood, I.14.i; III.23.ix.
[5] *Councils & Synods*, ii, 557; Lyndwood, III.23.ix.
[6] Lyndwood, III.23.viii.
[7] Ibid.

the entries in judicial records with the details of the monastic *horarium*, itself no uncomplicated or certain chronology:[1] to suggest that Terce was at 9 a.m., Sext mid-morning or even midday, Nones early afternoon, and Vespers and Compline perhaps combined in the late afternoon or towards dusk may not be too misleading, if it is constantly borne in mind that local custom and personal inclination rang many variations upon the broad requirements of the law. In Masham, for example, in 1519 it was arranged that from the Annunciation (25 March) to the Nativity of the Blessed Virgin (8 September) Matins should begin at 7 o'clock, and for the rest of the year at 7.30, Vespers at 2 o'clock in winter and at 2.30 in summer; to give due warning to the remoter inhabitants of a very extensive parish the first bell was to be rung half an hour before the service.[2] Although fixed hours were avoided in decrees, the incumbent or his deputy was expected to say the offices in due order and at hours customary or well known in the parish so that all who wished to could be present,[3] a rule violated by the vicar of Ospringe who kept no order 'but now he syngith at oon hower nowe at another at his owne pleasur and other whilis will doo all service by 8 of the clock and somtyme by alevyn of the clock', and at Stone where divine service was celebrated but once a fortnight and Matins and Evensong neglected even on holy days.[4]

As well as the canonical hours Mass was expected from the 'curate' of the parish each day. This was a custom which had developed since the thirteenth century when Pecham had insisted on Mass once a week.[5] No law necessitated Mass each day but by our period parishioners had clearly come to expect it: in 1472 the parishioners of Husthwaite complained that the chaplain who served the cure there celebrated Mass three days a week, Monday, Wednesday and Friday, in Carleton chapel, on which days no Mass was celebrated in the parish church 'to the great peril of the parishioners there'; and in Denton in 1511, it was complained, the parishioners had Mass only three times a

[1] D. Knowles, *The Monastic Order in England 943–1216* (2nd edn.), pp. 448–53.
[2] York Visitations, fo. 184r.
[3] Lyndwood, III.23.ix, note *r*: '*non reciproce sed gradatim*'.
[4] Reg. Warham, fos. 54v, 55r.
[5] E. L. Cutts, *Parish Priests and their People in the Middle Ages in England*, p. 203.

quarter and only on Sundays then.[1] Mass could not be celebrated before Matins and Prime were said and it seems to have occurred about 9 or 10 a.m; at Masham in 1510 the parishioners desired High Mass between 9 and 10 a.m. on weekdays and to begin at 10 a.m. on holy days.[2] It should have been said at the third hour on feasts, at the sixth on the eve of feasts, at the ninth on fast days, symbolizing respectively the hour at which Christ was condemned to crucifixion by the Jews and when the Holy Spirit descended on the Apostles, the hour at which he was crucified, and the hour when he expired.[3] There were exceptions to these rules, for on the four ordination days of the year Mass could be said with Vespers, and on Holy Saturday at the beginning of the night. Only at Christmas and Easter and in certain special cases could more than one Mass (apart from those for the dead) be celebrated in a parish on one day. At Christmas, indeed, three Masses were permissible: at night, in the morning, and at the third hour, betokening various mysteries; on Easter Day when one priest might have to communicate the whole of a parish, who could not all come at once, two, but only two, Masses were allowable.[4] Other exceptional occasions when one priest might celebrate two Masses were for funerals, for pilgrims, visitors, travellers, or the sick, for an anniversary, or an urgent marriage *ubi tempus laberetur*, or where one priest had to serve two parishes by himself.[5] Only on Christmas Day were *more* than two Masses permissible.

As well as the appropriate hours and the Mass, the priest had to celebrate the patronal feasts of the parish and the diocese and certain other feasts 'with the clergy and people present'.[6]

Among the non-liturgical duties of the incumbent or his deputy was the obligation to instruct his parishioners in their faith. It was the view of St. Augustine, repeated by a fifteenth-century writer, that the priest should study only Holy Writ, the law of Him whose minister he was, and should read all the books of the Old and New Testaments, but it is much more likely that

[1] York Visitations, fo. 16r; Reg. Warham, fo. 51r.

[2] Lyndwood, III.23.viii; York Visitations, fo. 119v.

[3] Lyndwood, III.23.viii, note *g*.

[4] Ibid., III.23.i, note *u*.

[5] Ibid.

[6] *Councils & Synods*, ii, 517, 1021–22; see also C. R. Cheney, 'Rules for the Observance of Feast Days in Medieval England', *B.I.H.R.* xxxiv, 117–47.

his acquaintance with his faith was derived from the service books and from the treatises described above than directly from the Bible.[1] It was from these sources and the considerable homily collections that he would have taught his subjects the rudiments of their faith four times at least in a year;[2] these were obligatory occasions for preaching, but there is persuasive testimony that other opportunities were frequently seized for the same purpose. So far as instruction was concerned—and not only in morality—there was no better occasion than confession. Each parishioner was bound on pain of excommunication to communicate at Easter and to confess beforehand; there was nothing to prevent a more frequent confession and, indeed, it had been advised at Easter, Pentecost and Christmas in the fourteenth century.[3] The simple confession of all his parishioners at Easter was in a populous parish no slight operation and the curate could license parochial chaplains to assist him. Some idea of its magnitude if properly executed may be gained from Myrc's lines of verse guidance;[4] the priest was to examine closely the parishioner's belief in the Pater Noster and in each article of the Creed, and to investigate his observance of the Ten Commandments, questioning him carefully about the venial and each of the deadly sins—an enquiry so particular as to leave the sinners with little concealed, though to some it must have revealed a range of experience outside their imagination. After this exhaustive and protracted interrogation, the priest had to think carefully of a penance suitable not only to the sin, but to its circumstances and to the character and attitude of the sinner, avoiding, for example, a penance which would betray a wife to her husband's disapproval, and eschewing penances which because of their severity had little chance of being faithfully performed.

Equally universal in its application was baptism, although in necessity midwives and layfolk could perform it. Some parts of the year, from the first Sunday in Advent until the octave of Epiphany, from Septuagesima until the octave of Easter, and from the first day of Rogation until the seventh after Pentecost,

[1] B. M. Burney MS. 356, fo. 106v. See below p. 88
[2] Wilkins, ii, 54–57.
[3] Lyndwood, IV.16.xvi, citing Simon Sudbury.
[4] *Instructions for Parish Priests*, pp. 21–53. Compare also the guidance for confessors among the sermons of *Speculum Sacerdotale*, ed. E. H. Weatherley (E.E.T.S. o.s. 200), pp. 63–68.

were free from marriages and nuptial masses,[1] but during the 'open season' the priest had to be careful, then as now, that all such formalities as the calling of banns and the presence of witnesses were observed.[2] The churching of women was a common but hardly an onerous chore. Far more exacting physically and emotionally was visiting the sick, especially during the frequent plagues; each Sunday and feast day in York diocese, but everywhere upon request, day or night, the priest, accompanied by the parish clerk, had to take the Host and blessing and comfort to the sick and, if necessary, confess them.[3] The last service the curate performed for his parishioners was their funeral mass and the utterance of prayers each day for the departed.

If these duties were conscientiously executed the average curate, except in the smallest of parishes, and despite the speed with which the hours can be completed, would not have excessive time remaining to cultivate his glebe and his mind. There were, however, within many, perhaps most, parishes more priests than the curate and it is easy to think that unless the assistant clergy of the parish occupied themselves in commemorative masses or teaching and other pastoral good works, they would have ample time in which to be lured from the ideal, the pursuit of sanctity, even supposing that they acknowledged such ambition.

III: *The Context: Oxnead, Kennington and Bowers Gifford*

The priest grappled with his vocation in a society of unrestrained passion and unseemly violence; not only was he surrounded by this context, he himself sprang from it; he was no alien to its emotions and traditions and his task was harder, in some ways, than the missionary's, for he had to seek detachment, moral and emotional, in two dimensions—from himself as well as from his parish. The brutality and the vice which challenged not merely his pastoral efforts but his own self-control will become more apparent later in this study, but since the parish clergy are too

[1] Lyndwood, III.16.i, note *e*.
[2] *Instructions for Parish Priests*, p. 7.
[3] *Councils & Synods*, ii, 346, 488; *Instructions for Parish Priests*, pp. 53–54, 57–59.

often considered *in vacuo*, as though they never lived and worked in a parish which had any other characteristics than those of boundaries, benefice and tithes, it is worth dwelling here on three different and difficult parishes.

The first, Oxnead,[1] in Norfolk, was typical of many. It was described in 1478 by its patron with the feeling, if not in the language, of an estate agent; he stressed its physical aspects and we must recollect that this was the picture which filled and fired a good many clerical heads. Oxnead like so many East Anglian parishes had an arcadian and reassuring charm about it. Of course, it had its economic value and the patron puts his price upon each item in turn, but the beguiling languor of this Norfolk parish is what remains in the mind: its small and pleasant church with the parsonage adjoining; the gardens and the fruit trees, the twenty-two acres of ploughland, pasture and meadow which belonged to the manse; the fresh river running near by; Aylsham, the market, two miles away, Norwich only six, the coast barely ten; and to distract the incumbent from all this were a mere score of parishioners. It is likely, however, that before the parson could succumb entirely to bucolic pleasures and agricultural exertions he would be distracted by the patrons, the Paston family, who seldom in this period wasted their livings on dedicated clergy; a variety of labours on behalf of the family doubtless fell to the lot of Oxnead's incumbents and such tranquillity as they enjoyed was punctuated by the internecine violence of Norfolk's grasping magnates.[2] The parsons there were particularly exposed to complacency or to secular preoccupations.

The vicar of Kennington,[3] in Kent, in 1511 was the victim of a much less subtle threat; his parish was a 'tough assignment' dominated by Richard Rickard, a lecher and a gangster. There seemed to be hardly a wife in the parish whom this Rickard had not ravished; William Christopher's had only escaped by the opportune arrival of one of her neighbours; Richard's children were born in several different houses. He frequented Thomas Hauter's home, beat him, killed another man in it, and threatened to take his wife overseas. With others of similar

[1] *The Paston Letters* (1904 edn.), v, No. 934.
[2] Ibid., ii, Nos. 50, 77, 81.
[3] Reg. Warham, fo. 53v.

THE ENGLISH PARISH CLERGY

inclination he was a great spender in alehouses, though he had no obvious source of income. He was a great slanderer of his neighbours, usually alleging treason, and the unlucky vicar was not safe from these malicious charges. In fact the vicar's immunity was much more limited than that: when he rebuked Rickard, an act almost of bravado, he merely provoked a threat of murder and Rickard and his associates so hindered the vicar's work that he eventually feared to reside and keep the cure. Rickard's gang so intimidated those who would help the vicar sing Mass that he could get no one to assist him; they obstructed his entry into the churchyard and when he did infiltrate they violently expelled him. It may have been the least of the vicar's troubles that one of the gang revealed in his attitude to the sermons and to images a trace of heresy, which at that time was overt a short distance away in Tenterden. Kent had a tradition of anti-clericalism brutally expressed, if not enacted, which goes back at least to the 1450s when a cry to kill pluralists and to castrate lascivious clergy was strident there,[1] but this 'puritan' element had vanished from Kennington, leaving mere mindless and vicious hostility. Not all parishes in the county in that year shared or even approached the discouraging barbarism of Kennington, but in most parishes in England it was a dormant habit awakened on frequent occasions; and it is a measure of how near the surface it lay that arousal could be effected by the most trivial incidents.

When on Ascension Day 1512 John Baker, the rector of Bowers Gifford,[2] in Essex, had finished Vespers and was going home for supper he met a youth of about sixteen years of age whom he recognized as the servant of one of his parishioners, William Hare; he proceeded to question the lad about if and where he had heard Vespers that day but got in reply a merry confession that he had been asleep; as the youth had not the good manners either to remove his hat or to conceal his mirth, the rector threatened to inform his master, William Hare, at which the lad guffawed and made a rude gesture; Baker thereupon struck him 'not maliciously, but lovingly for correction' (*non animo maliciose sed caritative corrigendo*) with a rod (*virgula*) which he had in his hand. Perhaps an excess of love—and

[1] R. L. Storey, *The End of the House of Lancaster* (London 1966), p. 9.
[2] G.L.C., MS. DL/C/206, fos. 215v–216v, 225r–226v, 230r–234r.

10

understandably—motivated him, for one witness tells how he found the youth, John Gilbard, on the highway between Pitsea and Bowers Gifford almost crippled by blows from a staff (*baculo*) about his ankles, where the evidence was still obvious; or perhaps the miscreant—like his kind—knew how to make the most of ill fortune, for about an hour after the incident, his master, William Hare, carrying a staff (*cum quodam le bille*), arrived to question the rector about the assault. After hearing the details, Hare reportedly said 'Thowe schall repent it' and Baker, fearing attack, put his hand on the sword (*gestrum*) at his side, or—as another witness stated—unsheathed it almost to the point. Whatever he did, he seems to have discouraged further attention from Hare. But his troubles were not over yet. About four days later, on the Sunday following Ascension Day, a number of boys, servants of Thomas Aleyn, were playing tennis against one of the rectory buildings and damaging some newly planted trees by shaking and breaking them. Baker warned them to stop and go away, and when one pert youth answered that he wouldn't, Baker—who as usual when confronted with small boys had a rod (*virgula*) in his hand—struck the offender lightly on the head with it and announced that he would complain to their master. He went that evening to Aleyn's house but finding him out told of the incident to Mrs. Aleyn, who promised to tell her husband and assured him that the boys would be punished. Evidently not content with this, he went in search of Aleyn, who with William Hare and two others had gone to Alan Cady's house in Pitsea for a drink and celebration (*causa bibendi et iocandi*). It was in this convivial and intimate mood, while sitting drinking, that they were disturbed by the uninvited arrival of John Baker, rector, who greeted them, according to Margery Cady, with the less than tactful words 'Miche gude do it yow, Masters'. Aleyn had evidently heard of his servant's fate, for he soon asked Baker why he had struck the youth; after this tempers were quickly frayed and Aleyn eventually exploited his authority as bailiff of Bowers Gifford to call on the assembled topers to witness that the parson intended an affray and to help keep the peace; with what exuberance they did this may be imagined, though they asserted that they merely took him by the arms without violence and removed him from the house, and—at the request of the rector of Pitsea—let him go away unharmed. It may have been between ejectment and the appearance on the scene of Pitsea's rector that Baker was put in the stocks on Aleyn's order. That, so far as the extant records show, is the end of the episode for the moment. Baker was undeniably a tactless man whose blood-pressure was soon raised by impudent youths, and he clearly carred a sword and usually a rod—if not a staff—which he was prone to use; he was also given to wearing a tippett and a tunic or 'Jakit' down to his calves; but whether he was, as one accusation stated, an apostate or anything worse than choleric and vain, testimony is lacking. What is more to the point here are the imponderable and trivial factors which impinged on clergy-laity relations; the neat analyses of textbooks—and even of this book—must be supplemented with the confusing and unpredictable element of individual human emotions. Impudent boys start a fracas which is entirely symptomatic of the age: the outraged priest wanting to see the rascals subdued; the masters insulted by the attack—if such it were—on their serving boys, who had doubtless invited and exaggerated it; the growing crescendo of rumour and feelings, reaching a climax in Alan Cady's house with the bailiff committing the rector to the stocks; the anticlimax perhaps was in the consistory court where Baker cited his adversaries for assault. These complexities and shallows of human and public relations are not peculiar to early Tudor England, but the course they take and the speed with which such paltry episodes run to violence are indicative of the age.

IV: *Entry: Orders and Ordination*

There would naturally be more men forthcoming who were tempted by the unfilled hours of a clerk's life than were inspired by the ideal or deterred by, or even aware of, the difficulties; there would also be more men who were moved and challenged by the vocation than would in fact be able to fulfil its demands, and others would earnestly, but rashly, underrate the obstacles to sanctity and pastoral success. The proportions of such categories were all the greater when the Church offered employment not only in the parishes, but also about cathedrals and chantries and private households, where life was much less demanding. Furthermore, the Church offered to a young man, if talent and good fortune were his, a prospect of advancement almost unequalled in other walks of life. It was this capacity to absorb, employ, promote and reward all ranges of ability and ambition which partly explains the numbers of candidates seeking entry to the Church. Another explanation is that the Church offered remuneration even for a man leading quite a different career, provided he were in orders. There was, however, some selection imposed at ordination.

This took place four times a year: the Saturdays in the third week of Advent, the first week of Lent, the vigil of Trinity, and in September following the octave of the Virgin's Nativity; if for any reason these days were impossible or another day essential, it could only be on the Saturday before Passion Sunday or on Holy Saturday. Although strictly no other times were permissible, they were sometimes expedient and necessary in a large diocese.[1]

There were eight stages in the progression from lay to priestly status. The first tonsure, although it was reckoned to confer upon its recipient clerkly status (*ordo clericalis*) and the duty of singing in church, was not regarded as an order or as a sacrament itself, but merely as a sign of pious intention.[2] Canon law prescribed no specific age limit for the first tonsure, merely that it could only be conferred on a child if he were entering religion,[3] and the most probable recipients would be the youths who, if not in the bishop's household, showed encouraging keenness in their local church. Far from enduring physically and with records of it only sporadically kept,[4] the first tonsure posed some difficulties of identification, especially of the clerks whose pious intentions melted away in the heat of adolescence and of those who sought it merely as a potentially valuable immunity. The tonsure made a boy or man a clerk, but it separated him from the lay world only by a presumed mental state of intention.

---

[1] *Liber pontificalis Chr. Bainbridge archiepiscopi Eboracensis*, ed. W. G. Henderson (Surtees Soc. 61), p. 44 (henceforth referred to simply as *Liber pontificalis*); M. Bowker, *Secular Clergy in Lincoln Diocese*, p. 40.

[2] Lyndwood, III.1.i, note *c*: '*sed solum dispositio ad ordines*'.

[3] *Liber Sextus*, I.9.iv.

[4] *Reg. Bourgchier*, ed. F. R. H. Du Boulay (C. & Y. Soc.), pp. 159–60; contrast their complete absence from the ordination lists ibid., pp. 358–455.

This ambiguity which belies our over-rigid distinctions between lay and ecclesiastical societies, pertained in fact to all the four minor orders. They, however, were considered sacraments; whereas the tonsure could be given privately, they required a Mass of ordination. Two minor orders could be conferred on the same day, together with the first tonsure, but no more, and certainly not with the major order of the subdiaconate.[1] The lowest of the orders was that of doorkeeper, *ostiarius*, whose duty was to ring the bell, to open the church and to hold the book for the preacher; and in token of his office, at his ordination he was handed a key. The *lector*, second in ascending order, was to turn the pages for the preacher, to sing the lessons distinctly and to bless the bread and all new fruits; as a sign of his office he received a lectionary from the hands of the bishop. The role of the exorcist, to abjure demons, is explicit enough, but he was also charged with organizing the communicant parishioners and with pouring water for the celebrant; he received a book of exorcism. The last of the minor orders was that of acolyte whose role was to carry the candlestick, to light the lights of the church, and to minister wine and water at the Eucharist, as a sign of which he received a candlestick and an empty ewer. This order was held to comprehend the other minor orders as well; though a candidate had to take each order in turn, he could accelerate the process by taking two minor ones simultaneously.

Until this time a clerk was very much a man who had left one foot in the door of the lay world: he could still marry with the approval of canon law and he might abandon—with some personal shame but no public scandal or legal obstacle—a clerical life altogether.[2] The subdiaconate, the first of the major, sometimes called the holy, orders changed all that, as the bishop's words to each subdeacon explicitly declared: 'If until now you have been slow to church, henceforward you must be punctual; if until now you have been somnolent, henceforth you must be alert; if until now intoxicated, henceforth sober; if until now incontinent, henceforth chaste'.[3] That a world of graver re-

[1] Lyndwood, V.11, particularly notes *x* and *c*. For the rest of this paragraph see *Liber pontificalis*, pp. 7, 9, 10, 11–13.
[2] Lyndwood, III.3.i.
[3] *Liber pontificalis*, p. 14.

sponsibility was entered with holy orders is clear from the specific age requirements for each: at least eighteen for the subdiaconate, nineteen for a deacon, and twenty-four for a priest.[1] With each of the major orders the candidate received by instalments the vestments of his priestly office. The subdeacon was to prepare the necessities of the minister at the altar, and to serve humbly the deacon; he received from the bishop as a sign an empty paten and chalice, and was clothed with a maniple and tunic.[2] The deacon, who was to minister at the altar, to read the gospels, to baptize and preach, received as a sign the gospels and was clothed with a stole and dalmatic.[3] Priests, who were to offer the host, to bless, to lead the prayers, to preach, consecrate and baptize, were given a paten with bread, and a chalice with wine and water, and were clothed with the chasuble.[4]

Candidates were not accepted into the clergy without submitting to some test of their fitness,[5] but that this examination was too perfunctory and superficial to be more than a scandalous waste of time deserves close study, for a galaxy of eminent and orthodox witnesses shared this view. Thomas Gascoigne, a chancellor of Oxford University, from whose vehement indignation few persons or institutions were safe, observed in the mid-fifteenth century that unworthy men were being ordained and beneficed.[6] William Melton, a Cambridge don before he became chancellor of York Minster, about 1510 lamented the ignorant hordes who in the recent past had entered and then shamed the Church by their inadequate learning and their notorious want of discipline.[7] A little later the dean of St. Paul's, John Colet, complained that the ordination examination tested competence but neglected devotion and godliness, a theme endorsed by More in his controversy with Tyndale: 'there should be more diligence used in the choice not of their learning only, but much more specially of their living'.[8]

[1] *Liber Clementinarum*, I.6.iii.
[2] *Liber pontificalis*, p. 14; B. M. Burney MS. 356, fo. 158v.
[3] *Liber pontificalis*, p. 27; B. M. Burney MS. 356, fo. 158v.
[4] *Liber pontificalis*, p. 34; B. M. Burney MS. fo. 158v.
[5] Lyndwood, I.5.
[6] *Loci e Libro Veritatum*, ed. E. T. Rogers, p. 18.
[7] William Melton, *Sermo Exhortatorius cancellarii Eboracensis hiis qui ad ordines petunt promoveri*, sigla A.iii.–A.iv.
[8] J. H. Lupton, *Life of Colet*, p. 300; *The English Works of Sir Thomas More*, ed. W. E. Campbell and A. W. Reed, ii, 219.

The examination for each order, major and minor, was bound by law to take place within the three days preceding the ceremony and to be conducted by the archdeacon. This was prescribed at a time when ordinands were few and the archdeacon truly *oculus episcopi*; if one examiner had had to cope in three days with the huge numbers who later and in our period presented themselves for orders in some dioceses,[1] laxity would have been inescapable, but it is plain from such fragmentary evidence as we have on the point that bishops could and did extend the time of examination and that usually several theologians or masters were commissioned as examiners, different ones being named for different orders.[2] In many sees, smaller or less magnetic than York or Lichfield, there were seldom more than thirty or forty ordinands at a time.[3]

Regardless of the numbers involved, laxity might be thought to result from official encouragement when we find a canonist (admittedly of the fourteenth century, but much read in the sixteenth) advising the examiners to conduct their enquiry briskly (*summatim cum quodam temperamento*), but this was clearly to discourage the examiners from searching for the ideal examinee rather than testing the candidate's competence for his duties.[4] Melton thought the examiners were not so much inclined to carelessness and cynicism as exposed to unscrupulous pressures and deceit; he stressed their need to explore the learning of the ordinand more thoroughly, but in this he was criticizing their criteria rather than their integrity; what alarmed him far more was the way in which candidates for orders got the socially eminent to write to the examiners on their behalf, or pleaded family poverty as a cause of urgent ordination, or hired an impersonator of greater talent for the occasion, or kept silent about canonical defects real or suspected.[5] The extent of this last practice is ill gauged from the numbers who sought papal absolution for defects successfully concealed at ordination, as

[1] See H. Maynard Smith, *Pre-Reformation England*, p. 39, n. 1.

[2] H. S. Bennett, 'Medieval Ordination Lists in English Episcopal Registers', *Studies presented to Sir Hilary Jenkinson*, ed. J. Conway Davies, pp. 22–24, citing thirteenth and fourteenth-century evidence.

[3] e.g. Bath and Wells, Hereford and London dioceses.

[4] H. S. Bennett, loc. cit., p. 31, citing the fourteenth-century *Pupilla Oculi*.

[5] Melton, op. cit., siglo A.ii (*verso*), A.iii (*verso*), A.iv (*recto*), A.v (*recto* and *verso*).

very few of these were English, as distinct from Irish and Scottish, clergy.[1] No records shed even this light on the other frauds. On one requirement, however, the examiners cannot be regarded as victims of deceit or acquitted of uncanonical and almost cynical haste. Every ordinand was supposed to have a title, that is a guaranteed source of maintenance, to sustain him until he found permanent clerical employment, and if a bishop ordained a man without an effective title he would by canon law become liable to support the clerk.[2] Yet by our period almost every ordinand, where the registrars even bothered to record the matter, offered as his title a religious house which professed thereby a readiness to sustain him; that it was often unable to do so must have been common knowledge when, as frequently happened, it was among the poorer, if not the poorest, establishments, and though a larger proportion of the ordinands then than previously would have had adequate means of their own, an incalculable number seeking in clerical opportunities an alternative to beggary must have been ordained.[3] More's complaint about this system was not that they remained unemployed and indigent but that they were too readily absorbed by household chapels where they lived in undemanding and unedifying ease to the embarrassment of their order and the clergy generally.[4]

More serious, however, than haste or fraud may have been the evasion of examination altogether by means of the system of letters dimissory, which licensed a man of one diocese to seek some or all orders in any other. This viewpoint is fostered by the decree of Canterbury Convocation[5] in 1529 which abolished letters dimissory and insisted that a clerk could only be ordained in the diocese wherein he was born, or already beneficed, or had been living for three years, and that at ordina-

[1] G. G. Coulton, *Medieval Panorama* (Fontana edn.), i, 174 misapplied this evidence; *C.P.L.* x–xiv, where only two English examples occur.

[2] *Liber Decretalium Gregorii IX*, I.14.xiii.

[3] An analysis of the ordination lists of Norwich diocese from 1413 to 1486 has shown that the larger and greater houses were hardly represented at all among the monastic titles, but that such an establishment as Molycourt between 1436 and 1445, when it had only one monk and no prior, provided titles for seven ordinands; it is pointed out that Molycourt and its like were hardly the sort of houses which attracted the trusts whereby A. H. Thompson sought to explain this phenomenon (J. F. Williams, 'Ordination in the Norwich Diocese during the Fifteenth Century', *Norfolk Archaeology*, xxxi, 355–7).

[4] *The English Works of Sir Thomas More*, ii, 219–20.

[5] Wilkins, iii, 718.

tion he had to produce letters testimonial from the curate or churchwarden of the parish in which he was born, beneficed or resident, sealed by the archdeacon or commissary, and stating the details of his life, birth, locality, character, faith and learning. Its implications about letters dimissory hardly seem justified by the evidence, for it is clear from some stray evidence of Hereford diocese that the recipient, if not scrutinized before the grant, was certainly not exempted from examination before next receiving orders.[1]

That the examination was uncanonically lax on the question of title and far from infallible on competence, that it did let through into clerical ranks men not entirely fitted for the Church needs no further demonstration than is made here and in the chapters which follow. Yet if legal requirements rather than vocation were sought, some idea of the ordinand's piety and sincerity may have been elicited from the testimony about his good character, though it is doubtful if this enquiry was—or could be—more than an attempt to exclude men of known depravity. The proofs of age, physique and title were primarily required to avert scandal. And the complaint is not that learning was unexamined—the substitution fraud denies that thought, but that a very little learning was deemed adequate. Yet some compromise with reality was unavoidable if the Church were to recruit personnel in sufficient numbers; it had to staff its organs, collegiate as well as parochial, and it had to acknowledge the requirements of laymen, moved ostensibly by piety, if in all too many cases by social prestige, for chaplains, obits and chantries; having sown the seed of such devotional habits, uprooting the resultant tree was an operation of extreme danger as well as difficulty. Until candidates were subjected to seminary training and observation before ordination, there was little chance of making the selection procedure more rigorous and less fallible.

[1] *Reg. Mayew*, ed. A. T. Bannister (C. & Y. Soc.), pp. 239–40, where the examination of 22 candidates for holy orders is recorded, 21 of whom had letters dimissory, all of whom were students or scholars at Oxford University. See also below pp. 72, 210.

II

The Chaplains

THE ecclesiastical work of the clerk in minor orders was distinctly part-time and unpaid, confined to divine service and involving no pastoral responsibilities and no cure of souls; its extent depended both upon the need of the parish for his assistance and upon his sincerity of intention; for the most part such clerks who were of age lived as laymen and worked their patrimony or found other secular employment. For the boys and youths who must have constituted a significant proportion of the minor clergy, their assistance would largely be in the choir and their other employment in study, if not at some local school, under the direction of the organist (as happened at a London church) or of a chaplain or of the parish clerk.[1] In the thirteenth century the office of holy water clerk had been regarded as a benefice reserved, as a kind of exhibition, from the alms of parishioners for scholars named by the incumbent; but by our period this had been assimilated, or had evolved, into the office of parish clerk, whose holders were often far from youthful and long since scholars: Richard Pond, *aquebaiulus* of Theydon Garnon in 1522 was also described as *clericus parochialis* and was then 28 years old, having occupied the office four years; John Trew was parish clerk of Burton Pidsea for at least thirty-seven years, Henry Newson at Bugthorpe for twenty-eight, Richard Eland at North Newbald for more than fourteen, and there were many more like them.[2]

---

[1] *The Medieval Records of a London City Church*, ed. H. Littlehales (E.E.T.S. o.s. 128), p. xxxiv; for the parish clerk see below.
[2] *Councils & Synods*, ii, 1026–7 (Exeter diocese, 1287); G.L.C., MS. DL/C/ 330, fo. 28r–v; York Visitations, *passim*.

Though commonly supported and nominated by the church-wardens, the parish clerk was appointed and removeable by the incumbent, whose factotum about the church and parish he was.[1] The deacon's office (*officium diaconi*) which he exercised usually entailed the preparation of the church for services and the assistance of the curate in singing divine office and in ministering the sacraments.[2] At St. Stephen's, Coleman Street, in London, which is probably typical, he had to lay out the service books in the choir open at the necessary places, and to collect them afterwards, to serve the curate and priests with copes, to kindle the censers, to light the tapers, to set the children to sing in the choir, twice a year to clean the font and renew the holy water, to inform the curate and churchwardens of all marriages, christenings and burials during each week, every Sunday to carry holy water to the sick, and to help the sexton—a very different character here as elsewhere—to ring the bells.[3] His supervision of the service arrangements and his choral responsibilities necessitated capacity in singing and reading and involved him, as we shall see below, in teaching the choir boys.[4] It was no doubt as these choir boys, who were growing more numerous as polyphony became more popular,[5] that the future clergy learnt to read and sing Latin and enlarged their understanding of the liturgy; that the parish clerks themselves were merely in transit to major orders is not unlikely in some instances, but much less common than Coulton thought, to judge by the long years many spent in this office.

Once in holy orders the clerk could join the ranks of chaplains

[1] The churchwardens at Lockington in 1527 found 26s. 8d. for the parish clerk ('Proceedings in Ecclesiastical Courts in the Archdeaconry of Leicester 1515–35', ed. A. P. Moore, *A.A.S.R.* xxviii, 632–5); see also Reg. Warham, fos. 49r, 58r, 55v; York Visitations, fo. 59r. In one parish at least the vicar shared the cost (Reg. Warham, fo. 48r). In some parishes there were two parish clerks, e.g. St. Stephen's, Coleman Street, London, and Masham, Yorkshire (E. Freshfield, 'Book of Records of the Parish of St. Stephen's, Coleman Street', *Archaeologia*, I(i), 49–51; York Visitations, fo. 80v).

[2] Reg. Warham, fos. 47v, 48v, 54v; *Archaeologia*, I(i), 49–50; F. F. Giraud, 'On the Parish Clerks and Sextons of Faversham 1506–1593', *Archaeologia Cantiana*, xx, 204–6.

[3] *Archaeologia*, I(i), 49–50; for similar duties see York Visitations, fos. 30v, 133r, 137r; *Archaeologia Cantiana*, xx and *A.A.S.R.* xxviii. On the sexton's office Reg. Warham, fos. 47v, 55v; *Archaeologia Cantiana*, xx, 206–7.

[4] *A.A.S.R.* xxviii; see below Chapter V for his teaching activities.

[5] F. Ll. Harrison, *Music in Medieval Britain* (London 1958), pp. 197–201, 213–14.

employed by incumbents about their parishes, or by laymen about their chantries or private chapels or gilds. Until such time as he found employment of this kind the cleric was supposed to support himself from his title. This should have been worth £5 a year and could be supplied by patrimonial lands or by a sponsor; by our period it was usually if not always of the latter kind, the sponsor almost invariably being a religious house, and most often a nunnery: at York in 1511, for example, all the titles were supplied by religious houses.[1] The idea that this reliance on monastic titles signifies the increasingly humble origins of the clergy is refuted elsewhere in this study, if it is not denied by the very universality of the practice;[2] but how so many religious houses, let alone poor nunneries, could in fact support the burdens apparently involved and why this change from patrimonial to sponsorial titles took place are questions which have so far eluded confident answers. It might be a loan arrangement, but more abundant and more accessible proof of this would be expected. Title for the present remains a mystery, but some such form of income or support was necessary to supplement the casual employment which marked the early stages of many a clerk's career. This employment could be singing occasional obits and masses for the dead, attending funerals and collecting as a result a few pence from the executors of the deceased; or supplementing in a gild or a parish where sickness or absence had caused a passing need. In due course, if he wished, he could become a hired priest of a parish, serving under, and later as, the parish priest, the incumbent's deputy.

For most men ordained to holy orders this service as a parish auxiliary was an unavoidable stage in their *cursus honorum*. Those who escaped it altogether were either graduates or the well-connected who were often provided with a living before they had either the necessary years or orders.[3] That it was the lot of a great many, however, is apparent from statistics: there were twice as many parish chaplains as incumbents in East Yorkshire in 1525, and in Holy Trinity, Hull, where—it being a chapel of ease of Hessle—there was no local incumbent, there were no less

[1] *Liber Pontificalis*, p. 270; J. S. Purvis, 'The Registers of Archbishops Lee and Holgate', *J.E.H.* xiii, 190–1.
[2] The idea was advanced by H. S. Bennett, 'Medieval Ordination Lists etc.', loc. cit., p. 27.
[3] For all this see the next chapter, especially pp. 33, 35–6.

than twenty-five chaplains![1] While a chaplaincy was usually of extended duration, for some it was even the summit of their careers; at Riston in 1494 Robert Wod, chaplain and only some ten years before vicar's proctor, was described as *senex et valetudinarius*.[2]

It is clear from this that, apart from the almost total absence of graduates and of the well born, the unbeneficed were in education and social origins no different from the vast majority of incumbents. It was not an invariable rule that the lower a chaplains birth was the longer he remained a chaplain, as we shall see below and as the dark origins of some bishops of that time bear witness. In Chester the kinsmen of barkers, carpenters, glovers, mercers, tailors, and even of a sheriff and a mayor can be found among the unbeneficed.[3] Whether Sir Piers Legh, knight and priest, who on his brass wears a chasuble over his armour and on his chasuble displays a shield of six quarterings, was ever active parochially or merely took orders as a widow took vows, there is no evidence, but he was certainly not beneficed.[4]

The remuneration of chaplains had been fixed by a statute in Henry V's reign which amended and slightly raised ceilings set during the wage crisis and 'freeze' of the mid-fourteenth century.[5] A parish priest was entitled to a maximum of 8 marks or 4 marks with food annually, unless the parish was particularly extensive, when by episcopal licence he could receive 9 marks; other chaplains, those without cure of souls, were permitted to receive 7 marks or 3 marks and food per annum.

The adequacy of these sums deserves careful consideration. No accounts survive of parish chaplains but Miss Wood-Legh has published the domestic accounts of two chantry chaplains of Bridport, extending over seven years from 1453 to 1460.[6] These

---

[1] 'The East Riding Clergy in 1525–26', *Y.A.J.* xxiv, 62–80.

[2] *M.C.A.* p. 8, n. 19.

[3] D. Jones, *The Church in Chester 1300–1540* (Chetham Soc. 3rd series, 7), p. 26.

[4] *A Collection of Lancashire and Cheshire Wills*, ed. W. Ferguson Irvine (Lancs. & Cheshire Record Soc. 30), pp. 31–40; H. Druitt, *A Manual of Costume as Illustrated by Monumental Brasses* (London 1906), p. 83. Compare Thomas de Grey of Merton, Norfolk, who lived for 41 years in priest's orders after the death of his wife in 1514 (Druitt, op. cit., p. 180).

[5] *Statutes of Realm*, 36 Edward III, c. viii; 2 Henry V, 2, c. ii; Lyndwood, III.23.xi.

[6] K. L. Wood-Legh, *A Small Household of the Fifteenth Century.*

two chaplains spent each year on food and fuel an average total of £8. 5s. They lived and ate quite well. Moreover, they entertained at table in the course of a year some hundred guests, many of whom fed there several days, some of whom were there for one week or more; so that in effect three persons were eating regularly in Munden's chantry throughout the year.[1] From this we may reckon that each of them cost for food and fuel £2. 15s. a year, or not much more than the four marks a year for food allowed to a parish priest by Henry V's statute. To this basic expenditure, however, must be added the wages of a servant, at its costliest in the Bridport accounts 26s. 8d. a year, and the cost of clothing.[2] In addition, some chaplains, as even the Exchequer acknowledged,[3] were supporting one or both parents. This latter burden could be advantageous if the chaplain lived in his parents' house, but many stipendiaries, where they were not accommodated in the parsonage or vicarage, had to pay for a room which in 1490 was reckoned in one parish at 6s. 8d. annually.[4] In the 1450s, therefore, a parochial chaplain, at best, living with the incumbent and not requiring a servant, would need £2. 15s. plus clothes money; at the most pessimistic estimate, when having to find a servant, accommodation, clothes and perhaps food and shelter for a parent or two, £4. 8s. 4d. would be an absolute minimum. The statutory maxima of 8 marks for the curate and 7 marks for his assistants met this basic need, the first adequately (particularly as the curate may be presumed to have resided in the manse), the latter by a narrow margin. But serious qualifications have yet to be added: firstly, the stipendiaries were now being frequently taxed; secondly, prices rose phenomenally in the early sixteenth century; thirdly, not all chaplains by any means were paid at the maximum levels.

From the mid-fifteenth century by the device of charitable subsidies levied ostensibly for the aid of the archbishop the stipendiaries of Canterbury Province were taxed, on at least seven occasions, when all the chaplains paid 6s. 8d.; the three

---

[1] In 1454–5 the equivalent of one guest on each of 349 days; in 1460–1 on each of 298, or possibly—for the text is ambiguous—384 days.

[2] Ibid., pp. xxii–xxiii for servants' wages; the cost of clothing is not given in these accounts.

[3] F. R. H. Du Boulay, 'Charitable Subsidies Granted to Archbishops of Canterbury 1300–1489', *B.I.H.R.* xxiii, 158.

[4] *M.C.A.*, p. 57.

23

charitable subsidies recorded in the Northern Province were not levied on the unbeneficed.[1] With Wolsey the example of the Southern Province was regularized into an annual levy of a fifteenth on each chaplain, by which most would pay at least 5s. 4d. p.a. out of an income of £4.[2] Not only would this seriously reduce any clear income which most curates could expect, and annihilate the margin of the stipendiaries' profit, as we have calculated it for the 1450s, but by Wolsey's time these margins had already been obliterated by the price rise.

Two scholars have recently shown that, except for a few isolated years, a long period of stable prices obtained from 1450 until 1518, but that from 1519 until 1530 prices rose to at least 30 per cent and often nearer 70 per cent above the 1450s level; an average increase for the 1520s had been calculated at 39 per cent.[3] The materials from which, and methods by which, these price levels have been calculated hardly allow such confidently precise conclusions to be drawn, but there can be little doubt that they do indicate a price-rise in the 1520s of around 30 per cent above the level of the 1450s. The basic minimum needed in the mid-fifteenth century would have to be revised in the 1520s from £2. 15s. to £3. 13s. plus clothes money, and from £4. 8s. 4d. to £5. 17s. 4d. These figures are offered merely to indicate the scale of the increased needs of the clergy.

Yet in the 1520s many assistant clergy were not receiving even the maximum rates laid down by statute. While the ceilings were very largely adhered to in Lincolnshire, in East Yorkshire in 1525 out of 298 chaplains only twenty-eight received more than £4 and only eight of these above £5; in the archdeaconry of Stafford in 1531 out of 166 chaplains 100 received only £4 p.a., thirty-two £4. 13s. 4d., and nine £5. 6s. 8d.[4] It may be that these tax lists are deliberately distorted to benefit the

---

[1] All those in Canterbury receiving the equivalent of four marks with board, but less than ten marks, that is (*B.I.H.R.* xxiii, 157–8). In York, on the accessions of William Booth, Rotherham and Wolsey (R.I.20, fo. 330v, R.I.23, fo. 294r and Durham Dean and Chapter MS. Reg. Quintum, fo. 156v).

[2] H. E. Salter, *Lincoln Subsidy 1526* (Oxford Historical Soc. o.s. 63), p. v.

[3] E. H. Phelps Brown and S. V. Hopkins, 'Seven Centuries of the Prices of Consumables, Compared with Builders' Wage-Rates', *Essays in Economic History*, ed. E. M. Carus-Wilson (London 1962), ii, 179–96; Y. S. Brenner, 'The Inflation of Prices in Early Sixteenth Century England', *Econ.H.R.* (2nd series) xiv, 227.

[4] *Lincoln Subsidy 1526*, pp. 1–3 for example, and *passim*; 'The East Riding Clergy in 1525–26', *Y.A.J.* xxiv, 62–80; Lichfield MS. B/A/1/17/1 (2), a tax list.

chaplain or else that they conceal from modern eyes payment in kind, but much more needs to be known—if it can be—about their compilation before their grim evidence is disregarded, and it is not to be supposed that gross evasion about a chaplain's stipend on so large a scale could be easily practised in the 1520s. More indigent even than the normal stipendiaries were those hired *ad hoc* in periods of need and paid at the standard rate.[1] It was possible, however, for a chaplain to supplement his income, if not from private sources, without much formality or difficulty by the occasional paid mass for a deceased, or by attendance at a funeral; there is no more eloquent testimony of the value of this last to hard pressed clergy than the funeral in 1524 of Lord Mounteagle who left a small dole to thirty priests who would attend his burial: eighty turned up.[2] In episcopal registers of this era there are few instances of bishops having to coerce chaplains to serve for a modest salary in parishes where the curates were legitimately absent.[3] The words of a fifteenth-century moralist that 'Some men would celebrate all the quicker if the eucharistic bread were turned into gold' lose some of their point against this economic background of the 1520s.[4] The morale of a good many priests must have been destroyed by the economic anxiety of their unbeneficed days or years.

The chaplain lacked the attributes of the rector or vicar: security of tenure, or the freehold of the benefice, and the rule of the parish. The parish priest was engaged by the beneficed clerk or his proctor; the assistant chaplains were hired by the *curatus*, that is the incumbent or the parish priest. We know little about the terms of their engagement beyond the legal provision that no chaplain could be removed without reasonable cause or retained once found guilty of immorality;[5] but it is likely that the parish priest survived as long as he wished or until the benefice changed hands, for there was no obligation upon a new incumbent to re-engage him;[6] the employment of the other chaplains was probably reviewed at more frequent intervals. Tenure would

---

[1] See below p. 64.

[2] *L. & P.* iv(1), No. 235.

[3] As bishops were canonically empowered to do (Lyndwood, III.23.10).

[4] B. M. Burney MS. 356, fo. 112r.

[5] Lyndwood, V.12.

[6] e.g. perhaps John Wilson, chaplain at Hornsea from at least 1481 to 1486, *M.C.A.* p. 7.

certainly depend upon the observance of an oath required of all chaplains before they could begin to work in a parish; this was an oath of obedience to the incumbent, or in his absence to his deputy, and a promise in no way to prejudice the rights and income of the parish church, or to encourage, sustain or favour hatred, scandal or gossip against the rector or vicar.[1] As well as acknowledging the authority of the beneficed over his parish and his assistants, such an oath was also designed to prevent a hired hand from usurping his principal's rights.

Economic pressure, personal insecurity, and social subservience stirred in many chaplains a frenetic desire for a benefice, but since it was the lot of so many clergy for so long in their lives to serve as chaplains, one need not deduce a special inclination among them to embittered negligence or disorder: some were too devoted, some too complacent; in some ambition was an impatient flame early replaced by the ashes of disappointment, whereas others would only gradually abandon hope. What even more than poverty and subservience might corrode their charity and diligence was the system of preferment to benefices.

[1] Lyndwood, I.14.i; Wilkins, iii, 604–5.

III

Preferment

I: *Finding a Patron*

THERE were some 9,000 parish churches in medieval England, though far exceeding the really able ordinands, barely enough to satisfy the innumerable clerics of that time.[1] Consequently competition was fierce, as a few examples will recall. Early in the sixteenth century Geoffrey Philipp of Paignton sent a messenger to inform the patron of Ringmore, who was in London, that the living was vacant; so hard did this messenger spur his horse to London that the creature died.[2] A little later George Hampton, on his way between Canterbury and Dover, met a scholar going from Oxford to Paris, who told him that the benefice of Melton had fallen vacant; Hampton soon struck off a letter to Wolsey, reminding him that Melton had been promised to his son, James Hampton, who was still at school.[3] It was for himself, perhaps, that Thomas Bennett, priest, sent to Wolsey brisk, bare details of the living of Brixton Deverill, just vacant, in the gift of Campeggio, and worth £10 a year.[4] Others put their trust in Cromwell. He was asked by George Lawson to 'be at some point' with the prior of Lewes to whom Lawson was sending his chaplain about a benefice.[5] A priest by the name of Copland

---

[1] D. Knowles, *The Religious Orders in England*, iii, 291, estimates the total at 8,838 of which 3,307 were vicarages, but it is notoriously difficult to be precise in these figures. Mrs. Bowker has shown that in Lincoln diocese there would in fact have been a shortage of qualified candidates but for pluralism which sharpened competition (*Secular Clergy in Lincoln Diocese*, p. 70).

[2] P.R.O., C 1/348/31.

[3] *L. & P.*, iv(2), No. 4660.

[4] Ibid., iv(3), No. 5660.

[5] Ibid., iv(3), No. 83.

ad been promised by Cromwell the parish church of Yardley, but the advowson was still in the hands of Sir William Gascoyne; Copland spent Christmas with two men who were going to use their influence, but he wrote to ask Cromwell, should he meet them, to stress the urgency of the matter.[1] Influence, vigilance and pertinacity were essential for the clerk in search of a benefice. Yet for some men the quest was ended easily and quickly, and there were even some benefices which excited no quest at all.

By far the greatest single patron of livings in England was the king. Not only did he possess many advowsons of his own, but those of tenants in chief so long as they were minors and of deceased bishops during the vacancy of the see also came into his hands. True the Chancellor had the gift of all crown livings valued at less than twenty marks, or during Wolsey's tenure of the office less than £20,[2] but he was not impervious to royal pressure and his chief beneficiaries were the king's clerks in Chancery. When no living was immediately available for one of his clerks, the king made a grant from the Exchequer or from the customs, or, more often, he obliged an abbot- or a bishop-elect to grant a pension until a benefice was vacant. In this way Master Thomas Medfield 'in consideration of faithful and acceptable service to the king [Henry VII] and his most dear mother heretofore performed to their singular pleasure' was granted a £10 annuity from the Exchequer until a living of like or better value could be conferred on him.[3] William Broun, Edward IV's 'continual orator', was to receive a pension of £8 annually from the abbey of Bruern until advanced by that abbey to a benefice of equal value, and William Barlee, Henry VIII's chaplain, one from Barking nunnery.[4] Bishop Stanbury of Hereford was called on to grant a pension to Ranulph Bird, chaplain, until the bishop could provide him with a living, and the bishop-elect of Durham was likewise persuaded by Henry VIII to pay a pension to Robert Vincent, who was still a scholar at Cambridge University, until a sufficient benefice was available.[5]

[1] Ibid., iv(3), No. 5268.
[2] A. F. Pollard, *Wolsey* (Fontana edn.), p. 322.
[3] *Materials for the Reign of Henry VII*, ed. T. D. Hardy (Rolls Series), i, 352.
[4] *C.C.R. 1461–68*, p. 47; *L. & P.* iv(2), No. 3869(17).
[5] *Reg. Stanbury*, ed. A. T. Bannister (C. & Y. Soc.), pp. 7–8; *L. & P.* i(1), No. 132(11).

Some revealing letters of Christ Church, Canterbury,[1] show how hard it was to ignore royal pressure. In one of 1483 the prior regrets that he cannot present the Duke of Gloucester's nominee to All Hallows in Lombard Street; the prior goes on to explain that at the last vacancy the king and queen wanted Thomas Brent presented, but agreed instead to the appointment of Thomas Langton, a singular benefactor of Christ Church, on condition that Brent should have it at the next occasion; the prior had pledged his faith and had renewed his oath after the king's death; he would, however, be pleased to present Gloucester's candidate at the succeeding vacancy. Another letter was written by Henry VII's queen to the prior; its style is gracious, but its tone imperious. After referring to her earlier letters asking the prior for the gift of All Hallows in Lombard Street at the next vacancy, and upon which he gave her the benefice 'at her liberty', she then stated that she had heard of the death of the present incumbent and requested the prior to send her the presentation deed, under the convent seal, 'with a blanke space in the same, to thentent we may name therin suche oon of our chaplayns as we shall think convenient for to be of abilitie to have the charge of the cure ther'. Wolsey himself was sometimes the recipient of these imperative letters: on one occasion Henry desired him, by virtue of his legatine prerogative, to confer the vicarage of Thaxted, in the gift of Stoke-by-Clare college, on the king's chaplain, Master Wilson; a week later Wolsey informed Henry that, being aware of the king's desire to promote Wilson, he had installed him in the vicarage of Wirksworth, valued at a hundred marks or more.[2] Royal patronage, therefore, is not to be measured by counting royal livings.

Meanwhile the king did not neglect his own resources, which ranged from bishoprics and prebends down to parish churches. For many royal clerks parish churches were but the beginning of a career, or a trifling, though not contemptible, addition to an already large income. John Morgan, who died in 1504 bishop of St. David's, twenty years before was presented by the king to Hanslope in Lincoln diocese; that was on 6 October 1485 when he was already a Doctor of Laws and a chaplain to the king.

[1] *Christ Church Letters*, ed. J. B. Sheppard (Camden Soc. n.s.19), pp. 44–45, 64. For similar attempts to exploit the patronage of Durham priory, see below pp. 33–34.
[2] *State Papers, Henry VIII*, i, 311, 318–19.

Three days afterwards he was appointed clerk of the parliaments for life with a grant of £40 a year out of the hanaper. Another nine days passed before he was granted the deanery of the free chapel of Windsor Castle. After a further lapse, this time of nearly two months, he became dean of the collegiate church of St. Mary near the Castle, Leicester. Although he seemed destined for a bishopric, he had to wait till 1496, and then content himself with one of the poorest.[1] By contrast a man who died in the same year as Morgan, but had enjoyed royal patronage much longer without obtaining a see, was Master Edward Underwood.[2] In 1466 he exchanged the vicarage of St. Michael outside Kingate, Winchester, for that of Kingston on Thames. This he left in 1468, also by exchange, on royal presentation to the rectory of St. Margaret Moses in Friday Street, London, which he held till 1482. Before his death in 1504 he had been or was, as well as incumbent of several parish livings, a canon and prebendary of Bridgnorth, master of Cobham college, dean of Middleham, warden of Bridgnorth hospital, and a canon and prebendary at York, St. Paul's and Crediton. Most royal gifts are less spectacular, but hardly less interesting. For example Master Geoffrey Elyse, B.C.L., king's chaplain, was presented to the parsonage of Shipton under Wychwood 'for faithfull service doon unto us, as well beyonde the see as in this owre royaume of England'; John London was not an administrator, but merely a clerk, 'the King's trusty chaplain', who was presented 'by way of charity' to the rectory of Petworth in 1485.[3]

Although royal patronage was extensive, its scope must not be exaggerated. In Hereford diocese during Myllyng's tenure of the see (from 1474 to 1492) 336 livings of all kinds, canonries and chantries as well as rectories and vicarages, were filled, yet the crown explicitly presented only eight candidates.[4] In Norwich diocese from 1503 to 1528 the king and queen filled directly only thirty-nine out of 1,187 vacancies.[5] In the diocese of London during the eight years when Tunstall was its bishop, the king presented seven and the queen two out of nearly three hundred

<hr />

[1] D.N.B., sub nomine; Materials for the Reign of Henry VII, i, 47, 77, 91, 597.
[2] A. B. Emden, Oxford, iii, 1930–1.
[3] Materials for the Reign of Henry VII, i, 47, 84.
[4] Reg. Myllyng, ed. A. T. Bannister (C. & Y. Soc.), pp. 185–202.
[5] Norwich Act Books XIII–XVI, passim. See on these statistics Appendix 1 below.

presentees to benefices vacated during those years.[1] Even accounting for the concealed royal presentations, other patrons were evidently by no means negligible.

Just as the king gave benefices for the support of his servants, so the bishops conferred livings upon their administrators and chaplains. Archbishop Bourgchier appointed Nicholas Bulfynch, chaplain, to be rector of Lambeth in 1472, and the next year, on his resignation, he appointed Master Thomas Aleyn; both these men subsequently became prebendaries of Wingham college, which was also in the archbishop's gift.[2] A few years later Edmund Lychefield, M.A., succeeded, at the archbishop's presentation, Thomas Wynterburn, Ll.D., as rector of Tring, a church later held by Richard Wareham.[3] Lambeth and Tring were reserved for archiepiscopal protégés and the way to their rectories led through Canterbury. Similarly, the bishop of Winchester kept Rimpton rectory in the diocese of Bath and Wells for his officers and the bishops of Worcester regularly presented their lawyers to the living of Henbury.[4] Occasionally there is a hint of sharp practice and sometimes of force on the part of the bishop to benefice his candidate: one of the witnesses in a case in the London consistory court in the early 1520s affirmed that Master Bodlay possessed his vicarage of South Weald *de facto*, 'But whether canonically, he doubted, believing rather the contrary to be true, for he had heard the abbot and certain of the monks of Waltham frequently say that Master Bodlay held this vicarage by presentation of the bishop of London against the will of the abbot and convent, the true patrons'.[5]

Within a diocese the bishop was sometimes the greatest single patron, having a wide variety of livings at his disposal, some *de pleno iure*, others by lapse when the true patron failed to present within six months of a vacancy occurring. On falling vacant every living reverted to the bishop's sequestrator-general who appointed administrators to see that services were performed and

[1] London Guildhall MS. 9531/10, fos. 1r–30v.

[2] *Reg. Bourgchier*, pp. 309, 312, 315, 322.

[3] Ibid., p. 335; *Lincoln Visitations 1517–31*, ed. A. H. Thompson (Lincoln Record Soc. 33), ii, 14.

[4] See the printed registers of Bath and Wells diocese (Somerset Record Soc.), *passim*; for the parish of Henbury, see A. H. Thompson, 'Notes on the Ecclesiastical History of the Parish of Henbury', *Trans. Bristol & Glos. Archael. Soc.* xxxviii, 140–52.

[5] G.L.C., MS. DL/C/207, f. 29r.

the fruits collected during the vacancy; if by the end of six months the patron had failed to present a suitable candidate, the bishop had the right of collation.[1] This usually happened where the living was too poor to attract applications or where the patron, perhaps because of death without direct heirs, was obscure or even unknown. By far the largest part, 101, of the bishop of Norwich's 172 collations to parish churches in the early sixteenth century resulted in this way, about half of the 101 being worth less than £5 and two thirds less than £8. The person to whom the undesirable living was collated no doubt found it unwise to spurn an episcopal offer, but such livings seem to have gone either to men greatly in need of sustenance, like scholars, or else to pluralists who might welcome a modest addition to an already adequate income.[2] Some bishops acquired occasional rights of presentation by the exertion of pressure, perhaps upon a religious house eager for episcopal friendship either because of the bishop's authority in the Church or because of his influence at Court.

To clerks who were neither royal nor episcopal servants laymen offered most hope of promotion, but they naturally looked after their own chaplains and relatives first. Sir John Tiptoft, Earl of Worcester, took care of his chaplain, John Hurleigh, by presenting him to the living of Hanslope in Buckinghamshire.[3] Wolsey had taught the three sons of the Marquess of Dorset at Magdalen College School and an invitation to spend Christmas with the family led to his acquirement of the living of Limington in Somerset.[4]

Quite often a layman purchased the right of next presentation in order to present an unbeneficed relative or protégé, as when Thomas and Margery Hampden in 1465 sought from Thomas Stonor the right of next presentation to any of his benefices worth £20 or more, or, if not, better than 20 marks.[5] The suspicion that the clerk himself may have found the money for the purchase of the advowson, a manoeuvre scarcely distinct from simony, is as hard to prove as it is to dismiss. In 1470

[1] R. L. Storey, *Diocesan Administration in the Fifteenth Century* (St. Anthony's Hall Publications, No. 16), pp. 10–11.
[2] Norwich Act Books XIII–XVI, *passim.*
[3] R. J. Mitchell, *John Tiptoft* (London 1938) p. 15; cf., *C.P.L.* xi, 166.
[4] A. F. Pollard, *Wolsey*, p. 12.
[5] *Stonor Letters*, ed. C. L. Kingsford (Camden Soc. 3rd series 29), i, 69–70.

Richard Counsell was presented to East Clandon rectory by Nicholas Counsell, who had bought the right of next presentation for that turn from Chertsey abbey.[1] For other clerks their families had no need to buy an advowson, being already in possession of one: a celebrated example is John Colet.[2] In 1485 he was presented to the rectory of Dennington in Suffolk by his cousin, Sir William Knevet, and five years later to the rectory of Thurning in Northants by his father, Sir Henry Colet; till 1505 he held the living of Stepney which stood near his father's house and was probably in his gift. But all of these examples are of small significance beside that of Prestwich rectory: it was in the gift of the Longley family and all its known incumbents, at least between 1445 and 1552, were Longleys.[3]

There was a small number of well connected men who were papally dispensed to receive benefices—usually *in commendam*—before, sometimes long before, they were eligible either by age or orders. Between 1447 and 1492 there were ninety-four English beneficiaries of such indults, or on average two a year.[4] Overwhelmingly, they were kinsmen of the great: George Vere, a sixteen year old son of the Earl of Oxford; John Bourgchier, nine years old, kinsman of the king, nephew of the Archbishop of Canterbury and of the Duke of Buckingham; Robert Langton, sixteen years of age and nephew of the Bishop of Salisbury.[5] James Stanley, kinsman of Edward IV, was dispensed when fourteen to receive one, when sixteen two, and when nineteen three benefices 'in administration' until of lawful age, provided no more than two were parish churches; but even before he was sixteen he held the parish churches of Winwick and Hawarden in the gift of a relation of his.[6]

A very large number of parish churches were in the gift of religious houses, but monastic patronage was by no means all a matter of free will. With the pressures exerted on Christ Church, Canterbury, we may compare those letters written to Durham priory by kings, nobles, prelates, magnates and burgesses on

[1] Manning and Bray, *History of Surrey*, iii. 50.
[2] J. H. Lupton, *Life of Colet*, pp. 116–17, 118, 119.
[3] F. Raines, *A Close Catalogue of the Rectors of Prestwich* (Chetham Soc. o.s. 103), pp. 29–30. See also Halsall rectory (*V.C.H. Lancs.*, iii, 189).
[4] *C.P.L.* x–xiv, *passim*.
[5] *C.P.L.* xi, 546, 565–6; ibid., xiv, 9.
[6] Ibid., xiii, 113–14, 617.

behalf of their relatives and clients who sought benefices; eighty-six letters of this kind are extant from the period 1380 to 1500, thirty-one from successive kings, thirty-one from local magnates, and it is indicative of the conflicting claims which the prior had to reconcile that only eleven of the royal and thirteen of the magnate petitions were successful. Clearly monastic patronage conceals the extent of royal and lay influence over the parish clergy.[1] Apart from acceding to *ad hoc* requests of this kind, a religious house could grant an advowson at the next vacancy to a layman or the king, usually in return for payment or goodwill; so common was this practice that Tutbury priory entered the formula of such a grant into its cartulary.[2] Some notable facts emerge from the institution lists in Tunstall's register for London. Of some ninety-six graduates presented to 113 livings, fifty were presented by religious houses. Since they presented 103 incumbents during that period, the non-graduates seem to have had an even chance of patronage from a religious house. If, however, we turn to particular houses we find that Westminster abbey presented sixteen graduates, one-sixth of the total, while of the six presentees of the abbess and convent of Barking, four had degrees. The usual inference is that the houses were bestowing their livings on lawyers and administrators and men of influence who would represent their causes in times of difficulty. This certainly might be alleged against St. Peter's, Westminster, which presented to the church of Sawbridgeworth, Geoffrey Wharton, the vicar-general of the bishop of London.[3] Likewise Peterborough abbey kept the livings of Cottingham, Bringhurst and Oundle almost exclusively for graduates of high repute, with legal skill or administrative influence.[4] Certainly the rectory of Ditcheat in the patronage of Glastonbury abbey had a succession of incumbents to support the usual inference: John Lax and John Gunthorp were humanists and royal ambassadors who spent most of their time in Rome and elsewhere

---

[1] R. Donaldson, 'Sponsors, patrons and presentations to benefices in the gift of the Priors of Durham in the later Middle Ages', *Archaeologia Aeliana* (4th series), xxxviii, 169–77.

[2] *The Cartulary of Tutbury Priory*, ed. A. Saltman (Historical Collections of Staffordshire, 4th series, 4), No. 349; see also F. R. H. Du Boulay's comments, *Reg. Bourgchier*, p. xlii.

[3] R. Newcourt, *Repertorium Ecclesiasticum Parochiale Londinense*, i, 881.

[4] A. H. Thompson, *The English Clergy*, p. 105.

on the continent; William Atwater became in due course bishop of Lincoln, while his successor at Ditcheat was Andrew Ammonius, papal collector in England; John Clerk was a Doctor of Laws and James Fitzjames a Doctor of Divinity.[1] Such a galaxy of learned and influential parsons suggests either that the abbot and convent were subjected to external pressure in their choice, or that they regarded Ditcheat, which was worth £46,[2] as an investment for security. It seems probable that most of the incumbents were acquainted with their successors and that they may even have nominated them to the abbot. Yet the extent to which a monastery preferred graduates to its livings would depend upon the value of those benefices and in Hereford diocese during Myllyng's episcopate there were only eight graduates among the eighty-nine incumbents presented by religious houses.[3]

It was doubtless advantageous when seeking preferment to be a graduate. If his college or university would send no letters of recommendation for him, and though petition rolls for provisions were no longer sent by the universities to the papal curia, the graduate was often, by virtue of his degree, the holder of an office which brought him to the attention of patrons and for which he was chiefly remunerated by a benefice.[4] The promotion of graduates had caused great anxiety earlier in the fifteenth century,[5] but in our period there are few echoes of this problem and graduates are almost unknown among the unbeneficed; very likely patrons were becoming more susceptible to the claims of the educated clergy; more of the laity were financing the studies of young clerks at the universities and themselves had sons who

---

[1] *Reg. Bekynton*, ed. H. C. Maxwell Lyte and M. C. B. Dawes (Somerset Record Soc. 49–50), p. 305; *Regs. Stillington & Fox*, ed. H. C. Maxwell Lyte (Somerset Record Soc. 52), p. 97; *Regs. King & Castello*, ed. H. C. Maxwell Lyte (Somerset Record Soc. 54), pp. 17, 170; *Regs. Wolsey, Clerke, Knight and Bourne*, ed. H. C. Maxwell Lyte (Somerset Record Soc. 55), p. 9.

[2] *Valor Ecclesiasticus*, ed. J. Caley and J. Hunter (Record Commission), i, 152.

[3] *Reg. Myllyng*, pp. 185–202.

[4] *Formularies which bear on the history of Oxford*, ed. H. E. Salter and others (Oxford Historical Soc. n.s. 5), ii, 381–2, a letter to the bishop of London in favour of a Master of Arts; ibid., ii, 395–7, to the pope seeking provision for a Doctor of Laws; ibid., ii, 400–1, from a student together with a testimonial from his master. This is a fourteenth century formulary, but it doubtless served its purpose in the succeeding century.

[5] On the earlier anxieties, see E. F. Jacob, *Essays in the Conciliar Epoch* (2nd edn.), pp. 223–39, and 'On the Promotion of English University Clerks during the Later Middle Ages', *J.E.H.*, i, 172–86.

went to Oxford and Cambridge. That the wealthier livings seldom went to those without degrees is true enough, but that graduates were reserved for the richer benefices is a mistaken notion, for they are found in the diocese of Norwich in the early sixteenth century holding livings worth less than £10 and in several instances even less than £5.[1]

So much for those who had little difficulty in securing a living. They were a minority, though a substantial one; most clerks had to wait considerably longer, according to an analysis of Archbishop Bourgchier's register.[2] How long it could in fact be is suggested by the career of Thomas Orchard, who took eight years to progress from a chaplaincy at Ditcheat in 1468 to his first benefice, the rectory of Weston Bampfylde in 1476; his subsequent career shows that he soon made up for lost time. He vacated Weston Bampfylde in 1478 and vanishes from the records for five years, until 1483; in that year he was described as chaplain and was instituted to the chantry of Sir Harry Hussee and others in Wells cathedral, which he continued to hold till 1497, despite the acquisition in 1484 of Evercreech vicarage. In 1490 he was described as Master Thomas Orchard, the first indication that he was a graduate. In 1509 he was again called Master, but he is also described as a Bachelor of Canon Law and as a priest; this was on the occasion of his institution to Frome vicarage. That year he was one of the proctors of the clergy of Convocation. The next year he died, not among the *sublimes et litterati* perhaps, but certainly among the better educated, although he had spent many of the early years as a stipendiary chaplain.[3]

II: *Simony*

Those who could not wait as long as Orchard for a benefice and had more money and fewer scruples than he had, caught a patron's attention by the glint and chink of gold and silver.

---

[1] e.g. Norwich Act Book XVI, fos. 52v, 62r, 63r, 63v, 65v–66r.

[2] *Reg. Bourgchier*, p. xli. In Lincoln diocese an average of five years elapsed between ordination as a priest and admission to a benefice (M. Bowker, *Secular Clergy in Lincoln Diocese*, pp. 72–73).

[3] *Regs. Stillington & Fox*, pp. 24, 63, 75, 122, 127, 163; *Regs. King & Castello*, pp. 2, 135, 140, 146.

Among the most blatant offenders was John Spynney, perpetual
chaplain of the chantry of St. Katherine in Bridport.[1] In 1457 he
entered into a bond to pay John Kyrkeby, clerk, 20s. at each
Michaelmas until £50 had been paid or until he had been advanced to a benefice valued at 20 marks a year; when beneficed
he was to pay 5 marks each Michaelmas until the £50 was paid,
or, if the benefice was worth £20, £5 a year; he further contracted not to refuse a benefice if offered to him. John Clerk,
priest of Salisbury diocese, was rather more dissembling:[2] when
seeking papal absolution for simony,[3] he alleged that 'for the
sake of greater safety, [he] gave in deposit certain money to
William Temmes, a layman, in order that he should preserve
it for him, and that the said layman, without John's knowledge,
paid part of it, namely seven English marks, to another layman,
the patron of the parish church of Hilperton in Salisbury diocese,
in order that he should present John thereto, then void'. John
was presented and instituted and held the church for six years
after he heard of that simony. It was an obvious stratagem to
conceal simony by giving the money to a middleman with no
advowsons to his credit. Perhaps, too, it was natural to approach
an unfamiliar patron through a common acquaintance. We have
seen above how simony might be disguised in the purchase of the
right of next presentation by a relative, and we shall note later
how a pension might conceal simony. Sometimes the simonist
was himself exposed to exploitation, as Robert More discovered:
he agreed to pay Athelstan Atley, vicar of Eastleigh, £6 for his
resignation and his own institution and induction; he bound himself in writing.[4] Alas, Athelstan had already been deprived of
the living before the transaction. More, with audacious frankness
about the whole transaction, sought the assistance of the Lord
Chancellor, who was at that time no less than the archbishop of
Canterbury! The extent of simony defies measurement, concealed as it often was by transactions such as John Clerk's
and by grants of pension and next presentation; moralists and
preachers, however, had no doubt of its serious dimensions and

[1] C.C.R. 1454–61, pp. 262–3.
[2] C.P.L. xii, 334.
[3] Papal absolution was only required when the incumbent himself had wittingly
purchased the living; if his friends had done so without his knowledge, the bishop
could dispense him (Lyndwood, I.4.ii, note a).
[4] P.R.O., C 1/340/28.

in 1509 the archbishop of Canterbury granted powers to ordinaries to investigate suspect simonists in their diocese, to try them and to punish the convicted.[1] Yet insidious as the practice of simony undoubtedly seems, it did not necessarily produce incumbents any worse than those who emerged by the normal and canonical processes of obtaining a benefice; indeed, it must frequently have resulted from the frustration and cynicism which the normal procedures provoked, if not from many a man's inability to distinguish the *officium* from the *benefiium*, a lay fee.

III: *Admission, Institution and Induction*

Patrons regarded advowsons as a source of profit through sale, or as a means of economy as maintenance for servants. There is little except an occasional vague reference in the letters of patrons to suggest that they were particularly exercised over the quality and suitability of their candidates: Gascoigne and Latimer, a century apart in time, acknowledged this.[2] It is true that the mayor and aldermen of London laid down careful directions for the appointment of suitable incumbents to St. Peter's, Cornhill, and St. Margaret Pattens,[3] but the average patron was not unlike the Pastons: in 1478 when Margaret's presentee to Oxnead was refused admission by the vicar-general, William Paston contacted the archdeacon, Nicholas Goldwell, and urged him to persuade the bishop to do Paston justice, and nowhere in his letter did William discuss the quality of the clerk, but he railed instead against the futility of delay and about the small value of the living.[4] This attitude was more ruthlessly and blatantly exhibited by John Neville, Lord Montague, who in 1471 imprisoned John Mason, rector of Richmond and prebendary of Norton, until he resigned both benefices in favour of Montague's chaplain, Oliver Bland.[5] Far more typical and perhaps more

[1] *Reg. Mayew*, pp. 107–8.
[2] J. Gairdner, *Lollardy and the Reformation in England*, i, 244–5; *Sermons by Hugh Latimer*, ed. G. E. Corrie (Parker Soc.), pp. 186, 290.
[3] *Cal. Letter Book 'K'*, ed. R. R. Sharpe, pp. 310–11 for St. Peter's, Cornhill; *Cal. Letter Book 'L'*, ed. R. R. Sharpe, p. 159 for St. Margaret Pattens.
[4] *Paston Letters*, vi, No. 937.
[5] *C.P.L.* xiii, 307.

innocent were the unconscious assumptions of Alice Hungerford, widow of a London draper; in 1484, when her late
husband's apprentice, Thomas Everard, then about twenty-two
years of age, revealed a wish to become a priest, she promised to
provide him with a benefice, because of the favour her husband
had had for him, and that same year sought out a living.[1] She
rode with Everard to Stourbridge[2] fair to meet there Robert
Gryme, rector of St. Olave's, Southwark; Gryme offered her the
vicarage of Tottenham, worth £20 a year, if she would pay
20 marks to Wyggmore, the vicar there, for the benefice and
other expenses; Mistress Alice thereupon addressed these revealing words to Everard: 'I give you this benefice that you
shall pray for the souls of my husband and your benefactors'.
Thomas, however, was a pious young man and sought advice
elsewhere about the legality of this simoniacal transaction; dis-
suaded from accepting it, he announced that he could have no
benefice by such a pact. Perhaps to avenge herself on Everard's
ingratitude she had him fetch to her, soon after Christmas,
Thomas Kirkham, curate at Tottenham, and concluded with the
latter (in Gryme's presence) an agreement whereby immediately
upon his institution and induction to Tottenham vicarage he
should pay her 20 marks (£13. 6s. 8d.)—for subsequent default
of which he was imprisoned in the debtor's prison at Ludgate.
The attitude of the clerics, Gryme, Wyggmore and Kirkham, is
as telling as Mistress Hungerford's; the scruples of Everard,
however, should not be forgotten in this context; eight years
later, by 1492, he was thirty years old and still unbeneficed, the
parochial chaplain of Isleworth.

It was necessary, then, that the presentees should be scrutinized by someone for their suitability, but even before this, if
there were the least doubt, the ordinary had to ascertain, by
local sworn deposition, that the living was in fact vacant and that
the presentee's patron was entitled to the *ius patronum*.[3] If the
rightful patron proved indifferent to the office and requirements
which his presentee was to fulfil, the Church could still exercise
discretion by means of the procedure for admission.

[1] London Guildhall MS. 9065, fos. 109r–v.

[2] Styrbridge in MS: no London fair is known by this name; perhaps the celebrated Stourbridge fair of Cambridge is indicated, improbable as this seems from the
context.

[3] Lyndwood, III.6.ii, note *l*.

A presentee had to be admitted by the bishop to his living within two months of presentation, unless he were found unsuitable or objections were raised against him. Before admission, therefore, some examination of his fitness was necessary. He had to be in major orders, a deacon at least for a vicarage, and would be expected to produce letters of ordination, although if he were of the same diocese these could be verified in the registers of the see. He had, moreover, to be at least twenty-four years of age, sound in body, legitimate in birth, and holding no other incompatible benefice. For any defect in these matters he would be required to produce appropriate papal dispensations. The enquiry, however, was very much dependant upon the candidate's own integrity since his want of orders, years, bodily soundness, legitimacy and the fact of plurality were not always readily apparent to examiners. It is plain from the case of Dominic Civi, cited below, and from others adduced by Dr. Oxley, that candidates were often tempted to make sure of their second cure of souls before incurring the cost of a papal dispensation, and that bishops perhaps were temporarily satisfied with assurances that a licence was being actively sought; the case of Civi makes it just as clear, however, that if a man was admitted in this way, the need of dispensation was not forgotten.[1]

Most of the clergy who were admitted to livings for which they were not adequately ordained were usually men of undoubted learning, men, for example, like Linacre, who held the livings of Mersham, Hawkhurst and Wigan before he was priested.[2] They were often the same men who, unable to appear in person for admission and institution, were represented by a proctor who bound them to attend subsequently for examination, though such men were rarely in need of close scrutiny: John Lax, rector of Street, whose brother was his proctor, would hardly expect to be tested for learning which had made him an abbreviator of papal letters.[3] Many of these men were already beneficed elsewhere and armed with papal licences for pluralism, so that the task of examining them again for admission was not unwisely neglected.

[1] See Appendix 2(a) below, and J. E. Oxley, *The Reformation in Essex*, pp. 34–35.
[2] G. T. O. Bridgeman, *History of the Church and Manor of Wigan* (Chetham Soc. n.s. 15), i, 73, 82, 83, 87.
[3] *C.P.L.* x-xii, *passim.*

Another group usually represented by proctors at admission comprised those who were dispensed to receive orders and benefices for which they were unfitted by their youth; numbering some ninety in England between 1447 and 1492, they could not be said to constitute a major abuse, and in so far as most of them were the sons of nobles, magnates, and even bishops, they were never likely to inflict themselves in person upon their parishioners.

Against papal dispensations the bishop was powerless; even against the lay, if not also the ecclesiastical, patron his authority, if ill-defined, had real limits. Had bishops punctiliously employed the admission procedure to eradicate patronal irresponsibility, it is unlikely that political, legal and constitutional conflict would have been averted. Nevertheless, some bishops and their deputies showed no hesitation in rejecting the scandalously unfit, as three examples will show. In 1479 Margaret Paston was eager to present to a benefice her son Walter, below the canonical age and untonsured; William Pykenham, the chancellor of the diocese, wrote to her that he thought it 'not goodly neither Godly', that a dispensation was unlikely to be obtained from Rome, and that he hardly dared to mention the matter to the bishop lest the latter should think it showed 'grete sympylness' on her part.[1] Some years later in York diocese Lord Clifford presented a clerk to the benefice of Londesborough which provoked the vicar-general to write to him, 'surely I cane not (of my conscience) admytte hym to itt, for his connynge is marvyllus slendur. I have seyne few prestis so symple lerned in my liffe'.[2] A year or two later a presentee for a church in Norwich diocese was found on examination by the bishop to be 'unfit for that church or any other in the diocese'.[3] Others, less objectionable, were admitted on condition that they studied at a school for a year.[4]

For the ceremony of institution a document known as a letter of institution was prepared beforehand, based upon information in the presentation deed.[5] During the ceremony, the clerk knelt

[1] *Paston Letters*, iii, 239.
[2] *Clifford Letters of the Sixteenth Century*, ed. A. G. Dickens (Surtees Soc. 172), p. 84.
[3] Norwich Act Book XIV, among the unfoliated memoranda inserted between fos. 60v and 61r.
[4] See below p. 77.
[5] For what follows in this and the next paragraph see K. Major, 'Fifteenth

before the bishop or his deputy and held in his hand the seal appendant to the letter from which the bishop read aloud the words, 'I institute you to this benefice to have the cure of souls; receive your cure and mine'. Canon law required that the clerk should be given a ring, cup, staff, or something in the nature of livery of seisin as a token of possession. When and where the institution took place, whether the clerk was there in person or by proctor,[1] what pension, if any, had been granted to the retiring incumbent or to a previous one—all these details were usually endorsed on the presentation deed by the registrar and later copied into the bishop's register. When the institution was over, now having the right to enter into his glebe and take the tithes of his benefice, the clerk was given a mandate of induction for the archdeacon or whoever was its addressee.

Induction gave the presentee freehold possession of the glebe and tithes of his benefice; that is to say he could grant them, and sue and be sued for them at common law. In most cases the archdeacon was ordered to induct, but usually he delegated another to perform the ceremony. In this he took the clerk by the hand, laid it upon the key or the ring of the church door, or, if there were neither, upon any part of the wall of the church or churchyard, and said, 'By virtue of this mandate, I do induct you into real, actual and corporal possession of this church C with all rights, profits and appurtenances thereto belonging'; he then opened the door and put the clerk into the church, after which it was customary for the latter to ring the bells to signify to the parishioners his possession.[2]

On the costs of these operations such fugitive documentation as survives discourages too much confidence in the commentaries of lawyers and the provisions of legislators. According to the Canterbury Convocation of 1421 institution should have cost no more than 12s., and in Norwich in the early sixteenth century we find that a fee of either 10s. or 12s. was required of the

[1] On 19 August 1511 at the Norwich palace of the bishop, Simon Fyncham was instituted to the church of Ringsted Parva in the person of Francis Mountford, *generosus* (Norwich Act Book XV, fo. 43v).
[2] For a vivid, though not a typical, induction see below, Appendix 2(a).

Century Presentation Deeds in the Lincoln Diocesan Record Office', *Studies in Medieval History presented to F. M. Powicke*, ed. R. W. Hunt and others, pp. 456–8, and R. Phillimore, *Ecclesiastical Law*, pp. 354, 357–8, 359.

candidate, some inscrutable differential operating.[1] The mandate
or certificate of induction should cost a shilling, but for the
induction itself the archdeacon was entitled to charge 3s. 4d., or
his official, needing a smaller train, 2s., which was to cover their
expenses and the cost of food for their servants; in the archdeaconry of Wiltshire, however, at the turn of the century 6s. 8d.
was the invariable fee.[2] In reality the cost to the presentee of
getting into his benefice may have been far greater, for the
Petition of the Commons against the Clergy in 1532 spoke of the
archdeacons' officials not only exacting large sums for institution
and induction, but also extorting bonds for the payments of first
fruits.[3] John Rand, priest, certainly entered into a bond to pay
first fruits at his induction to Scruton, and the case of Alexander Penhill who claimed that he was compelled to pay Master
William Piers, the official of the archdeacon of Cornwall, £20
before he could be inducted by him into the benefice of St. Logan,
Cornwall, raises suspicions of others where the victim was not so
astute, or so affluent, as to pay up and then seek redress in
Chancery.[4] In Norwich diocese, however, first fruits to the bishop
had long been a regular obligation upon each newly instituted
incumbent; Sir John Paston in a well-known letter recalled how
the parson of Oxnead paid first fruits of fourteen marks and
hinted that if the parson were 'wytty and have favour abowt the
Byschops offycers' he would have fourteen years to pay it at a
mark a year, so long as he could find sureties for payment;
but a glance at one of the more revealing Norwich registers
suggests that the bishop was both less forebearing and less
capricious than this, for rarely, whatever the sum, were more
than eight instalments at two a year exceeded and where re-
missions occurred they were usually to relieve hardship.[5] There
is no denying that it was a most substantial addition to the normal
burdens of an incumbent during his first years in a living.

[1] E. F. Jacob, *Reg. Chichele* (C. & Y. Soc.), i, p. cl; Norwich Act Book XIV,
fos. 71v–73r, 74r, 81v, 129v, 143v–144v, 147v, 148v, 162r, 163r.

[2] Lyndwood, III.6.iv; P.R.O., E 135/8/31 (an account book of the archdeacon of
Wiltshire 1497–1501), fos. 2r, 4v, 7v, 10r, where twenty-four inductions are recorded.

[3] *Documents Illustrative of English Church History*, ed. H. Gee and W. J. Hardy
(London 1914), pp. 149–50.

[4] A. H. Thompson, 'Registers of the Archdeacon of Richmond', *Y.A.J.* xxxii
137–8; P.R.O., C 1/255/9, 10, though this seems, from the sum alleged, a grotesque
charge.

[5] *Paston Letters*, v, No. 934, and the Norwich Act Books XIV and XV, *passim*.

IV: *Exchanges*

When all this was completed the clerk was beneficed. More than talent, wealth and good birth determined what benefices a man got, for vacancies might occur at inopportune times and in distant places and even without being known to any save local men. A cleric generally took what benefice he could and found means later of advancing his fortunes, if he wanted to, by simony, by connection, or by exchange.

Exchange was a practice which first became noteworthy in the thirteenth century and reached a climax verging on scandal towards the end of the fourteenth. During most of Courtenay's tenure of the see of Canterbury (1381–96) nearly all admissions were the result of exchange and the same was true of other sees; the frequency with which individuals were exchanging livings was becoming notorious; 'chopchurch' had become a common and unflattering colloquialism for men who engaged in, and particularly for those who arranged, these transactions;[1] the drift and progress of incumbents to London by means of exchange, and the existence of traffickers and 'rings' trading in benefices called forth condemnation in 1391, but the frequency of exchange was not significantly reduced until the third and fourth decades of the fifteenth century.[2] During the period 1450–1530 it is difficult to obtain precise figures, for though some exchanges were recorded in the episcopal registers, others only occur in the act books of vicars-general. In Tunstall's London register only eleven out of 271 admissions involved exchange; this figure may be slightly increased by consulting the concurrent vicar-general's act book to some sixteen, but the total is far from grave or scandalous.[3] In the first twenty-six years of Bourgchier's

[1] e.g; P.R.O., C 1/16/368; G. G. Coulton, *Medieval Panorama* (Fontana edn.), i, 156.

[2] I. J. Churchill, *Canterbury Administration*, i, 111–12; A. H. Thompson, *The English Clergy*, p. 107. In the registers of Lichfield, London and York, for example, no significant slackening in exchanges is observable until the 1430s and 1440s. See also for Norwich E. F. Jacob, 'Thomas Brouns, Bishop of Norwich 1436–45', *Essays in British History*, ed. H. R. Trevor-Roper, p. 73, where he notes a contemporaneous decline there too.

[3] London Guildhall MS. 9531/10, fos. 1–30; G.L.C., MS. DL/C/330.

tenure of Canterbury only sixty-seven exchanges are recorded, less than three a year, in fact.[1] The idea that clergy exchanged benefices for financial gain scarcely bears examination: of five licences in the London vicar-general's act book, permitting incumbents to negotiate for exchange, three contain specific reference to settling a pension, and the others imply that, for no licence would be needed merely to contact another incumbent and to propose an exchange;[2] when George Percy exchanged the living of Thame with John Parker for South Benfleet, they agreed 'that all the profites that shuld growe by reason of the seid benefices at Ester next after the seid permutacion shuld egally be divided betwixte' them.[3] A possible explanation for the exchange of pairs of benefices close to each other (e.g. Chaldon and Warlingham, Mickleham and Puttenham, and Clapham and Battersea in Surrey), may be that the incumbents found the parishioners unfriendly or uncongenial and wished to move, but not too far away from an area in which they may have been born:[4] there must have been several like the vicar who came to Margery Kempe to know 'whedyr he xuld mor plese God to Levyn hys cure & hys benefyce or to kepe it stylle, for hym thowt he profyted not among hys parysshonys'.[5] Or it may be that only one party was really interested in exchange; the man on his way to London or to a lucrative benefice found it easier, perhaps, to advance by short quick moves, and found that there were a number of incumbents willing to make a change which was refreshing, but not drastic. Perhaps William Mountforth, who exchanged Puttenham for Mickleham in 1507 and died in 1513 incumbent of Streatham, was one of these ambitious men.[6] Some of those who changed with him and men like him may have been graduates who at first accepted a living wherever they could find a patron and then, once assured of an income, looked round for a living nearer to (or further from) their home or family. Thomas Goldwell tried in vain and at great

---

[1] *Reg. Bourchier, passim.*

[2] G.L.C., MS. DL/C/330, fos. 2r, 90v, 95r, 108r, 164r.

[3] P.R.O., C 1/345/26.

[4] *Reg. Martival,* ed. K. Edwards (C. & Y. Soc.), i, 324–5, has several other useful references to the variety of reasons behind exchanges; though from the early fourteenth century, some of them are perennial.

[5] *The Book of Margery Kempe,* ed. S. B. Meech and H. E. Allen (E.E.T.S., o.s. 212), p. 53.

[6] Manning and Bray, *History of Surrey,* iii, 389, 395.

cost to exchange his living of Thaxted with the parson of Ayleston where he had been born.[1] Sometimes the exchange of benefices was merely to enable a translated bishop to take his favourite
administrators to his new see, and there is even one instance
where an incumbent was urged to exchange for disciplinary
reasons in order to remove himself from the jurisdiction of
York's dean and chapter.[2] Others, as Miss Churchill suggests,
may have exchanged to avoid the penalties for pluralism, but
this would hardly account for exchanging one cure of souls for
another.[3]

The nature of exchange, the survival of 'benefice agents', and
several other aspects of acquiring a benefice at the end of the
fifteenth century are well illustrated by the following case from
the diocese of London. Some time in July 1491 John Lyall, a
chantry priest (*divina celebrans*) in the church of St. James in
Garlickhithe, London, was eager to change his living, and
William Catcher offered to help him.[4] In Catcher's house a meeting was arranged with Thomas Kirkham, vicar of Tottenham,
and exchange was discussed. Kirkham objected that it would be
foolish for him to exchange a benefice worth £20 for one worth
£15, and when Lyall offered a pension he agreed to ask the
bishop for a licence to negotiate it. Afterwards Kirkham had
doubts about the wisdom of seeking a licence for a pension and
thus exposing the whole transaction to episcopal notice, and
when some six weeks later they met again, this time in Le
Taberd Inn in 'le Ryall' where Thomas Cape lived, he eventually
induced Lyall to agree to pay him £25 when securely possessed
of Tottenham; thereupon two witnesses were called into the
room to see Lyall hand over 6s. 8d. to Kirkham as the first of a
series of payments in token of the promised £25; Lyall, it

[1] P.R.O., C 1/27/425.
[2] R. L. Storey, *Diocesan Administration in the Fifteenth Century*, pp. 23–24;
R.As.55, fo. 187v.
[3] I. J. Churchill, *Canterbury Administration*, i, 111–12.
[4] London Guildhall MS. 9065, fos. 104v–105v, 107r–108v, 109r–v: depositions
in a case before the bishop's commissary in St. Paul's Cathedral, March 1492; we
have the testimony of several men, but since we are ignorant of the charge (except
that it concerned Kirkham) and since some of the witnesses may have been lying
for self defence and all of them were recording hardly memorable events which had
occurred several months before, it is not always easy to reconcile their conflicting
statements; the outlines of their stories, however, bear sufficient resemblance to
each other to make possible the above reconstruction.

seems, still had scruples for he refused to deliver the money directly, 'hoping to ease his conscience somewhat' by giving the 6s. 8d. instead to Cape who in turn surrendered it to Kirkham; on subsequent occasions in September Lyall handed over further instalments, apparently by his own hands, to a total of £8. Whatever the mysteries and scandals attaching to exchange, the effects on parochial life were far from sinister. If the persons exchanged in order to get away from an uncongenial parish, the result was probably beneficial; exchange was one remedy for incompatibility. And if one of the parties was merely *en route* to a wealthy living, the system of exchange made him no worse; it enabled parishes to be rid of him more quickly, even though more had to suffer his incumbency; the sooner an ambitious parson or vicar obtained his desired benefice, the better for all other parishes. Moreover, it is likely that such a man was often a pluralist and absentee; the brevity of his stay may scarcely have been noticed by his parishioners. Brief incumbencies were not uncommon and if any evils resulted from this, the practice of resigning one living in order to secure another is of greater significance than exchange. In short, in our period, neither in extent nor in effects were exchanges scandalous or detrimental.

V: *Conclusions*

These means by which the clergy secured the benefices which they desired were a principal obstacle to the Church getting the incumbents which it deserved. The abundance of clergy and the short supply of livings made an advowson a valuable, even a marketable, commodity, which could be used to indulge relatives, to remunerate servants, to please influential friends, or to beguile potential enemies; the owner could even sell it, or the right of next presentation, if not directly to a clerk, then to his relative. Yet so long as the advowson was construed as a lay fee and subject only to royal jurisdiction, so long as it was regarded legally and popularly as a piece of real property or merely as the appurtenance of a manor, over its disposition the Church could exercise no direct control. The ecclesiastical authorities took what precautions they could to ensure that it was not abused, that only suitable candidates were admitted to livings, but their real, as contrasted with their legal, power for thwarting patrons was distinctly limited, and if the candidate satisfied the letter of canon law in regard to his age, birth, physique, orders, and competence, no one challenged his sense of vocation and no one was curious about his piety. Indeed, ecclesiastical patrons were quite as indifferent to these two things as any layman. Nor was it only the beneficed who suffered by this system, for the way in which patronage was observed to be exercised must have had a demoralizing effect upon the aspiring unbeneficed; many must have concluded with a later commentator that 'yf a preest can flatter smothly, yf he wyll keape you [the patron] company at bankettynge, disynge and cardynge, runne with you of huntyng and hawkynge, whiche thynges draw after them al kind of vices, he shall be called a good felowe, & on suche ye wyll bestowe your benefices, yf money wyll let you gyve them frely'.[1] The astonishing thing is that this system of preferment was not more damaging to the religious life of the nation.

[1] J. W. Blench, *Preaching in England in the Late Fifteenth and Sixteenth Centuries*, p. 241, citing the words of Cuthbert Scott, Bishop of Chester in Mary's reign; compare the words a century earlier of Carpenter about clergy who 'tire and sweat to obtain church dignities, one in the king's kitchen, another in a bishop's court and a third in the service of a temporal lord' (G. R. Owst, *The Destructorium Viciorum of Alexander Carpenter*, p. 15).

IV

Absenteeism

I: *The Act of 1529*

In 1529 when the king was beginning his intimidation of the Church in England among the first objects of attack was non-residence. A statute of that year, which professed to be for the better service of ecclesiastical cures, dealt, in some detail and with some severity, with absenteeism and pluralism.[1] Henceforward these offences were to be tried in lay courts and treated with appropriate penalties; benefit of clergy was explicitly denied, and, as was the custom at that time,[2] the laity were encouraged to inform against offenders by the lure of half the fine. The fines were substantial: £10 for each offence of absence 'wilfully by the space of one moneth togather or by the space of two monethes to be accompted at severall tymes in any one yere'; £20 for obtaining from the court of Rome or elsewhere any kind of dispensation for pluralism or non-residence contrary to the act. Anyone who already held a cure of souls worth more than £8 per annum would automatically deprive himself of it by obtaining another cure of souls. Whether the statute was doing more than establish implicitly the right of the Crown to limit the application of the papal dispensing power in England, whether it was a serious measure of reform provoked by a scandalous abuse which the Church was unable or unwilling to curb, and whether in fact it would transform the scale of the practices which it purported to restrain are questions which deserve closer scrutiny.

[1] *Statutes of Realm*, 21 Henry VIII, 13, c. ix–xviii.
[2] G. R. Elton, 'Informing for Profit', *Cambridge Historical Journal*, xi, 149–67.

II: *The Men and Their Reasons*

That non-residence was extensive and not altogether unnecessary or unjustified will become apparent from a study of some typical absentees. Many of these were pluralists and the two problems of absenteeism and pluralism are almost inseparable: there was only legal objection to the latter when it involved absence from a benefice with cure of souls.[1] Many absentees who were pluralists would hardly have been resident had they held only one instead of several benefices: they were absent because they were engaged in some administrative or judicial work for some master, ecclesiastical or lay; for such work they were remunerated with more than one benefice. The truth of this was frankly acknowledged by the statute of 1529 which exempted from the penalties for its violators the chaplains of the royal household, of royal councillors, of prelates and of the nobility. There were, however, absentees who were simply pluralists, fulfilling no other offices within the Church or State; from the nature of preferment they were largely men of elevated social origins and with good connections among the patrons. Those from Lincoln diocese have been identified and illustrated by Mrs. Bowker and there they appear to form a significant proportion of the non-resident incumbents.[2]

It is impossible to estimate the numbers of beneficed clergy employed respectively by king, nobles and bishops. Although the king's patronage was extensive, incumbents who owed their livings to the service of nobles and knights were much more numerous than royal presentees. Bishops' chaplains, diocesan administrators and ecclesiastical lawyers, nearly all holding one parish church or more, amounted to a formidable number. Apart from the simple pluralists, the majority of non-resident rectors and vicars will be found in one of these groups; certainly other absentees occur much less frequently in contemporary records.

A royal clerk and master in Chancery, who was known, by

[1] A. H. Thompson, 'Pluralism in the Medieval Church', *A.A.S.R.* xxxiii, 63.
[2] M. Bowker, *Secular Clergy in Lincoln Diocese*, pp. 97, 101, 193–213. It is probable that were more information about their careers available, the extent of this group would not prove so impressive. See my review of her book in *E.H.R.*

name at least, in several parishes, was John Jamys. He appears in the records first in 1461, when, with another, he is ordered to deliver wheat, arrested by them, to the steward of the royal household.[1] In January 1484 he was presented to Mundesley parish church in Norwich diocese, in February to Balinghem in the Marches of Calais, and in November to a third portion of Crewkerne in the diocese of Bath and Wells. The following year he was presented to Little Cressingham in Norwich diocese, two years later to Berkswell in Coventry and Lichfield diocese and to Coston in Lincoln diocese. He held Coston till 1493; meanwhile in May 1492 he was presented to Old Romney in Canterbury diocese and before June he resigned Pihen in the diocese of Thérouanne. Ten years later he died. It is doubtful if he ever set foot in his benefices: none was in London or even nearby; two were across the Channel. A chancery clerk, servant of the Yorkists and Tudors, rewarded with parochial livings; he is typical of a whole class of absentees.

A more august example of royal servants is Alexander Legh, who was almoner to Edward IV, his ambassador to Scotland and his representative at the Council of Berwick.[2] In all, he held four rectories: Ditton in Ely diocese from 1468; Spofforth in York diocese from 1481 to 1499; Houghton le Spring in Durham diocese from 1490 to 1500; and St. Bride's in the City of London. They were widely scattered and held, for some time at least, simultaneously; furthermore, he had other livings, notably prebends at York (from 1471), Howden (1478–99), and Ripon (1481–91), as well as the mastership of Sherborne hospital (1471–1501); from 1490 he was temporal chancellor of Durham, and from 1491 so infirm that he had to resign his prebend at Ripon. Rarely could he have been resident. Legh was no mere clerk, but an active diplomat and administrator in the north of England, who was rewarded not only with parish churches, but also with the less onerous and often more lucrative prebends of cathedral and collegiate churches.

There was a third type of royal servant: the courtier. The

[1] C.P.R. 1461–67, p. 8; C.P.R. 1476–85, pp. 414, 410, 500; C.P.R. 1485–94, pp. 29, 170, 194, 373, 381, 449. He does not seem to have obtained Crewkerne: the registers of Fox and Stillington have no mention of him.
[2] For the following details of Legh's career see Acts of the Chapter of Ripon, ed. J. T. Fowler (Surtees Soc. 64), p. 189; and Plumpton Correspondence, ed. T. Stapleton (Camden Soc. o.s. 4), pp. 52, 104–6.

court poets, Carmelianus and Skelton, are notable examples, but more typical and more richly endowed with livings was Thomas Brent, who began his career at the court of Edward IV as a Licenciate in Civil Law and ended it in Henry VIII's reign a Doctor of Laws and a considerable pluralist.[1] He held Chilcombe rectory in 1469 and perhaps later, Great Chart rectory from 1473 until his death, the parsonage of Sevington until 1480, of Birdbrook from 1480 to c. 1494, the vicarage of Halifax until 1502, and the rectory of St. Olave's in Southwark 1502–7. In the course of his career he was almoner and later executor to Edward IV's queen, and chaplain to Henry VII; for these services he was also rewarded with the hospital of St. Bartholomew by Rye, the deanery of South Malling, and prebends in Warwick and London.

Royal presentees seem far more numerous than the domestic chaplains of the nobility and knight class because records of them are so much more accessible: the patent rolls abound with royal clerks; to identify the chaplains of nobles and magnates and gentry, however, requires a much more painstaking search. Nevertheless, this class of absentee may be found brilliantly illuminated in the *Paston Letters* where Thomas Howes and James Gloys, parsons respectively of Castle Combe and Stokesley, may be watched at work rarely concerned with, and sometimes far from, their spiritual duties.[2] Like the servants of the Pastons, Richard Danson, vicar of Carlton 1503–9, was busy about the estate affairs of his lord, Clifford.[3] In 1472 Master Henry Key was absent from his rectory of Handsworth in the service of Lord Talbot and in fact he had not been there once in a year.[4] Equally characteristic is Robert Gilberth, who while a clerk in the chancery, and a chaplain, of Edward, Duke of Buckingham, was presented by him to the living of Worthen in Hereford diocese in 1518; soon after the death of Buckingham Gilbert is found in 1526 (though still rector of Worthen) in the retinue of Lord Berners going to Calais.[5] The accounts kept by Richard Warde, steward for Lord John Hussey during the

---

[1] Emden, *Oxford*, i, 260, refers to him as Brente.
[2] *Paston Letters, passim.*
[3] *Clifford Letters*, pp. 90–92.
[4] York Visitations, fos. 34r–v.
[5] *L. & P.* iv(1), Nos. 1985, 2085; *Reg. Bothe*, ed. A. T. Bannister (C. & Y. Soc.), p. 331.

1530s, are still preserved in the Public Record Office, and though he notes there that he is a priest, he carefully omits all mention of his livings of Pickworth and Moorby which he had held since 1519, and Stickney which he held during the 1520s and perhaps into the 1530s.[1] So much for the requirement of canon law that no clerk beneficed or in holy orders (minor as well in Lyndwood's opinion), was to be employed as a bailiff or steward by laymen.[2] In view of the persons exempted in the 1529 act, Howes, Gloys, Danson, Key, Gilberth and Warde must represent a very large class indeed, elusive perhaps but by no means insignificant.

Archbishops and bishops, dignitaries of the State no less than of the Church, likewise had their officers and chaplains. John Perch, M.A., rector of Clapham in Winchester diocese from 1460, was chaplain to Wayneflete, bishop of Winchester.[3] A chaplain of the bishop of Ely in 1453, John Sugdon, M.A., was rector of Bishops Hatfield in Lincoln diocese.[4] Both were dispensed for plurality. Such examples, however, were overshadowed by the career of Thomas Tanfield, chaplain to Archbishop Kempe:[5] he was rector of Garveston 1428–35, of Gateshead 1435–74, of Oddington in 1442, of Gilling 1442–6, of Laxton from 1446 to 1465, of Sturton le Clay till 1459, of Castor 1466–74, of Gayton 1471–73, of Harpole in 1473, and portioner of Bromyard in 1450. Furthermore, he held consecutively and almost continuously four prebends at York from 1446 until his death in 1475. He was master of the hospital of Kinwalgraves near Beverley in 1449, and of one at Ripon in 1465. He was incumbent of at least nine parishes, usually holding two and occasionally three simultaneously. Some idea of the value of his livings may be gained from his will, in which he made bequests totalling over £150; £100 of this he left to the abbot and convent of Bourne in Lincolnshire towards an annual and perpetual obit for himself. That he was typical seems unlikely;

---

[1] P.R.O., E 36/95 (account book of John Hussey, Lord of Hussey, from 1529), p. 99; *Lincoln Visitations 1517–31*, i, 56, 66, 76.

[2] Lyndwood, III.29.ii, note *x*: '*nam laicis non licet advocare clericos a divinis officiis*'.

[3] *C.P.L.* xi, 165; Manning and Bray, *History of Surrey*, iii, 370.

[4] *C.P.L.* x, 140.

[5] For these details see *Testamenta Eboracensia*, ed. J. Raine (Surtees Soc. 45), iii, 213–14; Emden, *Oxford*, iii, 1848–9.

certainly most episcopal chaplains received rather more modest rewards. Most of them, however, were absentee and pluralist, if not on the same scale as Tanfield[1]

Not only were bishops' chaplains presented to parish churches, but officers of the diocese and personnel of the courts were also numbered among the parsons and vicars of the later Middle Ages. One who probably saw little of his parishioners was Thomas Martyn, Doctor of Decrees, in 1510 official of the archdeacon of Salisbury, vicar of Woodford and rector of Fugglestone St. Peter (both in Wiltshire), and prebendary of Chardstock.[2] Perhaps typical of the lawyers was John Jenyn, Doctor of Laws, in 1513 rector of Coulsdon and Blechingley in Surrey, vicar of Queen Camel in Somerset, and an advocate of the Court of Arches;[3] he was quite near, even for those times, to two of his benefices—a sturdy horse would soon carry him to Coulsdon or Blechingley—, but it is doubtful if he ever went to Queen Camel.

The absentees exemplified above have been given some prominence because they formed the vast majority of non-resident incumbents. They are alike in holding responsible offices and in being away from their parishes in order to meet those responsibilities. Though drawing their living from the fruits of a parish church, they are employed on other work elsewhere: such work was necessary for the good order of the church no less than of the State and society in general; such remuneration bore witness not only to the feudal origin of the *beneficium*, but also to the intricate relationship of Church, society and government which had developed in past centuries and was now, all unsuspected, on the verge of transformation.

There were other reasons for non-residence and though they have received more prominence and were sometimes the occasion for scandal, they were not nearly so frequent.[4] William Jonson, vicar of Wolfhamcote, who was nearly seventy years of age and afflicted with such a disease of the throat that he could hardly

[1] For a yet more remarkable example compare Thomas Magnus, archdeacon of the East Riding in 1536 (*Clifford Letters*, pp. 42–44).

[2] *L. & P.* i(1), No. 438(3), m. 28.

[3] Ibid., No. 1803(2), m. 2; *Regs. Wolsey and others*, p. 29.

[4] Lyndwood, III.4.ii, note *z*, gives other legitimate reasons for absence: debility, infirmity, remoteness from benefice, poverty, study and preaching. For poverty see below pp. 55, 165–6, and for study p. 80.

swallow and was unable to keep himself alive without doctors and good treatment, was licensed to absent himself for life while residing in any honest and becoming place, and Master Henry Burton in his sickness was allowed a year's absence from his rectory of Lockington in order to go to London '*ubi copia phisicorum existit pro corporali sanitate recuperanda*'.[1] In 1450 Master Robert Hoskyn, rector of SS. Mary and Bridget, Oxford, made his will before setting out on a visit to St. Peter's, Rome, and to other holy places.[2] John Wynstone was licensed to make a similar journey in 1475, provided his vicarage of Rickmansworth was laudably served and the cure of souls in no way neglected meanwhile.[3] In 1504–5 the incumbents of Witcombe, Stratton, Sporle and Woodmansterne were among the pilgrims to Rome.[4] Others were absent for less honourable reasons, though sometimes through no fault of their own. Thomas Dark, parson of Kettleburgh, was maliciously imprisoned by the keeper of the gaol of Melton and detained there chained and manacled without hope of release although he had offered good sureties; not only was it putting his life in jeopardy, but it also deprived his parishioners of his services, and this, he claimed, 'sore grevith hym'.[5] Also remote from their affluent benefices were foreigners like Erasmus, who held the living of Aldington,[6] but their number was negligible. It was not only the richest livings which were specially prone to absentee incumbents: in 1522 James Robynson, vicar of North Weald Basset, was licensed by the vicar-general of London to absent himself from his benefice for the next two years on account of its poverty.[7] Where the poverty was not chronic this limit of time may well have been precautionary: it meant that at the end of two years Robynson would have to apply for a further licence or risk the consequence of illegitimate absence; in effect it meant that his case would be reviewed again then. During the two years, it is

[1] *C.P.L.* xiii, 791; R.I.22, fo. 27r; cf. ibid., fo. 51v.

[2] *Munimenta Academica*, ed. H. Anstey (Rolls Series), ii, 604–7; also T. Madox, *Formulare Anglicanum*, No. DCCLXXX.

[3] *Reg. quorundam abbatum. . . . S. Albani*, ed. H. T. Riley (Rolls Series), ii, 118–19.

[4] *The English Hospice in Rome* (The Venerabile, xxi, 1962 Exeter), pp. 125, 128. Sporle is there wrongly transcribed as Sporsey.

[5] P.R.O., C 1/304/89, and a similar case in C 1/319/62.

[6] H. M. Smith, *Pre-Reformation England*, p. 34.

[7] G.L.C., MS. DL/C/330, fo. 33v, and below, p. 165–6.

implied, he could alleviate his poverty by singing Mass in a chantry or by holding some other paid office. Whether for poverty or not a number of absentee incumbents were serving chantry posts, but Miss Wood-Legh has shewn that they are not so often found as might be supposed.[1]

Unlicensed absence does not occur so frequently in the disciplinary records as extreme critics of the late medieval Church suggest. In London diocese in the 1520s, when the vicar-general kept vigilant watch on absentees, the number of unlicensed cases is notably small, as are the records in episcopal registers generally of men deprived for non-residence.[2] When it does happen, it is frequently explained by the incumbent's pursuit of a mistress: John Lambe, for example, who early in the 1470s was accused of adultery with Agnes Lambe and Katherine Martyn in London, although he was at the time rector of Wexham, is typical.[3]

III: *The Extent*

The extent of absenteeism at the end of the Middle Ages defies precise measurement. There were no returns for pluralists in this period as in the 1360s, and the registers of popes and bishops are by no means complete in their information. Yet the episcopal registers do contain sufficient entries referring to absenteeism to suggest some conclusions, which our knowledge of royal, ecclesiastical and domestic clerks and chaplains strengthens. In Norwich diocese in 1499 Morton found forty-eight absentees during his visit of 489 parishes; seventeen vicars and twenty rectors were absent from their livings when Warham visited 266 churches in Canterbury diocese in 1511; and in Lincoln diocese in 1518 about a quarter of the incumbents were non-residents.[4] During the eighty years prior to 1530 a great many parish churches must have been at some time in the possession of

---

[1] K. L. Wood-Legh, *Perpetual Chantries in Britain*, p. 196.
[2] See below, p. 114.
[3] London Guildhall MS. 9064(i), fo. 10v.
[4] C. Jenkins, 'Cardinal Moreton's Register', *Tudor Studies*, ed. R. W. Seton-Watson, pp. 67–69; Reg. Warham, fos. 45–83; *Lincoln Visitations 1517–31*, i. *passim*. See also M. Bowker, *Secular Clergy in Lincoln Diocese*, pp. 90–91.

absentee parsons or vicars, some parishes perhaps on a few occasions, others many times: Braughing had a long line of resident incumbents until John Kent set out on a pilgrimage to Rome; St. George's, Southwark, by contrast, was a favourite living for courtiers and officials with little opportunity, and perhaps less inclination, to serve the cure of souls personally.[1] Until much more intensive local research is completed—and it is doubtful if in any diocese there are adequate records for this— it is impossible to estimate precisely the incidence of non-residence and therefore to determine whether it was growing, declining or stagnating in scale. For all their hazards, visitation records are the only statistical guide that we have on this matter, and on their evidence it would be pessimistic to conclude that more than one benefice in four at any one time was possessed by an absentee. Some perspective is given to this when we recollect that throughout the land in 1827 an official survey—admittedly distorting but not grossly so—found less than half of 10,000 incumbents resident in their own parishes.[2]

IV: *Church Control*

Attempts to contain non-residence had begun as early as the Council of Chalcedon in 451, which forbade the holding of offices in the church of more than one city at a time.[3] Thereafter legis-lators, popes and councils, were concerned to ensure that absenteeism, where and as it became necessary, should be limited and, so far as possible, its dangers to parish life averted by the maintenance of services and charity. The Lateran Council of 1179, after denouncing pluralism, declared: 'let such a person be sought out for this purpose (i.e. the cure of souls) as can reside upon the spot and perform the cure thereof by himself'. Gregory

[1] G.L.C., MS. DL/C/206, fo. 304v, see Appendix 2(b) below; Manning and Bray, *History of Surrey*, iii, 645; among its incumbents were—William Hoper (see Emden, *Oxford*, ii, 958–9), William Moggys (ibid., ii, 1287–8), John Fox (ibid., iii, 714–15), John Giles (ibid, ii, 764–5), William Middleton (ibid, ii, 1279), and Carmelianus (ibid., i, 358–9, and *D.N.B.*, *sub nomine*).
[2] O. Chadwick, *The Victorian Church* (London 1966), i, 34.
[3] For this and the other continental legislation quoted see A. H. Thompson, 'Pluralism in the Medieval Church', *A.A.S.R.* xxxiii, 35–73.

X in 1274, endeavouring to ensure the satisfactory cure of souls in the benefices of pluralists, stipulated that the ordinary should 'make provision in such wise that neither the cure of souls be neglected in the same churches, parsonages or dignities, nor the benefices themselves be robbed of that service due to them'. In England in that century Langton, Pecham and the papal legates, Otto and Ottobuono, had issued decrees which Lyndwood was to turn to in the fifteenth century. Papal legislation reached its definitive form with the decree *Execrabilis* of 1317 which permitted dispensation only for the holding of one cure of souls at a time, but it could not abandon the papal *plenitudo potestatis* to dispense even from this; the legislation of 1363 and 1366 made no significant alteration to the law and very little difference to the practice. From this time, although dispensations for three or four cures of souls are only a small proportion, nearly all the licences granted permit two to be held simultaneously.[1] English legislators of this time were more concerned with absenteeism itself.

In 1455 Archbishop Bourgchier wrote to Blodwell, his commissary-general, a letter which depicted the Church very much as some Reformers later saw it, and urged on him the need for reform.[2] Bourgchier dwelt at length on the absentee incumbents, the illicit ones who spurned the cure of souls and spent their time in mundane pursuits elsewhere, especially in eating and drinking, adultery, fornication and other vices, so that meanwhile their chancels, rectories and vicarages fell into great ruin, and laymen farmed the fruits to the loss of the poor of the parish. He suggested, however, no new and, indeed, no precise remedies, nor did he produce any statistical evidence. Allowance must be made for rhetoric.

A provincial statue of Cardinal Morton in 1486 was concerned with the regulation of legitimate non-residence.[3] The man dispensed to hold two benefices must reside in each of them in turn; where a papal licence for absenteeism is sought careful inquiry into the grounds of the request is to be made; suitable hired deputies must be employed. Yet this decree of Morton contains no new sanctions; and indeed, the sanctions which the

[1] *C.P.L.* x–xiv, *passim.*
[2] *Reg. Bourgchier*, pp. 20–23.
[3] Wilkins, iii, 619–20.

Church could apply were limited. What is significant is the attempt to check papal indiscretion by examining the good faith of applicants for papal indults, though how far this was implemented, and how it could be, no evidence shows.

The problem of absence occurs again, this time in the decrees of York Convocation, in 1518.[1] At this a measure by Savage for sequestrating the fruits in the case of unlicensed absence, and another by Greenfield to compel the residence of vicars by the subtraction of the fruits were reiterated.

When Convocation next dealt with non-residence in 1529 it was primarily concerned with incumbents absent for the purposes of study.[2] The ordinary was to make careful inquiry on visitations and in chapter in order to prevent absence on a false pretext of study. Only those could be licensed who were known to be capable of, and suitable for, learning. A special check was to be kept of older men absent, though unfit, for study; only presidents of colleges and halls, public praelectors in theology or civil or canon law were exempt from such scrutiny. Chancellors or their deputies in each university, on admission to office, had to swear to examine twice each year for their suitability the inmates of all colleges, halls and hostels; if any were beneficed and yet passing the time in idleness and luxury, their ordinaries were to be advised with all possible speed to fetch the student back to his benefice and compel him to reside. A statute of 1536[3] in fact withdrew the privilege of non-residence for study from all those over forty years of age, with certain obviously necessary exemptions for college fellows and aspiring doctors; but there is no quantitative evidence to show that this problem of age was in fact a widespread or significant scandal.

This review has found no drastic changes in procedure or penalties, and no frantic attempts to cope with a problem almost beyond control. Current regulations are slightly modified and strengthened here and there. The legislators had done and were doing almost all they could. It remains to be seen if the administrators were as vigilant.

Absence from a cure of souls could always be licensed by the pope (or by his nuncios or legates) and, indeed, had to be when pluralism was the reason. In the thirteenth century, Dr. Moor-

[1] Ibid., iii, 665, 670.   [2] Ibid., iii, 719.
[3] *Statutes of Realm*, 28 Henry VIII, c. xiii.

man considers the pope's indiscriminate granting of dispensations was a primary cause of extensive and scandalous non-residence.[1] What, then, are we to expect of fifteenth-century popes? Some laxity in satisfying petitioners, no doubt, and this seems to be confirmed by the Canterbury provincial statutes of 1486[2] and by the numerous incumbents who obtained licences. Yet random checks in the *Calendar of Papal Letters*, so far as they are published for this period, induce not complacency but caution; with twenty-nine English recipients of dispensations for plurality and non-residence in 1450, thirty-three in 1460, twenty-four in 1470 and even sixty-five in 1480, should be contrasted the annual average of eighty-three such licences granted by the faculty office of the reformed Church between 1534 and 1549.[3] Moreover, not only could many of the petitioners at Rome hardly be refused dispensations, unless the pope were intent on disrupting government and society in England, but it had been a recognized principle at Rome and in the Church for three centuries that noble and lettered persons, *sublimi et litterati*, ought to be honoured with a plurality of livings.[4] The papal curia was not well placed to scrutinize the *bona fides* of applicants, and though Convocation envisaged a remedy for this, we have no evidence that bishops enforced it.

Non-residence for all other reasons could be licensed by the bishops or their vicars-general.[5] These dispensations cost the applicant money: in Norwich diocese varying from 2s. 4d. to 10s. with no consistent correlation to the time allowed, they were only given *gratis*, or the fee remitted, for pilgrimage or similar reasons, or to please the applicant's patron or employer.[6] It

[1] J. R. H. Moorman, *Church Life in England in the Thirteenth Century* (2nd ed.), pp. 218, 221, 223.

[2] Wilkins, iii, 619–20.

[3] *C.P.L.* x–xiv, *passim*; D. S. Chambers, *Faculty Office Registers 1534–39*, tables on pp. xxxvii–viii.

[4] A. H. Thompson, *A.A.S.R.* xxxiii, 43; Lyndwood, III.22.v, note *p*, '*nobilitate generis—hi dicuntur personae sublimes*'.

[5] Not always in writing: see Norwich Act Book XIV, fo. 40r, where a rector was licensed '*verbo et non scripto*' for three years' absence.

[6] Ibid., fos. 27v, 55v, 64v, 66r, 69r, 72r, 79r–v, 115r. A grant for two years cost 2s. 4d. (fo. 69r), for three years 6s. 8d. (fo. 79r), during the bishop's pleasure 6s. 8d. (fo. 115r) and 10s. (fo. 64v). The fee of Thomas Alen was remitted at the petition of Lord Rede, judge (fo. 115r), and the fee of Edward Ap Rise 'for the love of Sir Edward Howard, knight' (for. 27v).

may be that where a sponsor does not account for the inscrutable variations of the fees, the bishop's desire to extract however little or much the petitioner could afford was operative.

The vigilance of bishops against absentees may be explained by financial concerns, but it is silly to deplore this, for whatever the bishop's cupidity, he could only license what canon law permitted; it would, in any case, be facile cynicism to explain the vigour of such scrupulous men as Bishop Tunstall and his vicar-general, Geoffrey Wharton, by fees.[1] On 2 September 1523 John Harwood, stipendiary chaplain in a chantry in St. Michael's Queenhithe in the City, appeared before the vicar-general and confessed that he was also incumbent of Downham in the diocese of Norwich; he was ordered to withdraw from the London diocese before 29 September and after that date not to serve any cure or undertake any service within the diocese, on pain of suspension; the order was tantamount to deprivation.[2] That year six other similar offenders appeared before the vicar-general.[3] The following year Miles Jeffes, vicar of Eardisland in Hereford diocese, but not credited with any post or cure in London, was ordered to leave the London diocese or suffer suspension.[4] In June 1526 Master Nicholas Same, Doctor of Decrees, vicar of both Chishall Magna and Waltham Magna and rector of Radwinter, was arraigned in the consistory court despite his eminence; he was, however, able to produce letters granted by Leo X in 1517 authorizing plurality and others of 1524 from Wolsey, then legate *a latere*, licensing the union of Chishall Magna and Radwinter.[5] Three years later John Oterbury was absolved from the penalty of suspension for celebrating services in the parish of St. Clement's without the Bar at New Temple while, at the same time, being vicar of Farleigh in Winchester diocese; he had sworn that he had resigned the vicarage into the hands of the ordinary of Winchester and he had been asked to produce the instrument of resignation, or at least the notary public who had attested it, one of which he

---

1 A much more intimate knowledge of the ecclesiastical administrators of Tudor England than we have at present is badly needed.
2 G.L.C., MS. DL/C/330, fo. 52v.
3 Ibid., fos. 51v, 52v, 53r.
4 Ibid., fo. 74r; for other examples, see fos. 113r, 115v, 124v, 158r.
5 Ibid., fo. 114r.

evidently did.[1] A number of people, such as the vicar of Barking in 1529, were asked to show cause why they should not be compelled to reside personally according to the law, in view of their oath at the time of induction to reside or suffer deprivation.[2] This oath was very often taken for the incumbent by a proctor, and in some cases the irony is sharply pointed.

Without an earlier vicar-general's register, it is difficult to assess the novelty or continuity of these measures in London diocese, but there is scattered evidence from other sees and from other decades too of a general vigilance by ordinaries against the unlicensed absentee. The archdeacon of Richmond in 1471 called on rural deans to summon absentees to reside within six months; in 1506 the rural dean of Lynn was authorized by the bishop of Norwich to investigate all absentee incumbents in his deanery; similar steps were taken by Wayneflete, Courtenay and Fox in Winchester diocese; Stanbury, bishop of Hereford, deprived Robert Pery and Hugh Turnour, rectors of North Cleobury and Upper Sapey respectively, for non-residence, and a later bishop of that see, Bothe, was especially active in sequestrating the fruits of absentees' livings.[3] The penalties of suspension at the first warning and deprivation afterwards seem, in themselves, sufficient, for no man likes to lose all or a good part of his income, and actual cases of deprivation are in fact few. The evidence which has been adduced from Leicester archdeaconry to illustrate the futility of the efforts by ordinaries to curb non-residence is only superficially convincing;[4] while it shows that of thirty livings with absentees in 1518, twenty still had absent incumbents in 1526, no attempt has been made to show whether the living had changed hands, whether the parish was well or ill governed, whether the incumbent was licensed for such absence; and when all these questions have been answered, it is clear that non-residence in that archdeaconry had in fact declined, or been reduced, by a third.

[1] Ibid., fo. 188r; and Manning and Bray, *History of Surrey*, ii, 414.
[2] G.L.C., MS. DL/C/330, fo. 179r; another example is on fo. 199v.
[3] 'Reg. Archdeacon of Richmond', *T.A.J.* xxxii, 125–6; Norwich Act Book XIV, f. 52v; *V.C.H. Hants.* ii, 47; *Reg. Stanbury*, pp. 116, 125; *Reg. Myllyng*, pp. 100–1; *Reg. Mayew*, p. 190, a general monition to reside; *Reg. Bothe*, pp. 99, 133, 169, 170, 175.
[4] M. Bowker, 'Non-Residence in the Lincoln Diocese in the Early Sixteenth Century', *J.E.H.* xv, 43. See a fuller discussion in *Secular Clergy*, pp. 91–94.

V: *The Effects*

Absentees were obliged to provide a proctor to administer the temporalities of their benefice and a chaplain to perform the services in their church; part of the common form of their licences at the end of the Middle Ages is the phrase *sua cura bene servata*—provided the cure is well served.[1] Nevertheless, divine service was often left, it is said, to a poorly paid and none too diligent chaplain, while a farmer collected the fruits of the benefice, little, if any, of which he spent on the repair of the chancel and parsonage buildings. Even more neglect may be presumed on the part of the unlicensed absentee, except where he was anxious to conceal his irregularity. What this negligence amounted to in fact and what the significant consequences of it were may best be observed in the deposition books of the London consistory court.

In 1514 the parishioners of Thundersley were scandalized by the absence and incontinence of their rector, Miles Hogeson.[2] According to one witness he was absent from the Monday after Epiphany until the second Sunday in Lent, but when in fact the rector had resided in his cure he did not know. Another witness, who claimed that he usually accommodated the rector at Thundersley, said that Hogeson had not come to his house in all that time. Yet on the eve of Pentecost, a third deponent said, Hogeson did arrive in the parish and said Vespers there. Moreover, during Whitsun and the following days he celebrated other divine offices and even baptized one infant. One of the complaints of the parishioners was that, due to Hogeson's absence, the font had not been blessed either by himself or by a deputy; already two children had been baptized in it, though no deponent seemed very sure whether before or after Whitsun. The implication is that it was not and that the parishioners were naturally perturbed that baptism should be endangered by negligence and resulting irregularity. The cure of souls was served neither by Hogeson nor by a deputy at the beginning of Lent. True, a certain chaplain, John Wood, *ex sua benevolencia*, on the Thursday after Ash Wednesday blessed the ashes and

---

[1] Found many times in G.L.C., MS. DL/C/330, *passim.*

[2] G.L.C., MS. DL/C/206, fos. 262r–4r.

served the cure until the feast of the Purification of the Blessed Virgin. At the request of a group of the parishioners he had celebrated divine service for five days in the church, for which he was paid 20*d*. Another chaplain, Sir Robert, was hired by the parishioners to serve the cure for fifteen days for 6*s*. The inhabitants were evidently concerned to maintain services.[1] As for the church fabric, so ruinous was the chancel that the pyx and Eucharist were removed to the nave of the church. Hogeson had begun to see to the repairs by workmen and labourers, *tamen insufficientes et non expertes*; no doubt they were cheaper to hire.

It is likely that Hogeson's absence and presence were both determined by the whereabouts of a certain notorious woman, a Mistress Jane. She had already been warned by the constable to leave the area and never return, when one day he heard that she was at the house of the Petigrews. He went along, accompanied by a certain William Parder, and conducted a search which might have been in vain had he not, when on the point of departure, heard the sound of a large chest being closed; his suspicions and hopes were revived, and they were not disappointed. The chest was locked and the wife of Petigrew prevaricated until, under the threat of the stocks, she surrendered Mistress Jane. That very day Miles Hogeson was in Thundersley. When he died in 1519 he was vicar of Thaxted and he made no mention in his will of Thundersley, or of Jane.[2]

In Whitsun week, 1520, Robert Philipson was set upon in his own church of Braughing, where he had been vicar for nearly ten years, by some men in the service of Master Humphrey Fitzherbert.[3] The cause of the assault seems to have been personal animosity; the brother of Humphrey, Master John Fitzherbert, was described as an enemy of Philipson; one of the witnesses, John Lockyn, had been heard to favour Philipson's early death and was known to have carried reports of the vicar to John Fitzherbert. Several of the witnesses had been involved in a case

---

[1] The same concern is seen, among many other places, in Masham in 1473, where the parishioners, in default of the vicar, hired a chaplain at their own expense (York Visitations, fo. 19v).

[2] G.L.C., MS. DL/C/354, fos. 40r–v.

[3] G.L.C., MS. DL/C/207, fos. 3r–v, 26r, 30v–31r; see below Appendix 2(b) for transcript. Philipson was instituted to Braughing on the king's presentation 23 May 1513 (*L. & P.* i(2), No. 1948); he exchanged it for East Coker 23 March 1524 (*Reg. Clerke*, p. 31).

some years before against Philipson for withdrawing support of a chaplain. What is far more important for our purpose is that Lockyn is not reckoned to be well disposed towards Philipson because he was one of the 'Chekemaisters'[1] appointed by Humphrey Fitzherbert to record when the vicar was absent and how often he celebrated. Humphrey's motives in setting up this 'watch committee' may not have been entirely honourable; unfortunately too little is known of Philipson's career and residence to draw any sure conclusions. Checkmasters may have been known in other parishes; at least, in Braughing they indicate a serious, albeit malign, attempt by the laity to control non-residence.

In 1529 the people of Wennington promoted articles in the consistory court against their rector, John Marshall.[2] That he was also vicar of Aveley may account for his absence from, and neglect of, Wennington, which formed the basis of the parishioners' complaints against him. His replies to the charges give an interesting account of the disturbance which non-residence sometimes caused. He confessed, first of all, that he had been ordered by the bishop two years previously to provide the church of Wennington with divine service himself or by an adequate deputy.[3] He did in fact hire a chaplain, Sir John, who with the assent and encouragement of the parishioners, but without authority from Marshall himself, celebrated Mass and other offices one Sunday in the house of a certain Master Warham. This may not have been the only time when the parish celebrated in Warham's house, for Marshall told the court that rain pours into both the chancel and the nave. Whether these dilapidations were his or his parishioners' fault he did not know, but if the burden of repairs could be shown to his responsibility, he would 'willingly' undertake them. Marshall himself had said divine service there for a period up to Good Friday, but he had not celebrated Mass. Indeed, the Eucharist was not kept in the church because there was no pyx consecrated or suitable, merely

---

[1] Compare 'kirkmaster', a fifteenth-century term for churchwarden (C. Drew, *Early Parochial Organisation in England* (St. Anthony's Hall Publications, No. 7), p. 6, n.).

[2] G. L. C., MS. DL/C/208, unfoliated.

[3] G.L.C., MS. DL/C/330, fo. 117v, where in August 1526 the fruits of Wennington were sequestrated because of rectorial neglect. John Marshall had become rector of Wennington in 1522 (Newcourt, *Repertorium*, ii, 652).

an unblessed, copper one. The parishioners were clearly indignant at not receiving Mass, and at the deplorable state of the
church. It is evident that the people were not content merely
with divine services; the implications are that they had not
always been served either by the chaplain or by the rector, and
that they were troubled by the suspicion of irregularity in the
chaplain celebrating Mass in a house.

All the witnesses in the case against Dominic Civi, rector of
South Ockendon 1504–15, agreed that since he had been inducted
in the person of his father as proctor for him, five or six years
before, he had never been seen in the parish.[1] Some thought he
may have been studying at a university, as his father assured
them; indeed, his father had often promised them during the past
two years that they would see their rector upon a certain day;
many such promises and days had passed and still Sir Dominic
had not met his parishioners. They commonly assumed that he
was dead and had they begun to doubt his very existence it
would not have been surprising, for even the farmer of the parish,
Thomas Goodwyn, chaplain, had never seen him. But he was
alive and he appeared in the consistory court to answer charges
made by Master William Tyrel, patron of South Ockendon. The
charges concerned his induction, a violent and unruly affair. He
was earlier involved, if he did not appear, in an *ex officio* case
against him for neglect of his parish. It was widely agreed that
the church, both in the choir and the nave, was so dilapidated
that rain water was rotting the timbers and beams, and falling on
to the lectern and spoiling the books. Likewise the rectory
manse and all its buildings (except the barns and dovecote, on
repairs of which £24 had been spent) in roofs, walls and the
foundations (*le grouncellis*), whether of wood, stone or brick,
had reached such a state of decay that unless repairs were quickly
undertaken neither the damage nor the costs would be moderate.
Estimate of the costs varied between £12 and £30; the usual
figure was £20, and, as one witness pointed out, it was increasing daily. Some damage, it is true, had been caused at the induction when the doors of the church, found to be locked, were
battered down and the belfry broken into—damage which
William Tyrel had promised, and ever since neglected, to repair.
This, however, was a small item when compared with subsequent

[1] See below, Appendix 2(a).

decay. The farmer of the benefice, Goodwyn (himself the vicar of West Thurrock), thought the repair of the chancel roof would cost 4s. which was the rector's responsibility, since it was previously agreed that the farmer would not be burdened with this charge. The prospect of any repairs being done seemed slender. Gloomy conclusions seem to follow from such a picture. Yet the results for the parish were not disastrous: all the deponents testified that the divine offices and the cure of souls were quite adequately served by a parish priest, though all of them regretted that the services were conducted without music or singing, 'because there are diverse parishioners there who can and would sing if the curate would, but he will not'.

Here is a glimpse of what must have been the usual result of legitimate non-residence: the parish was quite well served by a chaplain. Unfortunately it is usually the parishes where absence had led to scandal of one kind or another which are described in the disciplinary and episcopal records of the time: parishes such as Didcot where the parson had gone to Oxford and left his flock without divine services and sacraments 'to gret unese to the parish', or Wrangle where the current vicar had never re-sided and the parish chaplain and the parish water-carrier were equally negligent, or Mixbury whose rector was living in London and whose curate was living in sin.[1] The orderly parish of an absentee is rarely described; yet such parishes must have been numerous. Many parishes had as well as the incumbent a number of assistants who would mitigate the effects of absence: quite typical was Chipping Norton where, beside the vicar, who was absent in Paris, there were Henry Davy, *curatus*, John Grass, *cantarista*, John Reynold and John Smith, stipendiaries.[2] In the visitation returns of the archdeaconry of Leicester in 1526 five benefices, ruinous and ill served, were held by pluralists actually residing there, while twenty-three also held by plural-ists, who resided in other livings, were well served and repaired; in Norwich diocese in 1499 there were forty-eight parishes with absentee incumbents, but only in two of these was non-residence accompanied by neglect.[3]

[1] *Stonor Letters*, i, 67–69; *Lincoln Visitations 1517–31*, i, 71, 123.
[2] *Lincoln Visitations 1517–31*, ii, 45.
[3] 'Leicester Archdeaconry Proceedings', *A.A.S.R.* xxviii, 215–17; C. Jenkins, Cardinal Morton's Register', *Tudor Studies*, pp. 67–69.

Just as derelict chancels and rectories cannot be regarded solely or inescapably as the consequence of non-residence, so it is equally misleading to regard the leasing of tithes to laymen as a practice unknown among resident incumbents, who may have sought by such means to gain more time for the cure of souls.[1] Although farming may have compounded the sin of the absentee in the eyes of his parishioners, it is doubtful if the farmer was a more objectionable recipient to them. What was far more dangerous in this habit of lay farming was the encouragement it gave to laymen to compete for a lease and to develop a proprietary interest in ecclesiastical revenues, a habit of mind which gained full scope and successfully thwarted the re-endowment of livings when the monasteries were dissolved.

There is another important consequence arising more exclusively from non-residence. When incumbents were absent from, and indifferent to, their parishes and when the services and rites were neglected, the parishioners became anxious, not because they were greatly concerned with clerical discipline, but from fear for their own souls. Since the thirteenth century parishioners had been responsible for maintaining the nave fabric, for providing the ornaments and utensils necessary for services, and for these purposes they were represented by the churchwardens who in time hired priests for obits and annuals and often were called upon to administer a sequestrated benefice.[2] It was doubtless through these representatives that the parishioners began to hire their own parish priests and to celebrate services as best they could; if the latter were irregular, so much the greater was their anxiety, and their anger at the incumbent; they even, in one parish, appointed 'checkmasters' of their own to coerce the recalcitrant incumbent. In fact, the laity acquired, not always willingly, but by default of the incumbent, a sense of responsibility for the functioning of the church for the good of their own souls. This was a very subtle, perhaps neither a conscious nor a widespread, transformation. People were assuming responsibility for their own salvation, albeit within the framework of the Church and through the medium of a priest administering the sacraments. The change of emphasis was slight but fundamental. Moreover, it should be remembered

[1] J. E. Oxley, *The Reformation in Essex*, pp. 35–36.
[2] C. Drew, *Early Parochial Organization*, especially pp. 5–6, 16–18.

that when an incumbent was suspended and the revenues of the living sequestrated, their administration was often, as at Wennington in 1521, granted to one cleric and two parishioners —perhaps the churchwardens—who were to see that the cure was served, the income collected and the expenses met; again we see the laity, this time actively encouraged, participating in their parochial government.[1]

VI: *The Significance*

While absenteeism was certainly common among the late medieval clergy, its extent, which defies precise calculation, seems to have been far less than is usually assumed today. Bishops and their officers evinced diligence and some success in keeping its incidence near to that permitted by canon law. The English church authorities could not prevent applications for dispensations to Rome, still less to Wolsey, and though they saw the need to ensure that no fraudulent or unjustified appeals arrived at the papal curia no evidence witnesses their efforts or success in this; the discrimination exercised by the Curia and by Wolsey's faculty office cannot be accurately judged from the materials at present available, but there is little to suggest that they were more prodigal of licences than the Anglican authorities subsequently. Most non-residence was as essential to society as to the Church, which was both powerless and unwilling to eliminate it. Moreover, so long as the numbers of unlicensed were kept to a minimum, the effects of non-residence upon the parishes was both less spectacular and more subtle than is usually recognized. The assertion of private spiritual responsibility and initiative, which we saw emerging in the neglected parishes of Thundersley, Braughing and Wennington, was one important element, which has other and wider sources, of the English Reformation; the assertion of national sovereignty, which the statute of 1529 attempts, was another: in both instances the laity was taking control of its spiritual welfare and destiny, with reference to the same problem, but in an ambivalent way. The ambivalence of the English Reformation, the dualism of Establishment and Non-Conformity, was already implied.

[1] G.L.C., MS. DL/C/330, fo. 12r, one example from several.

V

Clerical Learning

I: *The View of the Humanists*

A CRUCIAL element in the late medieval Church was the emergence of the literate layman and along with this, partly as a consequence, the development of printing. It was an age which produced labourers who could read, tradesmen who could write, merchants who compiled commonplace books, and gentlemen who composed poetry; books were being bought and bequeathed by men who were neither nobles nor clerics; Bibles were being read by artisans.[1] The year 1500 saw fifty-four new titles issued from the presses of England, and though the career of Wynkyn de Worde is exceptional among the printers of his day, his production of some 700 books from 1492 to 1532 is symptomatic of the age.[2] More than ever before, to elicit respect and to defend the faith, the parish clergy had need to be learned or, at least, capable of learning, teaching and preaching. That they were not so, evidence is not lacking, even ignoring the tendentious witness of men like Tyndale and St. German.

Among the books printed by de Worde about 1509–10 was the sermon addressed to ordinands and their examiners by Dr. William Melton, chancellor of York, a friend of Colet, and

[1] L. C. Gabel, *Benefit of Clergy*, pp. 82–84, and below, p. 128; J. W. Adamson, 'The Extent of Literacy in England in the Fifteenth and Sixteenth Centuries', *Library* (4th series), x, 164–5; S. Thrupp, *The Merchant Class of Medieval London*, pp. 156–8; R. H. Robbins, *Secular Lyrics of the Fourteenth and Fifteenth Centuries* (Oxford 1952), pp. xxviii–xxxii; see also the article by Robbins on Newton and his circle, in *P.M.L.A.* lxv, 249–80; G. R. Owst, 'Some Books and Book Owners of 15th Century St. Albans', *Trans. St. Albans and Herts. Architectural and Archaeological Soc.* (1929), 175–94; *Reg. Stanbury*, pp. 123–4.
[2] H. S. Bennett, *English Books and Readers, 1475–1557*, pp. 29, 179. 190.

owner of a fashionably humanist library.[1] Basically his sermon is an appeal for men so dedicated, that despite their patent educational fitness they would not be permanently discouraged from seeking orders, if the examiner were to consider them at their first attempt, or after several, insufficient on other grounds. The first requirement, in Melton's view, was idealism and dedication; equally indispensable were intelligence and learning. Melton emphasized this second need not merely for fulfilling the pastoral obligations of the priest, but also as a bulwark against sloth and sin. The priest who had not 'a deep-rooted and almost perfect grasp of the theory of (grammatical) construction' which would enable him to read easily, accurately and with pleasure any Latin book, would be exposed over several hours of each day to other distractions, stultifying or vicious; once without the constant nourishment of devotional reading, what virtue there originally was in the priest would quickly be overwhelmed by the temptations of the world. The capacity to read Latin fluently was vital, therefore, to the priest's moral and spiritual development; from this private study and personal contemplation he would the better inform and kindle the faith of his parishioners:

> the chief remedy against idle sloth is the constant reading and conning of the books of the laws of God and of the Scriptures, which holy fathers and teachers before us have published. In their works, which are now plentiful in print, even the moderately learned can gain a pleasant solace of various kinds. Such study belongs to the true priestly art. Every craftsman who uses his hands has, besides the stall for his wares outside, a workshop for his craft within, and if he does not work diligently in it for many days, he will not easily earn for himself through his craft the necessities of life; similarly, besides the temples and the shrines of God in which by daily prayer and psalms we, as it were, display our wares to passers by, we must make use of our inner workshop or study with sacred reading and teaching, that we may become rich in learning and have no lack of the necessities of life eternal . . . Nor may we have any other source to expound to the people the holy consolation of God's Word.

[1] William de Melton, *Sermo Exhortatorius cancellarii Eboracensis hiis qui ad sacros ordines petunt promoveri;* it has seemed unnecessary to give page references for the argument of this brief treatise. On Melton, see A. G. Dickens, *T.R.H.S.* (5th series)xiii, 53–54.

71

A variety of considerations induced examiners to admit to orders men far removed from this ideal, as Melton himself revealed. He argued that men who had the slightest misgivings about their learning, apart from other factors, should withdraw before they took subdeacon's orders, for after that no other employment than ecclesiastical was legitimately open to them.

Colet, in whom Erasmus heard the authentic voice of Plato, shared Melton's views on clerical learning and sponsored de Worde's edition of the sermon to ordinands; in his own celebrated discourse to Convocation Colet dealt briefly with the same topic in the same vein. He too was gravely dissatisfied with the way in which ordination examiners exercised their office and his remarks are more directly addressed to them:

> the brode gate of holy orders opened, every man that offereth hymselfe is all where admytted without pullynge backe.[1]

Colet urged a more stringent test of what a fourteenth-century canonist had loosely called *litteratura sufficiens*;[2] not the ability 'to construe a collette, to put forth a question, or to answere a sopheme', but 'metely lernynge of holye scripture, some knowledge of the sacramentes' should be sought by the examiners.[3] He is no more precise than that, but the 'metely lernynge' is the equivalent of Melton's accurate fluency. Though Colet indicates that even such learning as this would be inadequate unless accompanied by 'a good, a pure, and a holy life', it is clear that he, like Melton, thought this an unlikely accomplishment without a deep knowledge of the scriptures.

Sir Thomas More lacked the occasions to comment on clerical shortcomings which occurred to dignitaries of the Church, but when he was called upon to defend Catholic institutions against another layman, Tyndale, he acknowledged that while so many clerics were employed outside parochial needs and examiners of ordinands had to bear such employment in mind, there was little

---

[1] J.H. Lupton, *Life of Colet*, pp. 299–300. On Colet's Christian-humanist approach to education see ibid., p. 271 and J. K. McConica, *English Humanists and Reformation Politics*, pp. 31, 48, 70. One should bear in mind the comment of H. C. Porter— 'Some of Colet's savage indignation was a reflection of the tensions in his own spirit' (*Essays in Modern English Church History*, ed. G. V. Bennett and J. D. Walsh (London 1966), p. 26).

[2] See p. 16, n. 4 above.

[3] Lupton, op. cit., p. 300.

chance of higher standards among the clergy; he had made the same point long ago and more succinctly in Utopia, where the priests were laudable, simply because they were few.[1] He expressed his pessimism more mirthfully when he wrote the epigram on a fat, ignorant priest who fondly quoted St. Paul's words about learning puffing up a man.[2]

What Melton, Colet and More feared was not merely the contempt in which the ignorant clergy might be held by their parishioners—for they were doubtless aware that men despised by their teachers and examiners have often been esteemed by their own pupils and subjects; far graver than this was the threat which such clergy formed to piety, since the unreading priest would have little of personal reflection, insight and experience to offer his people; he would be a man only sufficient to keep dogmas alive, and not able to make them move; a man who, in the language of the Christian humanists of that time, was better equipped to proclaim the 'Law' than to induce 'Faith'. It was this sterile preoccupation with the 'Law' that the Catholic humanists, and the Lutherans, particularly resented and assaulted.

II: *Quantitative Evidence*

In London immediately upon his consecration to the see in November 1530 Bishop Stokesley conducted an examination of curates 'in letters and in their capacity and suitability for those things which pertain to the cure of souls'.[3] Only a fragmentary record survives, but what it reveals is telling. Altogether fifty-six men were examined, and of these, twenty-two (which included two M.A.s, two Frenchmen and one Irishman) were barred from practising in the London diocese on account of their ignorance, while six more (among whom were two M.A.s and two canons from Waltham Abbey) were allowed to remain only

---

[1] *The English Works of Sir Thomas More*, ii, 215, 219; *Complete Works of St. Thomas More*, iv (ed. E. Surtz and J. H. Hexter, Yale 1965), 227.

[2] *The Latin Epigrams of Thomas More*, ed. L. Bradner and C. A. Lynch (Chicago 1953), No. 244. His story of the priest who thought *Te igitur* was a saint is of thirteenth-century origin (G. G. Coulton, *Europe's Apprenticeship*, p. 67). For his dissatisfaction with clerical learning briefly but seriously indicated, see above, p. 15.

[3] G.L.C., MS. DL/C/330, fos. 265r–266r.

provided that they studied and later convinced the bishop of their competence. Half, therefore, were found insufficiently educated and these included four M.A.s. Nor is this all: six other curates (three of them Irish) were barred as unsuitable (*propter inhabilitatem*), nine were rejected for reasons which are not recorded, and of two others there is no indication whether they were admitted or not. Out of fifty-six, therefore, only eleven were explicitly admitted. The criteria applied in this examination are unstated, but they may be inferred from the academic and humanist background of Stokesley.[1]

No less disturbing is the declaration in 1535 by Edward Lee, archbishop of York, a man of more traditional learning, that in the whole diocese he could not think of a dozen secular priests capable of preaching, and those few were non-resident.[2] He ascribed this fact to the poverty of most livings which deterred learned clerics from accepting them; so poor and unattractive were the benefices that Lee and his officers were content to find incumbents who could understand what they read and administer the sacraments in due form, although in other things they would need counsel. There is assuredly a touch of rhetoric about Lee's figures and his testimony comes in a letter excusing himself on the grounds of a dearth of competent preachers from a charge of negligence in propagating the new doctrine of Royal Supremacy: such evidence needs careful appraisal, but its argument was clearly one which Lee thought would find easy credence.

Perhaps no record affords a more telling critique of the medieval criteria of clerical learning—the criteria which the humanists were attacking—than Bishop Hooper's visitation returns for the see of Gloucester in 1551.[3] He examined the parish clergy on the Ten Commandments, the Articles of the Christian Faith, and the Lord's Prayer. He expected them to know how many Commandments there were, to recite them and to locate their text in the Bible; similarly with the Articles of Faith; not only were they to recite and locate the Lord's Prayer, but they were also required to name its author. The findings of Hooper's enquiry of 311 clergy were that 168 were unable to

[1] *D.N.B., sub nomine.*

[2] J. Strype, *Ecclesiastical Memorials*, i, 291–2.

[3] J. Gairdner, 'Bishop Hooper's Visitation of Gloucester in 1551', *E.H.R.* xix, 98–121, and F. D. Price, 'Gloucester Diocese under Bishop Hooper', *Trans. Bristol and Gloucester Arch. Soc.* lx, 51–151.

repeat the Ten Commandments accurately, nine unable to count them, and thirty-three unable to locate them; ten were unable to repeat the Articles of Faith and 216 unable to prove them by Biblical references; ten could not repeat the Lord's Prayer, thirty-nine failed to find its Biblical location, and thirty-four were ignorant of its author.[1] Allowing for the pre-Reformation rarity of Bibles in clerical possession and indeed for the rare use made of them even in the services,[2] remembering the numerous non-Biblical texts of these items available to medieval clergy— as a result particularly of thirteenth-century legislation,[3] we should expect clergy of this vintage to be weak on Biblical references; as for their inability to repeat the Decalogue, this is possibly more a commentary upon their memories and their sense of priority than upon their ignorance, for they were markedly better on the Articles of Faith.[4] Though neither illiterate nor, within the requirements and context of the late medieval Church, incompetent, the Gloucestershire clergy reveal a woeful unfamiliarity with the scriptures and an absence of those habits of reading and recollection so warmly advocated by Melton: their workshop was certainly not their study, and with so tenuous a grasp of the basic essentials of their faith they were patently ill equipped to cope with the increasingly curious layman.

III: *Selection Procedure*

The means whereby the Church attempted to separate the wheat from the chaff before ordination and the obstacles to success in this operation have been described above; it remains, however, to scrutinize the process more closely. The best witness would be a list of candidates who failed their pre-ordination tests, but no purpose would have been served by such a record and none is,

[1] Figures from F. D. Price, op. cit., 101.
[2] M. Deanesly, *The Lollard Bible*, pp. 199–202.
[3] W. A. Pantin, *The English Church in the Fourteenth Century*, Cap. ix.
[4] F. D. Price, op. cit., p. 103. These figures need further qualification before they are accepted too readily as a commentary on the clergy of medieval England; they include 129 curates, among whom (as among the beneficed) were many ill-trained Welshmen; though such men were probably common among the clergy of the border shires, the figures are apt as a consequence to be misleadingly pessimistic for England generally.

or perhaps ever was, extant. Melton, Colet and More, indeed, suggest that there was great reluctance to turn away anyone who offered himself and no documentary evidence impugns this. We do hear, however, of a few 'conditional passes', candidates enjoined to study before being admitted to orders, or being admitted on condition of a year's study afterwards, but the signs are not encouraging: thus the order of subdeacon was conferred on John Hardyng of Ely in May 1459 on his oath to study grammar for a year; even before this year was up, in December 1459, he was created deacon and renewed his oath; in March 1461, he was ordained priest and no oath was demanded.[1]

How far the good intentions of the examiner were defeated by the system of letters dimissory is less certain from this distance than it was to the Canterbury Convocation which in 1529 abolished them. It is clear, for example, that very few cases of ignorance can be traced to men who received such letters; that many of the grantees were graduates of, or students at, Oxford or Cambridge; and lastly, leaving aside the probability that such letters were neither obtained without prior, nor exempted from subsequent, examination, a large proportion of such recipients were already acolytes, subdeacons or deacons who had been ordained and examined once before at least. Of 2,962 men who received letters dimissory under seven archbishops of York from 1452 to 1530, 2,241 fell into these last two categories, and though a breakdown of figures shows a vast increase in these letters under Wolsey, especially in grants to acolytes, the proportion of recipients without even that order was only a thirtieth, 34 out of 1,065.[2]

Against those clergy who secured presentation to a benefice a further test of fitness was applied, albeit with equally uncertain results. Before a presentee was admitted to a living, he was examined for his capacity to instruct parishioners according to the canonical injunctions: a grammatical understanding of letters and the scriptures, and a knowledge of the Articles of Faith, the sacraments and the seven deadly sins were essential, all of which should have been required at ordination. It is therefore a damn-

[1] Ely Diocesan Records MS. G/1/5 (Reg. Gray), fos. 202v, 206r, 207v, 208r.
[2] See below, Appendix 3. Wolsey may have been swayed by the fees for these letters, which in Norwich diocese at the beginning of the sixteenth century cost 2s. 4d. if one example is representative (Norwich Act Book XIV, fo. 68v).

ing commentary on the ordination processes that Bekynton, bishop of Bath and Wells 1443–65, admitted John Wigguemor to a living only on the condition that he would study to master letters and submit to a further examination within a year, failure then entailing resignation of the benefice: Wigguemor was already a priest.[1] After Bekynton's day and in other sees the figures of conditional admission are too few and too haphazard to allow any confident conclusions.

Serious objections could be levelled against each piece of evidence so far marshalled to demonstrate the clergy's inadequate learning: Melton, Colet and More could be charged with the rhetorical exaggeration and statistical vagueness symptomatic of righteous indignation, Lee with special pleading on his own behalf; the text of Stokesley's inquiry might be considered too fragmentary, and the answers to Hooper's too complicated by personal and social factors, for valuable deductions; the very futility of recording rejections from orders and benefices may be thought to have distorted and concealed the truth for ever. Yet cumulatively this varied evidence overwhelms objections and dispels complacency. Even the rarity of charges of ignorance in visitation records—as in 1511 when in 266 churches Warham found merely three curates and one chaplain insufficiently lettered[2]—set beside the previous testimony merely raises doubts about the criteria applied, the questions asked and the witness given during the visitations. Yet there are signs that the evidence needs careful qualification.

IV: *Training the Clergy*

(a) *The Universities*

Inescapable—and familiar—as the preceding conclusions may seem, they are none the less surprising, since the late fifteenth and early sixteenth century saw an unparalleled expansion in the opportunities for education; not merely were the institutions increasing in number and diversifying in character, but there was

---

[1] *Reg. Bekynton*, p. 340. For examples from other dioceses, see *V.C.H. Cambridgeshire*, ii, 163; A. H. Thompson, *The English Clergy*, p. 242; *Register of Butley Priory*, ed. A. G. Dickens, p. 35.

[2] Reg. Warham, fos. 45–83.

an enthusiasm and enterprise about the methods of instruction, the content of curricula, and the endowment of scholars which had not been equalled in England before. In addition to this the occasions for self-improvement by continued private study were enhanced beyond measure by the advent of printing and the consequent multiplication and diffusion of texts. England was to see far more significant—and better remembered—achievements in education and general culture in the mid- and later sixteenth century, but the early Tudor period, too, witnessed a dramatic change, not confined to, though epitomized by, its distinguished grammarians and by the avid purchase of Erasmus's pedagogic works.

While the number of colleges founded at Oxford and Cambridge during the last decades of the fifteenth and first years of the sixteenth century would be a legitimate index of this educational 'boom', it would be a misleading guide to the learning of parish clergy, for colleges then were confined to fellows and implied no augmentation of undergraduate numbers. A more accurate index would be the numbers of halls, or inns, which accommodated the students; this evidence immediately looks discouraging, for halls during this period steadily declined in total, from some seventy at Oxford in the mid-fifteenth century to thirty by 1500, and twelve by 1514; these figures, however, are explained by the growing process of amalgamation, exemplified by the twelve halls which once stood on the site later occupied by Christ Church College and which by 1500 had been combined into three large ones.[1]

There seemed to be no difficulty in entering a university: age and qualifications (so long as one could speak Latin) were not too carefully scrutinized; men too old and too inept to learn and boys too boisterous to do so were welcomed with their fees. Canterbury Convocation in 1529 drew attention to those sere and feckless incumbents who preferred to sojourn at Oxford and Cambridge.[2] Historians have dwelt on the outrageous youth of other students there, but whether in fact the age of the undergraduates was so disturbingly low has recently been questioned.[3]

[1] W. A. Pantin, 'Before Wolsey', *Essays in British History*, ed. H. R. Trevor-Roper, pp. 36–37; *V.C.H. Oxfordshire*, iii, 17.

[2] Wilkins, iii, 719.

[3] E. F. Jacob, *Essays in the Conciliar Epoch* (2nd edn.), pp. 210–11.

Youth, indeed, was an advantage for anyone who aspired ultimately to the very protracted study necessary for a degree in theology or law.

A major deterrent, of course, was the cost of living and the fees, which could together amount to fifty shillings a year even in the early fifteenth century.[1] This not only prevented some aspirants from entering altogether, but also compelled a very significant proportion of those who did to depart before they had completed the seven years necessary for a master's degree, let alone the fourteen required to incept in theology or to take a doctorate in law.[2] Many parish clergy had studied at Oxford or Cambridge without waiting to graduate, or had contented themselves with the B.A. after four years, and though Rashdall suggests that they left little better than when they arrived, there is just as much reason for supposing that their time at the university, though unavoidably curtailed, was beneficial.

Of those who went to the university some did so at the expense of wealthy parents or patrons: Masters Edmund, Flynte and Kyckhall were three of many who had reason to be grateful for Sir William Stonor's liberality to students;[3] some, as Latimer recalled in 1548, were indebted to the generosity of Londoners— 'In times past, when any rich man died in London, they were wont to help the poor scholars of the Universities with an exhibition . . .';[4] others were indebted to abbeys like St. Mary's, York.[5] Clergy themselves were important patrons: John Warde, incumbent of Snailwell, provided £4 a year for nine years for a student of divinity at Cambridge, and £2 yearly for seven years for the exhibition of a poor scholar of St. John's College there;[6] Robert Pacoke, a London clerk, in 1513 left 40s. to support a poor scholar from Newcastle upon Tyne or Northumbria at Cambridge.[7] But many students already had

---

[1] H. E. Salter, 'An Oxford Hall in 1424', *Essays presented to R. L. Poole*, ed. H. W. C. Davis (Oxford 1927), p. 428.

[2] Emden, *Oxford.* i, p. xviii; H. Rashdall, *Medieval Universities* (1936 edn.), iii, 331–2, 343.

[3] *Stonor Letters*, ed. C. L. Kingsford (Camden Soc. 3rd series, 30) ii, 35, 118–19, 137.

[4] *Sermons by Hugh Latimer*, ed. G. E. Corrie (Parker Soc.), p. 64; he goes on to lament that now, when the universities are at last centres of true religion, the Londoners are more renowned for their parsimony.

[5] J. Gairdner, *Lollardy and the Reformation in England*, i, 247–8.

[6] P.C.C., Porch 8.   [7] G.L.C., MS. DL/C/354, fos. 23v–24r.

livings before they went up: a beneficed clerk, like Lawrence Hosky, vicar of St. Wendron in Cornwall, would farm his church to the parish priest, though it could be to a layman and even to an illiterate so long as the services were adequately performed and a competent proctor left to answer for him.[1] Hosky leased his vicarage for seven years at a rent of £12 per annum, £40 of which he took in advance; deeds of the transaction were made and signed. Perhaps for economic reasons he left Oxford prematurely and, on returning to St. Wendron, expelled the farmer, seized the copies of the deeds, and refused to repay the £40. It was customary for the mature student to manage his own finances and Hosky may have regretted not entrusting the £40 to the principal of his inn to dole out by careful instalments to him.[2] In financial difficulty he could have had resort to one of the university loan chests, an expedient which William Kettyl, a Colchester incumbent, was glad enough to make use of, but on several occasions these chests were nearly empty—testimony of their importance.[3]

A growing number of the graduates had enhanced their learning in Italy at Bologna, Ferrara or Padua.[4] Most of these held parish livings, usually after they had left the university, and acquired as well important legal, diplomatic or administrative posts, or ecclesiastical dignities. Some, like John Helier, rector of St. Michael's, Oxford, and student at Bologna, and John Kebil, parson of Glemsford, Suffolk, and also studying at Bologna, held the livings before and during their residence in Italy.[5] A few very likely came back to reside in one of their benefices. Thomas Alcock, after a distinguished career as rector

[1] P.R.O., C 1/269/44, 45.

[2] E. F. Jacob, *Essays in the Conciliar Epoch*, pp. 211–12; G. Pollard, 'Medieval Loan Chests at Cambridge', *B.I.H.R.* xvii, 113–19.

[3] For their emptiness see Jacob, op. cit., p. 212, and *V.C.H. Cambridgeshire*, iii, 164. In the church of St. Mary at the Walls, Colchester, there is a thirteenth century bible, once the property of William Ketyll, rector there 1467–76; the last page records the pledging of the bible in 1452 by William Ketyll and its deposit in the Chichester chest at Oxford; this was a security for a loan of 14s. which he repaid by annual instalments of roughly 1s. 8d. so that by 1458 the balance was 5s 4d. In 1452 the bible was valued by the stationer, John Dore, at 20s.

[4] R. J. Mitchell, 'English Law Students at Bologna in the Fifteenth Century', *E.H.R.* li, 270–87; 'English Students at Padua, 1460–75', *T.R.H.S.* (4th series), xix, 101–18; 'English Students at Ferrara in the Fifteenth Century', *Italian Studies*, i, 75–82.

[5] R. J. Mitchell, *E.H.R.* li, 272; P.R.O., C 1/328/44.

of both jurist universities at Bologna (1488), as a Doctor of Civil and Canon Law there, and as master of Jesus College, Cambridge (1515–16), retired to a small country living and died in 1523 as parson of Shipden in Norfolk.[1] He was kinsman to the bishop of Worcester and Ely and appears to have shared the bishop's characteristics of intellectual distinction, personal humility, and piety. William Latymer was an Oxford man; a B.A. there in 1489 and a Fellow of All Souls, he went on, via Padua, to Ferrara, where he took his degree in arts in 1502; four years later he came back to England and in 1513 was incorporated Master of Arts at Oxford.[2] One of the outstanding Greek scholars of his age, friend of Tunstall and Erasmus, tutor of Pole, he nevertheless finished his days as a parish priest in the church of Saintbury, even though he was a prebendary of Salisbury and possessed a living elsewhere.

That the graduates in this period formed a statistically significant proportion of the parish clergy is clear from some sample figures: about a fifth of all the clergy instituted or already beneficed in the Canterbury diocese during Bourgchier's tenure of the see were graduates;[3] about a tenth of the parish incumbents of Surrey at this time had degrees;[4] in 1522 of fifty-two incumbents in the City of London, six were doctors and thirty-three masters, and one-sixth of the unbeneficed clergy there were masters;[5] about a third of those admitted to and vacating parochial livings in the whole diocese of London while Tunstall was its bishop were graduates,[6] and out of 1,454 presentees to parish livings in Norwich diocese between 1503 and 1528, 256 were graduates—or just over a sixth.[7] A chronological analysis of the institution lists of different dioceses would no doubt support this picture and reveal a gradual increase in the number of graduates. Yet apart from statistics their importance is less certain. Among the unbeneficed, after the anxieties of the early fifteenth century and except in London, they were almost unknown; with the

---

[1] *E.H.R.* li, 279.

[2] R. J. Mitchell, *Italian Studies*, i, 81.

[3] *Reg. Bourgchier*, p. xxxix.

[4] This proportion is arrived at by the admittedly incomplete lists of incumbents in Manning and Bray's *History of Surrey*, but the proportions need not be misleading for that.

[5] *V.C.H. London*, i, 245.

[6] London Guildhall MS. 9531/10, fos. 1–33r.

[7] Norwich Act Books XIII–XVI.

encouraging presence of Latymer must be contrasted the total absence of graduates from the great archdeaconry of Richmond in 1525–6, and from the lesser archdeaconry of Stafford in 1531.[1] Even as incumbents they must be chiefly numbered among the absentees, for they acquired at Oxford and Cambridge skills and contacts which led them into courts and palaces to administer laws instead of the sacraments, to rule a diocese or a kingdom instead of a parish, or to lecture instead of to preach. This survey of university education, therefore, has little bearing upon the Church's instruction of the faithful in the parishes, except to underline a lost opportunity. In this loss, the Church was not wholly culpable: graduates in all ages have expected more than average rewards of status and money for their extended study and the Church in England had had a difficult struggle under Archbishop Chichele (1414–43) to provide this;[2] only as graduates became more numerous and opportunities for their employment in secular government became more restricted would parishioners begin to encounter the graduate parson and vicar (the graduate curate was still a long way off), and the encounter may not have fulfilled the expectations of reformers.

IV: *Training the Clergy*

(b) *The Schools*[3]

As a preliminary or as an alternative to university education the majority of parish clergy, beneficed and unbeneficed, acquired their learning from local schools and teachers. Those living in the vicinity of a monastery might attend the almonry school, which was not intended exclusively for novices; Roger Belle, a layman of Laughton en le Morthen, recalled in 1496 how some twenty years or more before he had attended the school held

[1] P.R.O., E 35/61 (taxation list for archdeaconry of Richmond). Lichfield MS. B/A/17/1(2), a tax list for Stafford archdeaconry 1531.

[2] E. F. Jacob, 'On the Promotion of English University Clerks in the Later Middle Ages', *J.E.H.* i, 181.

[3] The best brief introduction to schools at this time is John Lawson, *Medieval Education and the Reformation* (London 1967), and the most authoritative recent work Joan Simon, *Education and Society in Tudor England* (Cambridge 1966). The following pages, except where otherwise indicated, rely heavily on these two books.

within five feet of the old font in Kirkham priory church.[1] Boys living near a cathedral or a collegiate church might learn Latin in the grammar school (from no less a grammarian than Robert Whittinton at Lichfield or William Lily at St. Paul's in the second decade of the sixteenth century),[2] or a lad bent on a clerical life from an early age might master singing, spelling, the Articles of Faith and a few anthems and psalms in the song school; by canon law each cathedral and college was obliged to maintain these two schools. Nevertheless, the role of these institutions in education was not always as sound or as continuous as it should have been.[3] Apart from these, theoretically, permanent schools there were others more ephemeral, depending for their endurance, once begun, on the adequacy of the endowment and the ability and dedication of the teacher. In 1439 William Byngham, rector of St. John Zachary, London, had complained that seventy schools of this kind in the Midlands were empty for want of competent teachers and he had founded— with the aid of William Gull, rector of St. Peter's, Nottingham— God's House at Cambridge to train teachers in grammar.[4] By the 1470s and 1480s no such pessimism was possible, as free grammar schools were being founded and endowed in considerable numbers by bishops, laymen and parish clergy. Wayneflete's school appended to his college, Magdalen, at Oxford was the seedbed of English grammarians in the last decade of the fifteenth century; Alcock re-endowed an ancient school in Hull, Rotherham established a grammar school at his birth place, and Stillington at Acaster.[5] Laymen endowed other schools in which the master was also to be a layman; Stockport, Macclesfield and Manchester yield examples.[6] The part of chantries and their priests in education has recently been criticized by Mrs. Simon,

[1] R.VII.F.307, fo. 1r.
[2] See E. L. Pafort, 'Tudor Grammarians', in *The Thought and Culture of the English Renaissance*, ed. E. M. Nugent (Cambridge 1956), pp. 107–55, especially pp. 107–35.
[3] *Visitations of the diocese of Norwich 1492–1532*, ed. A. Jessop (Camden Soc. n.s.43), pp. 54, 73, 107, 124, 137, 156, 160, 165, 192–3.
[4] H. Rashdall, *Medieval Universities*, iii, 312; K.S.S. Train, *The Clergy of Central Nottinghamshire* (Thoroton Soc.), ii, 43.
[5] A. F. Leach, *Schools of Medieval England*, pp. 270, 275; John Lawson, *A Town Grammar School Through Six Centuries* (Oxford 1963), pp. 22–42; Rashdall, op. cit., iii, 225.
[6] J. Simon, *British Journal of Educational Studies*, iv, 32.

but she is more concerned with, and more successful in, demonstrating their comparatively small, rather than in proving their negligible, importance:[1] in Staffordshire in the early sixteenth century schools were kept at ten out of eighty-five chantries;[2] the priest of Barnard's service at Campden in Gloucestershire kept a free grammar school which was reputedly attended by sixty to eighty scholars;[3] at Newland, in the same shire, by the terms of its foundation the chantry provided a school for all who would learn letters, and its foundress thought carefully about its organization;[4] a chantry with a free grammar school attached was endowed at Wareham by John Rodger, a priest.[5] As well as the chantry priests and the incumbents, like John Faukeys,[6] who, to counter their poverty, were licensed to keep grammar schools, there were other parish clergy instructing their parishioners. In London a priest is found teaching grammar to some thirty local boys and girls; in Braughing at least one parishioner learnt letters (presumably English) from two successive parish chaplains; and a parish priest of North Creake left in his will 2*d.* each to 'all my skolers'.[7]

Apart from all these founts of knowledge and grammar there was supposed to be in every parish a 'deacon' or parish clerk, able to sing and read the lesson, who was to help in the services, ring the bell, and teach those who wanted to learn; this was usually glossed as meaning to teach them to read the psalter and to sing.[8] Coulton concluded that this was merely a pious ideal, and it is true that most of the instructions for parish clerks extant from the period 1450–1530, those of Louth, Lockington and St. Stephen, Coleman Street, for example, do not mention teaching.[9] Nevertheless, it had not disappeared from all, and

---

[1] Ibid.

[2] W. N. Landor, *Staffordshire Incumbents and Parochial Records 1530–1680* (Historical Collections of Staffordshire, 1915), pp. xxxiii–xxxiv.

[3] *V.C.H. Gloucestershire,* ii, 28.

[4] *Reg. Stanbury,* pp. 21–33, 105–10.

[5] *V.C.H. Dorset,* ii, 27.

[6] *Reg. Bekynton,* p. 393.

[7] C. T. Martin, 'Clerical Life in the Fifteenth Century', *Archaeologia,* lx, 359–60; Appendix 2(b) below; Norwich County Record Office, Will Register 'Haywarde', fo. 48r–v.

[8] *Liber Decretalium Gregorii IX,* III.1.iii.

[9] *The First Churchwardens' Book of Louth,* ed. R. C. Dudding, pp. 13–14; Leicester Archdeaconry Records, *A.A.S.R.* xxviii, 632–5; 'Records and History of St. Stephen, Coleman Street', *Archaeologia,* 1(1), 49–51.

the parish clerk of Faversham was expected 'to teche childern to rede and synge in the quyer and to do service in the churche as of olde tyme hath be accustomed'.[1]

Often clergy who did not themselves teach nevertheless endowed students: Richard Wolaston, a parson of Aldwinkle, left 20s. to John Bett the younger 'yf he will goo to the schole elles not'; and the parson of Moor Monkton bequeathed 10s. for Roger Robynson 'to fynd hym to the scole, and it to be paid as he haithe nede upon it'.[2] Henry Lucas, a London priest, in his will of 1517 left £20 to Thomas Swetyng's son Leonard, to continue his schooling for seven more years, but if he absented himself a week, or twelve days in a quarter, except for sickness, the executors were to devote the money to the poor and sick.[3]

We can seldom show at which schools or from which people a priest acquired his learning, but a rehearsal of the possible sources may leave us little doubt that he did acquire some; schools were varied, widespread, increasing in number and diminishing in fees; the endowment of teachers and students was fashionable and frequent. It is well to note that the aged London priest who had some thirty pupils would never have appeared in the records but for a malicious charge of rape, and that the two Braughing parish chaplains who taught some of their parishioners to read would not have been noticed but for the garrulity of a witness in a lawsuit and the fortuitous survival of the depositions.

As for the liturgical aspect of his training, that would have been nurtured by youthful and lifelong attendance at church, before he began his apprenticeship as an ordained assistant first in the services and then in the cure of souls. Much he would learn by imitation and by conversation with other clergy, but for a satisfactory knowledge of theology and canon law requisite in one who was to have the *regimen animarum* he would need to be literate. From most of the schools and teachers enumerated above he could learn to read, and probably write, English, and from many of them he could acquire some familiarity with Latin,

---

[1] F. F. Giraud, *Archaeologia Cantiana*, xx, 203–10.
[2] P.C.C., Porch 23; and *Yorkshire Star Chamber Proceedings*, ed. W. Brown (Yorks. Arch. Soc. 41), i, 166–72.
[3] G.L.C., MS. DL/C/354, fo. 25v.

though often perhaps no more than enough to understand or translate the scriptures and the litany. Thus equipped he could complete his education from books, such as had been written in the vernacular as well as Latin from the early fourteenth century for the guidance of just such a priest.

V: *The Mentality of the Clergy*

How often with the equipment thus attained the clergy did retire to their studies to read and write, what they read and what effect this had upon their thoughts are questions by no means easy to answer. For one thing the records of the books which they possessed or had access to are exasperatingly capricious. What in fact they read of the volumes to hand they seldom if ever record and though this might be deduced from their own compositions or from their own copies, it is well to remember that their own creative exercises are as yet relatively unexplored.

Probably few clergy entered upon the cure of souls so usefully prepared as that confessor or companion of Margery Kempe who for seven or eight years read to her from the Bible, from biblical commentaries, from St. Bridget, Walter Hilton, Bonaventura, Richard Rolle and others; 'aftyrwardys he wax benefy-syd & had gret cur of sowle, & than lykyd hym ful wel that he hadde redde so meche beforn'.[1] There were, of course, the academics and lawyers who had parish livings and whose libraries reflected their extra-parochial activities, men like Hugh Damlet, rector of St. Peter's, Cornhill, and Henry Caldey, vicar of Cuckfield,[2] but most clerical libraries of the time, if they are worthy of the name, were much less voluminous and varied. William Moreland, with benefices in Devon, Lincolnshire and Surrey, is, unusual in combining works relevant to his career in Chancery, a book of statutes and a register of writs, with a commonplace sermon aid, the *Legenda Aurea*, and the very rare sermons of the contemporary Flemish mystic, the Franciscan, Henry Herpe.[3]

---

[1] *The Book of Margery Kempe*, pp. 143–4.
[2] *Munimenta Academica*, pp. 609–11; *Catalogue of Cambridge University Library Manuscripts*, v, p. 253.
[3] P.C.C., Doggett 11.

For the most part clergy who owned books could only afford the popular aids.

A closer look at the clerical book owners whose wills were proved and registered in the consistory court of Norwich between 1500 and 1550 will bear this out.[1] By confining our attention to the consistory court we immediately eliminate that group of incumbents who because of the extent and distribution of their property came under the jurisdiction of the Prerogative Court of Canterbury; but since these were usually pluralists and dignitaries of Church and State, their reading habits have little relevance to our theme. Many and possibly all of the men covered by our survey must have grown to maturity in the age of the printing press and most of those who died in the fifth decade of the sixteenth century would have been at their peak on the eve of the schism.

The first thing to note is that out of 869 wills of parish clergy, books are mentioned in 158.[2] Considering that only twelve of all the testators were graduates, the proportion of book owners, almost one in five, is remarkably high. Yet it must be emphasized that such a figure is only a pessimistic assessment: many testators, like the graduate rector of Walpole St. Peter, Nicholas Robynson, were not in a condition to itemize or remember their books; like Thomas Lemanne, parson of South Acre, even those who had time and energy for quite extensive wills often made no allusion to considerable libraries which are only revealed in probate inventories, a type of document rarely extant for this area at this time. Not only were few of these book owners graduates, nine in fact, but seventy-two of them, almost half,

---

[1] Now kept in the Norfolk County Record Office. As there is a comprehensive alphabetical index of testators in print (M. A. Farrow, *Index of Wills Proved in the Consistory Court of Norwich 1370–1550* (Norfolk Record Soc. 16 in three parts)), no manuscript references are given here.

[2] These 158 clerical wills and 1 inventory are distributed through the fifty years as follows:

1500–10	: 66
1511–20	: 23
1521–30	: 22
1531–40	: 30
1541–50	: 18

That all of them are of parish clergy as distinct from collegiate, chantry and private chaplains it is impossible to be sure but such men have been excluded from this survey where identification was possible.

were unbeneficed clergy, generally thought of as the most ignorant. Among the resident, active local clergy, therefore, it would not be unjustified to think of a significant proportion as book owners; a quarter, to the present writer's mind, would be a very cautious estimate.

Less optimism is permissible when the character of their libraries is examined. In twenty-one, or almost a seventh of the total of book owners, no clue is given to the titles of their books, but bequests are made by such formulas as 'all my books', 'two of my books' or 'my books at Norwich'. In fifty-eight other wills service books only are left: manuals, missals, processionaries and so forth. Sermon aids alone are left in nine wills. In almost half these wills, therefore, if they do in fact record the whole truth of the testators' books, the mental horizons of the clergy may be drawn very closely around their liturgical obligations. Nor is the vista much widened by the remaining wills or by noting the occurrence and frequency of various works. By far the most common are books of sermons: ten *sermones discipuli* and six *sermones parati*, exceeding in popularity Myrc's *Festial* of which only five copies are noted. By contrast copies of the sermons of Augustine, Bede, Albertus Magnus and Bishop Fisher appear only once each. As well as sermons there were a variety of ancillary aids: that source of innumerable *exempla*, the *Legenda Aurea*, was named in fourteen wills; that theological encyclopaedia, the *Destructorium Viciorum*, appeared in four wills; the more voluminous and miscellaneous work of Bartholomew, *De Proprietatibus Rerum*, in five; the dictionary, *Catholicon*, was left by four testators. Such guides to pastoral work and teaching as the fourteenth-century *Pupilla Oculi* and *Manipulus Curatorum* add another eleven volumes to the list of works directly or obliquely relating to preaching. Altogether it is impressive evidence of the homiletic interest and activity of some pre-Reformation clergy.

Bibles, though not always complete, occur in seventeen wills; all but five of them are prior to 1540, but in proportion to the number of book owners in fact a significant increase has taken place by 1550.[1] Five of these Bibles were accompanied by commentaries and five clergy left commentaries without Bibles. What is most remarkable is that all the exegetical works are

[1] See p. 87, n. 2 above.

medieval; as late as 1541 Haymo of Faversham on the Gospels and Epistles, and in 1547 Nicholas de Lyra are named in wills. No sign betrays acquaintance with, or even awareness of, the dramatic advances in Biblical scholarship and interpretation which characterized this half century.

The conservatism which marks the theological libraries left by these clergy is equally apparent in other fields. History is represented by two copies of Geoffrey of Monmouth, mysticism by four of the *Vita Christi* of Ludulphus Saxonicus, the works of Boccaccio and Chaucer each appear only once in these wills; in 1515 Thomas Bevys, B.D., parson of a Norwich church, left a book of rhetoric by Alanus de Insulis, entitled *De planctu naturae*, and in 1541 George Boteler, parson of Melton, bequeathed a book of surgery. Only two of the 159 clerical book owners reveal anything but the most narrowly conventional and medieval tastes. In 1500 William Gage, S.T.B., left, alongside his legal and medical books, a *Vocabularium Cornucopie*, two books of Plutarch, the *De Tabulis* of Guido Bonati of Forli (the thirteenth-century astrologer) and a philosophical work by Aristotle with a commentary by Averroes; the picture of his outlook is completed by the three astrolabes and the clock which he also left. The interests of William Levyng, a priest of Sudbury at his death in 1510, are less varied and intellectual, more literary and musical; beside the books of 'prick-song' he bequeathed apparently several books of Virgil's work and some of the poetry of Terence and Ovid. These are the nearest to, though still far from, Renaissance men among our sample and yet they are also the least certainly parish clergy; Gage at his death was a chantry priest and apparently had no parish living,[1] Levyng was probably an inmate of the collegiate church of Sudbury.

In an area of rapidly growing prosperity, easily accessible and fully exposed to the radical influences of London and the Continent, not to mention those of Cambridge University itself, and in an age of tumultuous upheaval and profound intellectual changes, the parish clergy of Norwich diocese, though possibly more actively literate than is often conceded, were astoundingly conservative and narrow in their tastes. So innocent do they appear not only of the burgeoning Erasmian humanism of their time but even of the primitive humanism of fifteenth-century

[1] Emden, *Cambridge*, p. 255, *sub nomine* Gedge

England, that it is probably not unfair to allow them to be represented by Richard Torkington, parson of the Norfolk living of Mulbarton and author, *c.* 1517, of an account of a pilgrimage to Jerusalem.[1] Pilgrim journals are a special literature written by and for the preternaturally pious, but in so far as they are travel literature they may be nonetheless revealing for that. The aim of the pilgrim was to collect along the route indulgences for the remission of sins and Torkington never omits to record where and how plenary remission may be obtained, yet he avoids the crushing and exclusive obsession with images and relics which mars other writings of this genre and he has an eye for other things in early sixteenth-century Italy as well as the numerous fingers of Mary Magdalen.[2] He spends eight pages recounting the hospitality which the pilgrims enjoyed and the sights which they saw in Venice; he notes how Sicily had to import its cloth from England, 3,300 (sic) miles away by water; and he comments on the climate of Crete, its six month absence of rain, its temperate winter, and its immunity from frost and snow.[3] Yet his curiosity had distinct limitations and there is little sign that his mind was in any way unconventional or his interests humane. The stone in the church tower at Mount Olivet, from which Christ ascended into heaven, for Torkington still bore 'the prynte of hys holy foote . . . and specially of the ryght foote'; no Erasmian scepticism touches this passage.[4] Still less is his curiosity aroused by the 'ix Diverses Sectis of Cristen men' who share the use of the temple of the Holy Sepulchre; this diversity provokes no comment or speculation from the Norfolk parson.[5] In short, this survey of East Anglican clergy amply confirms the conclusions drawn by Professor Dickens from different sources about the predominantly medieval and narrow mentality of Tudor clerics.[6]

[1] Edited by W. J. Loftie, *Ye Oldest Diarie of Englysshe Travell* (London 1884).
[2] For another example of this kind see *The Pilgrimage of Robert Langton*, ed. E. M. Mackie (Cambridge, Mass. 1924). See also on Langton A. G. Dickens, *The English Reformation*, p. 5.
[3] *Ye Oldest Diarie*, pp. 7–15, 21, 65.
[4] Ibid., p. 30.
[5] Ibid., p. 39.
[6] A. G. Dickens, *The English Reformation*, pp. 1–8; 'Aspects of Intellectual Transition among the English Parish Clergy of the Reformation Period', *Archiv für Reformationsgeschichte*, xliii, 51–70, and 'The Writers of Tudor Yorkshire', *T.R.H.S.* (5th series) xiii, 49–76.

VI : *The Defects and their Causes*

On the statistical and documentary evidence available, it would be unjust to stigmatize the pre-Reformation parish clergy as overwhelmingly and abysmally ignorant; they were on the whole neither illiterate nor incompetent. Yet it is clear from the most discerning critics of the time and from the more searching episcopal enquiries that many clergy were nevertheless inadequate. Basically they were men who, if they read at all, read the wrong books; they were totally unaware of the New Learning even where it touched upon the very core of their faith, the life and values of Christ. Not only did they lack the modern guides to Christianity, the works of Erasmus foremost, they were rarely in possession of the very source of inspiration and contemplation, the Bible. Their unfamiliarity with this central work, the very Word itself, was emphasized by the evidence of their wills as well as by Hooper's findings. The clergy wanted, then, not so much the capacity as the opportunity to deepen and vitalize their faith and that of their parishioners. To a large extent this was due to the negligence of Church authorities in exploiting the printing press to distribute Bibles among the clergy; an imaginative initiative here, or even, following Colet's advice, a fierce insistence at ordination on 'metely learning of Holy Scripture' could have transformed the situation, but no legislation defined the scriptural learning needed for orders. It is possible that had the English Church not discouraged vernacular editions of the Bible the clergy might have proved themselves worthy of their times, but only the most vague and polemical testimony permits us to believe that Latin was the stumbling block to a well-informed clergy. The ill acquaintance of clergy with modern movements in theological and secular learning is likewise to the discredit of the Church authorities who left the clergy to get their education where and how they could, in schools and from teachers that varied enormously in their fitness for the task and in their view of it. There was plenty of private educational enterprise by bishops but no concerted plan and no blueprint even of how a priest should be trained—or even that a priest should be trained at all *as a priest*. It is not unhistorical to blame the English

Church for these failings: both Melton and Colet appreciated and demonstrated how the printing press could be employed deliberately for clerical improvement; an official vernacular Bible was commonplace on the Continent before ever Luther wrote his and whatever the anxieties inspired by Lollardy the English prelates who feared the publication even among the clergy of the fundamental Christian text cannot be exonerated; even the training of the clergy, though it seemingly occurred to none, was not a project impeded by unyielding social and mental patterns. Such patterns, however, do excuse the system, endorsed by Church and society, which usually prevented the graduates, those best equipped by ability and education to cope with the increasingly articulate and earnestly curious laity, from being present and active in the parishes. The clergy who remained to serve the parishes, neither commonly illiterate nor grossly inept, nevertheless had too few resources to strengthen their own and their parishioners' faith against the vigorous and radical challenges of Protestantism; a survey of their preaching will demonstrate this.

VI

Preaching

In 1281 Archbishop Pecham prescribed an outline of Christian doctrine and morals, which parish priests with the cure of souls should expound in the vernacular to their parishioners four times a year.[1] This decree, the *Ignorantia Sacerdotum*, enumerated the fourteen articles of faith, the ten commandments, the two precepts of the gospel, the seven works of mercy, the seven deadly sins, the seven principal virtues, and the seven sacraments of grace, and was, in fact, a very adequate teaching manual for the parish priest. In 1357 Archbishop Thoresby repeated it for the York Province, and had a vernacular translation made for the profit of lay readers.[2] After that time *Ignorantia Sacerdotum* was reissued at York Convocation in 1466 and 1518 and was sold in an English version at Oxford in 1520.[3] It bore fruit in sermons like the *Quatuor Sermones*, which were first printed by Caxton 1483 and by 1500 had gone through eleven editions and been issued by all the notable printers in England.[4] These four sermons in English dealt systematically with all the essentials of Christian faith: the Pater Noster, the seven short petitions, the Ave Maria, the Articles of Faith, the Commandments, each of the sacraments, the deeds of mercy, the virtues and the deadly sins, the pains of hell, the three elements of penance, and the general sentence of excommunication. Wholly without *exempla*,

[1] Wilkins, ii, 54–57.

[2] W. A. Pantin, *The English Church in the Fourteenth Century*, pp. 195, 211–12.

[3] Wilkins, iii, 599–601, 664–5; *The Daily Ledger of John Dorne 1520*, ed. F. Malden (Oxford Historical Soc. o.s. 5), p. 109; D. L. Douie, *Archbishop Pecham* (Oxford 1948), pp. 138–42.

[4] E. G. Duff, *Fifteenth Century English Books* (Oxford 1917), pp. 84–89; for text see *Quatuor Sermones* (Roxburghe Club, 3).

they were comprehensive, concise and lucid; indispensable as a summary of doctrine to the parish priest. They were often printed with, and some might think this an explanation of their popularity, John Myrc's *Festial*.[1] These sermons for Sundays and feast days throughout the year abound with explanations, often fanciful, and anecdotes, often sensational, and are clearly aimed at a parochial audience; it is all the more significant then that the early printers, with their keen sense of the market and their economic realism, saw fit to print nineteen editions of Myrc's *Festial* between 1483 and 1532.[2] In more than a few parishes, to judge from this fact and from the extant manuscripts of *sermones de sanctis et temporibus*, through Advent, Epiphany, Lent and Pentecost, the people would be regaled with homilies much like John Myrc's. There is other evidence too that the clergy were not lost for sermons or disinclined to preach. Certainly Margery Kempe had many occasions for weeping, as was her habit during sermons, and found the parish clergy rather more tolerant of her than the friars.[3] Pews and pulpits had begun to appear in parish churches in the thirteenth and fourteenth centuries, and they became more numerous and opulent in the fifteenth.[4] All those who had preferment and the cure of souls were allowed to preach; chaplains and students were often licensed, as the Bath and Wells registers show, and it seems probable that those whom Owst calls auxiliaries were very frequent preachers.[5] Interesting confirmation of curates preaching comes from Cheshunt, where in 1523 Richard Godd, it was complained, enlivened his accustomed sermons on Sundays and feastdays with many opprobrious words about the stews once kept at Waltham Cross and now at Cheshunt church, presumably the nunnery.[6] The frequency of preaching was noted by Alexander

[1] *Mirk's Festial*, ed. T. Erbe (E.E.T.S. e.s. 96).

[2] P. Janelle, *L'Angleterre Catholique à la Veille du Schisme*, p. 19.

[3] *The Book of Margery Kempe*, pp. 149, 165.

[4] J. C. Cox and A. Harvey, *English Church Furniture*, pp. 148–50 for pulpits, pp. 261–83 for seats, benches and pews; G. R. Owst, *Preaching in Medieval England*, pp. 160–4 for pulpits, pp. 165–7 for pews; see also F. R. Raines, *Vicars of Rochdale*, ed. H. H. Howarth (Chetham Soc. n.s.1), i, 26, and *V.C.H. Leics*. iv, 343. A whole series of elegant, richly decorated octagonal pulpits were produced in a late fifteenth century Somerset workshop and frequently ornamented with the Tudor rose (*Proceedings Somerset Archaeological and Natural History Soc*. xciv, 71–80, and cv, 106–9).

[5] G. R. Owst, *Preaching in Medieval England*, pp. 1–3.

[6] G.L.C., MS. DL/C/330, fo. 39r: '*solet predicare in diebus dominicis et festivis*'.

Carpenter who wrote that 'now, in many places, there is greater abundance of preaching of the Word of God than was customary before our time'.[1]

But whether the sermons which they delivered were altogether fitting, adequate and efficient vehicles for communicating to the laity fundamental Christian truths has been questioned recently. The criticisms are threefold: that their plethora of crude and sensational anecdotes, or *exempla*, and their preoccupation with hagiography have lured the attention of parishioners away from the figure and meaning of Christ; that their elaborate conventions of sermon making and Biblical exegesis, their addiction to tropological, anagogical and allegorical, rather than to literal, interpretation, often results in a wholly misleading exposition of the text; and that their emphasis is morbidly ascetic and their tone extravagantly minatory.[2] Each of these charges is pointedly illustrated by the critics and it would be foolish to deny them, but it deserves emphasis that there were healthier and more positive features also present. There are two just ways of revealing the quality and character of the average parochial sermon in this period and since it is a subject of crucial importance they are both worth adopting: firstly to examine a whole collection somewhat less naïve and lurid than the *Festial*, but more exuberant than the *Quatuor Sermones*; and secondly to compare the treatment of Easter, the most vital feast in Christendom, in three representative collections which are easily accessible in print.

The author of the *Speculum Sacerdotale*[3] began by urging priests with all their might to bring due and needful teaching and doctrine to the people,[4] and then provided nearly seventy sermons for feasts and saints' days. This collection certainly has its share of fancy and fiction, not least when narrating the fate of St. George, St. John the Baptist and St. Michael;[5] all the sermons on saints in fact are scarcely more than heroic stories with no Christian relevance explicit or elicited; beyond an enduring

[1] G. R. Owst, *The Destructorium Viciorum of Alexander Carpenter*, p. 21.
[2] J. W. Blench, *Preaching in England in the Late Fifteenth and Sixteenth Centuries*, pp. 1–7, 232–3, 257–8; G. R. Owst, *Literature and the Pulpit in Medieval England*, p. 48 about the preacher's preference for themes of denunciation and terror rather than of love and sweetness.
[3] *Speculum Sacerdotale*, ed. E. H. Weatherley (E.E.T.S. o.s. 200).
[4] Ibid., p. 3.
[5] Ibid., caps. xxxii, liii, lvii.

loyalty to Christ no remotely Christian virtue, still less any doctrine, is glimpsed. The unreality and irrelevance of these homilies could only have been underlined when they dwelt upon saintly victories over dragons.[1] The perverse avoidance of Christian essentials is best revealed by the sermons on the Holy Rood and the Exaltation of the Cross;[2] this last exemplifies the tendency to miss the point, being a narrative about the fate of a fragment of the Cross and not at all concerned with the significance of the Crucifixion. Yet for all this, the morbid asceticism and implacable deity alleged by modern critics to characterize medieval sermons are far from evident; rather is abundant hope of salvation offered to those sunk in sin. The sermon on St. Paul's Conversion tells how Paul was steeped in the sin of pride, as David was in lechery, and Matthew in avarice, and how all three are now high among God's servants, and it goes on: 'no man who would be converted should despair of forgiveness and of the mercy of God, seeing that such grace was extended to such sinners', a theme expounded again in words only slightly different in the sermon on St. Matthew.[3] Elsewhere in the collection doctrine and practice are from time to time explained: the three Masses of Christmas Day are accounted for, and devotion to Mary set in its place after that to Christ; Lent witnesses sermons on the seven works of mercy, on the necessity of confession and the nature of fasting; on Good Friday the preacher explains the symbolism of the liturgy, for example the absence of the introit and invitatory from the office that day; the origin and purpose of the Litany is outlined in one sermon, a definition of the Trinity given in another, and the feast of the dedication of the church occasions an eloquent account of the Church's function.[4]

The Easter Day sermon of the *Speculum Sacerdotale* is a long and systematic treatise.[5] The preacher begins by emphasizing its pre-eminence over all other feasts of the year, because by rising from the dead on this day Our Lord 'gave us a certain hope of our again rising'; each true Christian should communicate this day for by communion he receives the body and blood of Our Saviour who joins the communicants to him. After adjur-

1 Ibid., pp. 132, 143, 214.
2 Ibid., caps. xxxvi, lv.
3 Ibid., pp. 22, 210.
4 Ibid., pp. 6–8, 108–9, 135–40, 161–2, 163–4.
5 Ibid., pp. 117–29.

ing them to attend divine service in the week to come (before temporal work), the preacher turns to philology. Following St. Augustine, he derives 'Pascha' from 'passin', passion, and 'phase', passing, and concludes that 'Pask' connotes the time of Resurrection. He then expounds 'Pask' by history, allegory and tropology. By history 'Pask' was first celebrated when the Red Sea parted and the Israelites passed from, and the avenging angel through, Egypt. Allegory represents that in the time of 'Pask' (from Palm Sunday to the octave of 'Pask') the Church passed from infidelity to a new life by baptism. Tropologically we pass from vices to virtue. Anagogically Christ passed from death to life. The preacher next explains why the psalm *Confitemini* is said at Matins that week instead of *Quicumque vult*. He then expounds how Christ rose from the dead mightily, that is by his own will; marvellously—from a closed sepulchre and from Hell; truly—in his very own body—as the gospel for the day proves; and profitably, since he took out of hell all those who had been there since Adam's fall. A most dramatic account of the harrowing of Hell and Christ's imperious opening of the gates is followed by an appeal to the congregation to 'rise spiritually with Him if you will be with Him in Heaven'. To rise thus from sin needs three things—contrition of heart, confession of mouth, and satisfaction of deed: the greatness of her contrition won forgiveness even for her sins for Mary Magdalene; confession is a medicine for the sickness of sin and will cope with any so that there is no need to despair and hang oneself as Judas did—even he, had he confessed, would have been forgiven 'for the mercy of God surpasseth his wrath'. All sins, however, must be forsaken, for who keeps to one is 'like to a shipman that stoppeth all the holes of the ship except one, at the which all water cometh in and drowneth the ship'. Satisfaction is achieved by worthy penance which is abstinence from future sins in addition to repentance for past ones. This seems to end the sermon for what follows is more a selection of cautionary tales to buttress the foregoing.

Likening the soul (the spiritual temple) to the body (the material temple) the preacher urges that we should shave away sins and vices as we shave off beards, which grow from excess of humours. The temple of the Church is described in its three parts: walls, choir, altars, and their Easter decoration is explained. Then he states how reconciliation with enemies must precede communion, which is obligatory on Easter Day. At communion it is very necessary that the priest should preach, moving the discordant to concord; unworthily to receive Christ's body is a deadly sin. There then follows a story, which reappears (with very slight variations) in Myrc, about a bishop and the complexions of communicants, the purpose of which is to emphasize the unlimited mercy of God who could forgive two such women as Mary Magdalene and Martha and 'set them in dignity and virtues', and who gave his only begotten Son for the world. The reverence necessary at Easter is next described: to leave temporal works this day, to fast (and so fast always in spirit), and to keep sober and merciful are stressed. Care when taking the Host, the avoidance of spitting, belching and sneezing afterwards are urged. The preacher next records how husbands and wives are to abstain from intercourse for three days before taking the sacrament, and tells a savage little story in support.

The preacher tells how and why the three days following 'Pask' are also kept holy, and concludes with little apparent connection by explaining the three kinds of processions.

Clearly all this sermon was not delivered at one time, but its basis leaves little to be desired; if its explanations are curious, they are adequate, and if its tales are crude their point is wholesome. Comprehensive and systematic, it makes clear what Easter Day is about, and what part in it confession and communion should play; above all it is about the mercy of God.

Myrc,[1] too, begins with philology, deriving Easter from 'astyr', hearth, and he recalls that as this is the time when most householders clean out their winter fires from the hall and spread green rushes and sweet flowers about, so should all men now clean out from the house of their soul the fires of lechery, wrath and envy, strewing in their place the flowers of meekness, love and charity; for Christ departs from the dwellings of wrath and envy. At that point the preacher reverts to philology, interpreting Pase (sic) day as the passing day, when 'surpassing all others' you should love all men, and the day when God's children pass from evil to good living, from each vice to its opposite virtue. Above all this, however, it is God's Sunday because this day God's Son rose from death to life and the Church therefore rejoices and celebrates; no one should come to

[1] Mirk's Festial, pp. 129–32.

98

this feast unless clothed in God's livery of love and charity, not
the Devil's of lust and envy. For this, confession and the renunciation of sins are first necessary. To stir the parishioners further
to such renunciation Myrc recounts an example of the bishop
who prayed to God to know which of the communicants came
worthily and which unworthily; whereupon the bishop saw some
coming with faces as red as blood and with gore falling from
their lips—they were the envious, the backbiters and the oath
swearers; others came with faces as black as pitch—the lechers,
male and female; some had faces as white as snow—those who
had sinned greatly but had been contrite and washed white by
the weeping of their eyes; yet others came, fair and ruddy and
pleasing of appearance—the common folk who by their hard
work are kept out of sin (a proletarian sympathy often obtrudes,
as well as the notion of the orders of society, into medieval
sermon collections); lastly came two women with faces as bright
as the sun, two whose repentance and avowal never, with God's
help, to sin again, won them his forgiveness for their previously
evil lives.

Though the tale is coarse its moral is orthodox, merciful and
wholly encouraging; though the doctrine of the sermon is slight
and naïvely presented, it has a simplicity which is commendable
and doubtless was meaningful to its audience. The mystery and
need of Resurrection are unexplained and even unacknowledged
—but they were less of a mystery to the medieval imagination;
the emphasis is upon contrition and the mercy of God is stressed.
There is also an emphasis upon charity and meekness towards
one's fellow men, an exhortation to gentleness and kind intentions not wholly unnecessary before a congregation of early
Tudor men. There are undoubtedly some assumptions here
about the background knowledge of parishioners and before
criticizing its scope some attention should be paid to the sermons
which immediately preceded Easter Sunday and which were
delivered on such related feasts as Christmas and Pentecost.

Myrc's sermon on Passion Sunday[1] is a brief tale of how
Christ began to be persecuted by the Jews for pointing out their
sins and for calling himself the Son of God—though which was
more significant is left unclear; Myrc explains why the book of
Jeremiah is read this week, prophesying as it does Christ's

[1] Ibid., pp. 110–11.

passion, and finally concludes with a warning to those who persecute Christ today; in illustration of this and as a deterrent two repellant *exempla* are appended on treachery and oath swearing.[1]

Palm Sunday calls forth an unobjectionable exposition from Myrc[2] and an explanation for the day's procession and its reverence to the Cross 'that was the cause of our salvation and of the joy that we all hope for to come'. He concludes that 'palm' also refers to Christ's victory in driving the merchants from the temple in Jerusalem. Again an *exemplum* follows, from the *Gesta Romanorum* about an emperor's knight, which was designed to encourage humility and vigilance in order to avoid sin.[3]

The sermon on *Tenebrae*[4] explains why for three days the service is done without lights in the eventide, signifying Christ's evening travail in the Garden, his betrayal at night and the darkness on his Crucifixion. It briefly recounts Christ's mercy to the thief seeking forgiveness on the cross, and it comments on the suicide of Judas, which was unnecessary 'for Christ is so merciful in himself that he would have forgiven him had he asked it with a contrite heart'. Myrc then explains the service of *Tenebrae*, the extinguishing of the candles symbolizing the disciples leaving; the relighting of one, the Resurrection of the Lord; the blows on the book representing the thunder as Christ broke the gates of Hell. It concludes with an *exemplum* from Alexander Neckham about a lion bound to a tree by an adder and cut free by a knight; this, to Myrc, represents mankind bound to the tree of disobedience by the fiend and released by Christ.[5]

On Good Friday[6] most of Myrc's narrative was concerned with the genealogy and career of Pilate, illustrating the theorem that 'all evil beginnings have foul endings'. A terse and surprisingly restrained account of the torture and Crucifixion of Christ is followed by two *exempla* of blood-curdling horror.[7]

These related sermons fill out the details of the Easter Day oration, but Myrc clearly is addicted far less to doctrinal explanation than to cautionary tales of savage butchery. His sermons

[1] Ibid., pp. 111–14.   [2] Ibid., pp. 114–16.   [3] Ibid., p. 116.
[4] Ibid., pp. 117–18.   [5] Ibid., pp. 119–20.   [6] Ibid., pp. 120–2.
[7] Ibid., pp. 122–4.

leave the modern reader with a sense of revulsion and disappointment, but it is a modern anachronism to protest at these unwholesome fables and the present writer prefers to believe that they were a way of attracting attention in order to dispense morality; and here as in the other collections the loving mercy of God rather than a morbid asceticism obtrudes.

In the third series there are three sermons for Easter Day. The first[1] begins by quoting the words of Christ about the Mass —'who eats my flesh and drinks my blood will remain in me and I in him and therefore I will go to the place that I come from'. A caveat—with text from *I Corinthians*—about taking communion unworthily follows; next a lurid story of a woman who feigned to forgive her enemy and was strangled emphasizes the need for sincerity. Then the homilist gives a warning against those who worthily receive the sacrament but a few days later forget and return to their sin. A tale of the Christian clerk with a Jewish brother, recounts how a crowd of Jews cut the Host out of the clerk's entrails, how it transfixed them, became a child, spoke to the people, reverted to a Host so that the clerk was restored and thousands converted; a gruesome illustration of the power of the Host. More than this, as the preacher concludes, it demonstrates the meaning of the first words of the sermon. It might seem a silly and gross aberration from Christian essentials, but how else would one explain such a mystery as communion with all its attendant problems of transcendance and immanence to an unlettered and simple audience; what part of the audience would have understood—or would even today—a serious exploration of the theology? There is nothing in this sermon about Crucifixion or Resurrection; it is all about communion and is concerned to explain its importance and power, and to emphasize the need for being worthy of it.

A second Easter sermon[2] begins with the words of Christ, 'who eats this bread shall live eternally'. The story of the lion and its dead born whelp awakened after three days by the lion's roar introduces the theme of Christ awakening those, his children, dead in sin during the past year, for Christ this day feeds them with his own flesh and blood in the form of bread—'which bread is full good medicine to thy soul'. Christ succeeded where

---

[1] *Middle English Sermons*, ed. W. O. Ross (E.E.T.S. o.s. 209), pp. 61–65.
[2] Ibid., pp. 125–33.

other physicians, the prophets, failed to make man whole; for by his cry to the Father when on the Cross this day he gave life to man's soul—as the lion's roar did to the whelp. As the gospel tells us, the same body that died on the Cross and on the Sunday rose as God and man; this very body, is on the altar in the form of bread: 'I am the bread of life, and whosoever eats of me shall have eternal life'. With the Lollards perhaps in mind, the preacher next warns the congregation of the devil who tries to deceive them and to corrupt their beliefs; thcy should accept the Church's teaching unquestioningly and beware of their senses which tell them the Host is merely bread, for it is Christ's flesh and blood and 'ful mekell' filling heaven and earth; trust holy Church, therefore, and not the misleading senses. The story of the loaves and fishes symbolizes how this day Christ with one loaf—'his own precious body in the form of bread, feeds many hundreds of thousands of men'. The story of St. Thomas the Doubter and Christ's words 'Blessed are those who have not seen and yet believe', shows how those shall enjoy heaven's bliss who 'leave those things that pass their wit'. Further to persuade the parishioners that it really is Christ's flesh, the preacher re-counts the tale of the Jew whose disbelief in transubstantiation induced him to wager that his dog would eat the bread of the Host if it were put before him; a Christian who accepted the challenge went to communion and afterwards brought the Host to the Jew who had meanwhile starved his dog; despite its hunger it fled from the Host and when caught by the Jew fell down on all fours before the Host in reverence; when, to defeat fear and reverence, the Jew beat the dog, it leapt up and seized him by the throat.

The preacher concluded by saying that from Genesis all men have a body and a soul, and as the body needs food so does the soul: 'Unless you eat of the flesh of the Son of Man you shall not have life in us'. You must make a house for God with foundation, walls and roof: the foundation is steadfast belief in the sacrament of Mass and that the same body that died arose; the walls are the hope that whatever your sin God will forgive it; the roof is charity, honest charity towards others.

The third Easter sermon in this collection[1] begins by recalling how the three Marys sought out the dead Jesus with sweet

[1] Ibid., pp. 135–7.

ointments, just as we should with sweet prayers. We do this
when we believe firmly that he died for us to be our help and
succour. We seek him in heaven who believe that he ascended
there by his own might and are neither by fear nor favour nor
love deterred from God's laws. Not finding a body, the three
Marys found instead an angel in white, betokening a clean life
and joy in heaven. To redeem man Christ became man and rose
from the dead to life and he never fails them that seek him with
good will. After an unexpected digression on the role of women
and a defence of them—'for it is not wisdom to despise what God
loveth'—the preacher declares that Christ called Peter three
times and that this is another cause of hope to us, even if we have
denied Christ. We see Christ in Galilee, he says, when we
forsake our sins and therefore we should receive the sacrament
this day.

These sermons may lack the Renaissance and Reformation
emphasis upon the humanity of Christ and they seem to stray
towards a crudely materialistic view of the Host (it was not only
Lollards who fell into this error), but as an account of the meaning of Easter and of communion they are remarkably efficient;
they stress Christ's unlimited mercy to the truly penitent, and
they try to translate into the uncompromising vernacular of their
audience the intractable subtleties of incarnation and trans-
substantiation. It may be, however, that the more common
sermons of the year with their violent fantasies and pagan
narratives, insensitively marshalled to support Christian doctrine, and not always even that, in fact smothered Christian
truths in the minds of artless congregations, and that the Easter
message was too infrequently and, for the rest of the year, too
equivocally proclaimed or even remembered. A more serious
criticism of even the best parochial sermons of that time is of
their stale and hackneyed structure, their derivative and ossified
mode of interpretation; in other words, the singular absence of
any personal insights into, or any direct contemplation of, the
scriptures. The sermons, though functional and wider in scope
than is often allowed, were uninspired and uninspiring; the
parishioners could hardly have mistaken them for a declaration
of personal conviction by the preacher, unless he were an outstanding orator.

VII

Clerical Discipline

I: *Introduction*

THE evidence for clerical behaviour at the end of the Middle Ages has a Delphic ambiguity about it: the *detecta* and *comperta* of visitation records speak only of shortcomings; depositions in court are testimony and, for the historian, not proof; verdicts and penalties are often unrecorded; most ambiguous of all is the significance of purgation. It is hardly possible, therefore, to say whether crimes and misdemeanours among the clergy were increasing, not only because the sources are equivocal, but also because they are fortuitous, and before 1400 much less abundant. It is impossible to speak in modern parlance of a crime wave: conditions in the fifteenth century may or may not have been normal; what is certain is that they were not ideal. The aim of this chapter, therefore, is to see how far the Church tried to improve discipline and if and why these attempts failed: whether the bishops or their deputies were aware of a new situation, or whether they failed to perceive the critical nature of a familiar condition, whether they yielded to panic or complacency, whether they misjudged the relative gravity of different abuses, and whether their weapons were inadequate for the task of correction.

II: *Clerical Offences*

The most serious, because the most notorious, problem confronting the Church was incontinence. After the Gregorian Reform no

104

clerk who had been ordained subdeacon could take a wife.[1] The enforcement was slow and partial and while the intention was to avoid the very real danger of ecclesiastical property and goods being diverted, deliberately or inadvertently, to the support of a family and heirs, the effect was to drive many clergy into an illicit and scandalous relationship, or to expose them to scurrilous and malicious accusations. That some candidates for holy orders and for benefices were of a kind unlikely to be intimidated by ecclesiastical law or conscience, entering the life with no sense of vocation, is obviously true, but for others the strain must have been agonizing and debilitating, so great indeed for a Worcester priest in 1448 that to extinguish his lust he mutilated himself.[2] The parish priest of Swalecliffe, hesitating between vice and virtue, 'drawith to oon John Potters wif and she cannot be ride of hym' and he 'doeth stand herkenyng under menys wyndowes at 10 of the clock in the nyght'.[3] Master William Kemp, parson of Orsett, was reputed to have clandestine meetings in his chamber in the London Charterhouse with William Radley's wife, while Rose Vinfrey, a bawd of Orsett, waited in the garden below to see Kemp.[4] The rector of St. Mary Axe consorted with several prostitutes, and Adrian and Margaret Harrison kept a brothel in the parish of St. John Zachary for priests and friars.[5] Away from London and the south-east the rector of Bolton by Bowland, William Pudsay, of a substantial local family of that name, had a child by Mariane Burgh of Stammergate.[6] Yet it was not only 'commodious drabs' and village maidens who lured young clerics to disaster: the prioress of Kilburn committed fornication with John Wryght, *curatus*, and the nuns of Stratford were suspiciously familiar with John Lubbenham, a chaplain of St. Mary le Strand and vicar of Kimberley in Norwich diocese.[7]

[1] Lyndwood, I.8.i; III.2.i; III.12; III.13.i. See also C. N. L. Brooke, 'Gregorian Reform in Action: Clerical Marriage in England, 1050–1200', *Cambridge Historical Journal*, xii, 7; for its partial enforcement in subsequent centuries see H. G. Richardson, *T.R.H.S.* (3rd series) vi, 99, 120–3; *V.C.H. Norfolk*, ii, 219.

[2] *C.P.L.* x, 401.   [3] Reg. Warham, fo. 47r.

[4] G.L.C., MS. DL/C/206, fos. 24v–28r. It was not uncommon for clerks and even for laymen to lease rooms in the London Charterhouse; see P.R.O., E 326/B 7050 (Ancient Deeds) for such a lease in 1512.

[5] London Guildhall MS. 9064(iv), fos. 18v, 21v.

[6] *Acts of the Chapter of Ripon*, p. 90.

[7] W. H. Hale, *Precedents and Proceedings*, p. 83; G.L.C., MS. DL/C/330, fos. 123v, 128r, 155r, 84r.

About the children in which these unions often issued the records are singularly laconic, a feature which suggests that they were accepted without much difficulty or embarrassment by society.[1] Though priests sometimes name sons and daughters in their wills, it is charitable and perhaps accurate to think that they are usually referring to their god-children. This conclusion is difficult to accept about the will of Richard Leyfley, rector of Evedon, who in 1508 left his houses in Ewerby Thorpe to 'my son', Hugh, and if Hugh should die without heirs, 'to Margery, my daughter'.[2] The evidence is still more unequivocal that John Cowper, vicar of St. Leonard, Shoreditch, begat three boys from Elizabeth Cort, and that Robert Worthington, vicar of Bringhurst, had one child by his servant, Alice, and two by another servant, Elizabeth.[3] Thomas Hayns, a regular canon and vicar of Layston, had carnal knowledge of at least two women and in successive years was ordered to remove his two bastards from Buntingford and to keep them at least ten miles away from his parish of Layston.[4] This illustrates the official view and fears, not the lay attitude.

The picture above is undeniably sordid, yet much is more suspicious than notoriously scandalous. When William Sawge, vicar of Braughing, was ordered to expel the woman he accommodated in his house and consort no more with her, he claimed that she was Agnes Sawge, his sister.[5] Most incumbents had a servant or housekeeper, usually a woman, but canon law decreed that no clerk was to retain in his house any woman who aroused suspicion, not even his mother or sister, for the Devil turns even these to scandal.[6] Yet contact with women could not be avoided; some incumbents doubtless enjoyed without abusing the friendship of women in the parish; and many, no doubt, had occasion to give confidential advice to women in their cure. For these reasons, when some girl, or even some wife, of the parish was suspiciously with child, the culprit would find it easy to promote accusation of the incumbent or his assistant; the

[1] As in the fourteenth century (H. G. Richardson, *T.R.H.S.* (3rd series) vi, 99, 120–3).
[2] *Lincoln Wills*, ed. C. W. Foster (Lincoln Record Soc. 5), i, 37–38.
[3] London Guildhall MS. 9064(iii), fo. 33v; *Lincoln Visitations 1517–1531*, i, 11.
[4] G.L.C., MS. DL/C/330, fos. 97r, 100r, 101r–v, 114r, 149v, 150v, 152r, 171r.
[5] G.L.C., MS. DL/C/330, fo. 226r.
[6] *Liber Decretalium Gregorii IX*, III.2.i.

parishioners would find it easy to believe, if only because it was sometimes true.[1] Just such an attempt to implicate a parson occurred in London in 1492: Thomas Jurdan was charged with 'Falsly and dampnably' defaming and slandering Sir George Brownhill, priest, saying that 'he shulde carnally have to do with his wyff Marget Jurdan, she thene being quick with childe', although it was protested that she 'was gone quicke with childe a quarter of a yere or [ere] ever the preste knew her or the saide Jurdan'[2] John Roo, curate of St. Christopher next the Stocks, London, persistently denied paternity when a woman of his parish—incited, he claimed, by the chantry priest—accused him before the bishop of being the father of her child and sued him before the sheriffs of London for £800 (sic) maintenance; discontented with the slow processes of law, in the middle of divine service she walked up to the chancel and laid the no doubt raucous babe before him; her extravagance suggests derangement, but we cannot be absolutely sure of malice.[3] If the apocryphal story about John Skelton, poet laureate and parson of Diss, is true (and it is consistent with his character) no doubt was left in the minds of his parishioners, for when challenged about his offspring, he held the naked child up before the congregation in church and proudly acknowledged his fatherhood.[4]

Clearly to permit clerical marriage would have abolished these scandals; clerical self-discipline would only have achieved the elimination of legitimate accusations. Not only is there no sign in England of that episcopal tolerance of 'hearthmates' which characterized the Welsh Church then,[5] but the English

---

[1] The dispensations from illegitimacy granted in *C.P.L.* x–xiv to the sons of priests who themselves wished to take orders does not support the gloomy conclusions sometimes alleged. Between 1447 and 1492, 586 such dispensations are recorded, but only 8 of these concern England, the rest being for Scottish and, far more numerously, Irish recipients. Of course, not all such sons, and no such daughters sought dispensations of this kind and some figures are concealed by occasional grants to papal collectors in England to dispense a certain number—varying from ten to fifty—of bastards; what is stressed here is that *no* conclusions should be drawn from these papal letters about the scale of clerical procreation in England.

[2] London Guildhall MS. 9064(iii), fo. 93r.

[3] *L. & P.* iv(2), No. 2754.

[4] *Merrie Tales newly imprinted made by Master Skelton Poet Laureate* (London, Thos. Colwell (1567)), sigla B.i.

[5] Glanmor Williams, *The Welsh Church from Conquest to Reformation* (Cardiff, 1962), pp. 338–9.

Church attempted to assist clerical self-discipline: in 1518 the York Convocation cited a statute of Greenfield, which decreed that women living as the wives or *focariae* of priests were to be punished by excommunication, or, if they persisted in their offence, were to be seized by the secular arm and denied ecclesiastical burial as well;[1] but its repetition two hundred years after its first publication held little promise of its efficacy now. Furthermore, the keeping of hearthmates, though it may have complicated such chores as the collection of tithes from resentful contributors, in itself certainly seems to have caused far less scandal and was less damaging to clergy-laity relations than mere irregular promiscuity with women of ill, or good, repute; nor did sexual irregularity necessarily entail negligence of the priest's other duties.[2]

After incontinence the subject which perplexed the Church's legislators and lawyers most was dress. It seems an odd inversion of values that from the twelfth century onwards the records of Convocation had far more to say about clerical dress than clerical negligence.[3] The clerk was not distinguished then from the layman by a uniform, but was entitled to wear any dress not expressly forbidden, provided it avoided extravagance of colour or style; he was to avoid the voluptuous colours of red and green—though Lyndwood was not sure why these specifically—and the style of knights, adhering instead to simplicity and soberness.[4] Clergy were to avoid knives, swords, gold purses, padded shoulders, curly toed shoes, and long unkempt hair, all of which caused the Elizabethan antiquary, Harrison, to recall that in his youth 'to meet a priest in those days was to behold a peacock that spreadeth his tail when he danceth before the hen'; but even the simpler dress of the average layman could give an equally false impression, as Bishop Alcock noted: 'if thou se a preest go lyke a lay man, with his typpet, slyppers and grete sleves, it is to presume that he repenteth hym that ever he forsoke the habyte of a layeman and therfore he useth it'.[5] Doctors

---

[1] Wilkins, iii, 670.

[2] See M. Bowker, *Secular Clergy in Lincoln Diocese*, p. 121.

[3] For the period 1450–1530 see *Reg. Bourgchier*, pp. 92, 109–10; Wilkins, iii, 619–20, 651, 666 et seq., 697, 712–13, 717, 721.

[4] Lyndwood, III.1.i–iii: *'medium tenere honestum est et commendabile'* (iii, note *f*).

[5] *Reg. Bourgchier*, pp. 61–63, 109–11; *V.C.H. Essex*, ii, 36; J. W. Blench, *Preaching in England in the Late Fifteenth and Sixteenth Centuries*, p. 239.

were permitted, in accordance with their status, rather more opulence, but they, of course, were rarely active and resident parish priests. The contents of innumerable clerical wills confirm that the simple moderation of the ideal was frequently exceeded; the effects and dangers of this might well be imagined at that time when a crucial part of the priest's income came from tithes and offerings yielded by people who could ill afford them or, being able to, yet gave with increasing reluctance and resentment. The prelates of Convocation were naturally alarmed when they contemplated such consequences, but it is significant that in no court or visitation records known to the present writer is there a single case of a cleric presented for extravagance of dress; the legislation was either ignored by the administrators, or the laity were indifferent. Legislation, indeed, could hardly stop people leaving the clergy gowns of exuberant quality and colour as gifts or as mortuaries (the best or even the second best gown was not always particularly sober), and it may be that the irritation caused by their ostentatious dress was mitigated by the frequency with which the clergy in their turn left such gowns to the poor and elderly of the parish.

More important than dress and more attainable than chastity was diligence, and in some ways the Church's most important disciplinary task was to ensure that the parish clergy executed their office conscientiously. There is no reason to believe that where an incumbent was absent the morale of the assistant clergy was lower than elsewhere, for the parish priest, the incumbent's deputy, exercised no less authority than his principal over the other clergy; he could dismiss them, a sanction no doubt of some persuasion in the competitive world of the assistant clergy and in times of economic hardship. The deputy himself enjoyed much less security of tenure than the incumbent. Neglect of the rectory and chancel buildings was the most common feature of negligence, but this was far more a problem of finance than of the will; not so the damage at Ridlington, whose parson made a bonfire in the chancel of its timbers, 'sparres and byndyngs', and threw stones at the parishioners who approached to stop him.[1] The procedure in cases of dilapidations is clearly seen in the London records: in November 1530 the vicar of Thurrock Grays and the rectors of Downham,

[1] *N.C.C.D.* No. 289.

Dunton and Woodham Ferrers were summoned to shew why, because of dilapidations, their benefices should not be sequestrated; all of them appeared early in December by proctors who were warned to complete the repairs—by the following Easter in two cases, by the second Sunday after Easter in one, and by Pentecost in another; in two instances they were to certify, with the witness of two honest parishioners, that the repairs had been done, and in all if they were not done the proctor was ordered to appear on the third or fourth court day after the expiry date and show again why the benefices should not be sequestrated.[1] So far as sheer want of cash was not the cause, this procedure doubtless worked, and in any event, if the defendant could show mitigating reasons, sequestration would not follow.

Not all negligence was of this kind. The rectors of Candlesby and Gunby were typical of many in their failure to keep hospitality.[2] Clerical indifference to divine service was not so frequent as to be typical—Archbishop Warham found only eleven instances in 266 churches[3]; it could range from neglect by the rector of All Saints in the Wall, London, to sprinkle holy water on his parishioners at divine service on Sundays, to the priest and clerks of St. Thomas Magnus, London, who 'in tyme of dyvyne service, be at tavernes and alehousis, at fyshing, and other trifils'.[4] Others disregarded the tiresome formality of certificates necessary when a person from another parish sought marriage, negligence arising from indolence or impatience, if not from some hope of profit by fees.[5] Avarice may also explain refusal of the priest of Bishopton to hear the confession of a dying parishioner, as it explains the refusal of a London curate to administer to the sick until he had received a fee,[6] but one must bear in mind the morbid hypochondriac who was probably just as much a nuisance and embarrassment to the medieval priest as his modern counterpart is to the general practitioner.

[1] G.L.C., MS. DL/C/330, fos. 199v, 201r, 202r, 203v; the proctors were lawyers—in two instances of the Court of Arches—and are not to be confused with the proctors which absentees left in their parishes.

[2] *Lincoln Visitations 1517–31*, i, p. xxxviii.

[3] Reg. Warham, fos. 45–83; excluding the results of poverty and absence.

[4] London Guildhall MS. 9064(iii), fo. 61v; *Customs of London or Arnold's Chronicle*, p. 278.

[5] W. H. Hale, *Precedents and Proceedings*, p. 65.

[6] *Acts of the Chapter of Ripon*, p. 22; W. H. Hale, op. cit., p. 62.

It may seem odd that Convocation was so much more concerned with the neglect of buildings than with neglect of persons
or offices, for this second category was clearly more damaging to the repute of the clergy and the Church, but in so far as
dilapidations jeopardized the economic value of the living, they
represented a far more urgent problem, threatening the incumbent with repairs so expensive, or accommodation so decayed,
that the cure could not be efficiently served, or possibly even
filled. The other sort of neglect would disappear with the offender
and could be erased by his successor; it was a less complex
problem and its solution depended, if not on better selection, on
the summary powers of correction discussed below.

A great variety of other offences was open to the clergy as a
miscellany of examples will shew. The curate of Hawridge who
played football in his shirt and on occasions played dice was a
man no doubt much in demand, though perhaps not least for
divine services, most of which he was accustomed to finish
before 8 a.m.[1] The vicar of Doddington, finding the vicarage
uninhabitable, betook himself, not without raising suspicions, to
lodge at alehouses in the town.[2] Some incumbents kept their
horses in the churchyard, and the rector of Kencott even arranged
a couple of tombstones to form a trough for the calves which he
kept there.[3] Disclosures of confession were much more serious
and disruptive of parish life, but they were, for an age so prone
to back-biting, remarkably rare.[4] The clergy themselves were
by no means inarticulate when defaming their neighbours, and
least of all when pronouncing on the evil character of other
clergy. Words, however, sometimes failed them; certainly they
did John Saull, priest of Chislet parish, who 'came violently
upon Sir Aleyn Bukster and strake (him) unpreestly with a
nakid sword openly in the strete and was likely to kyll the said
Sir Aleyn'.[5] The rector of East Barming did kill Nicholas Hunt,
but in self defence, and John Roche, vicar of Sarratt, in 1462 murdered and secretly buried his parishioner, Richard Glowcestre,

[1] *Lincoln Visitations 1517–31*, i, 44.
[2] Reg. Warham, fo. 55v.
[3] Ibid., fo. 53r, and *Lincoln Visitations 1517–31*, i, 134.
[4] For two of these rare examples see *Archaeologia*, lx, 361–3, and London Guildhall MS. 9065, fos. 219v–220r.
[5] Reg. Warham, fo. 47r; and for other examples see G.L.C., MS. DL/C/330, fos. 77r–v, 95v.

and then fled.[1] The vicar of Tilmanstone, John Smale, was a persistently violent individual, who lavished blows gratuitously upon a variety of people and even employed his servant to do so; when he appeared at the alehouse one night and ordered his man to 'Go yn and geve a blowe', it is not surprising that 'there was a fray and lykely to a bene manslawter'.[2]

At the most personal level the discipline of the parish clergy was regulated by their fellow clergy. The assistants confessed to the incumbent or, if they wished, to the bishop; rectors and vicars were bound to confess to the bishop or his deputy. This episcopal deputy was almost certainly the penitentiary: in each deanery one rector or vicar of good fame, sufficiently lettered and endowed with grace, was to be appointed to this office by the bishop to hear the confessions of and enjoin penance upon the rest of the secular clergy, beneficed or unbeneficed, in the deanery; although the penitentiary's competence extended over most of the cases reserved to the bishop and his original *raison d'être* was no doubt to reduce this burden upon the bishop, he very probably dealt with unreserved cases too.[3] It is clear that to a considerable extent the parish clergy were hearing each other's confessions; the efficacy of the system therefore depended upon the careful selection of the penitentiaries and upon the conscience of their subjects.

At a different level the parish clergy were subject to correction by the bishop and the archdeacon. The commonplace view that bishops of this period were mostly absent from their sees, busy serving the king and indifferent to their diocesan responsibilities must be qualified by the records of such episcopates as Praty's at Chichester, Carpenter's and Morton's at Worcester, Atwater's and Longland's at Lincoln, not to mention the visitation records of Archbishop Morton in Norwich diocese and of Warham at Canterbury.[4] And even where the bishops were largely absent, as was Tunstall of London and the archbishops of York, their vicars-general performed their duties with dili-

---

[1] *L. & P.* ii(2), No. 3948; *Reg. quorundam abbatum . . . S. Albani*, ii, 11.

[2] T. S. Frampton, 'List of Forty-Five Vicars of Tilmanstone', *Archaeologia Cantiana*, xx, 107.

[3] Lyndwood, V.16.i, especially notes *z* and *f*.

[4] *V.C.H. Sussex*, ii, 16; *V.C.H. Worcestershire*, ii, 38–39; *Lincoln Visitations 1517–31*, i, ii; C. Jenkins, 'Cardinal Morton's Register', *Tudor Studies*, pp. 66–74; Reg. Warham, fos. 45–83.

gence and vigour, as the London Act Book and the registers of York clearly show.[1] Occasional entries in many registers—of Hereford, Lichfield and Lincoln, for example[2]—indicate that if episcopal visitation was no longer, as the law required, a triennial affair, neither was it as rare as is sometimes alleged. In the intervening years archdeacons were to visit the parishes within their jurisdiction, a duty which they usually performed by deputy at the end of the Middle Ages. Their obligation on these tours was primarily to record each year all the ornaments, utensils, vestments and books in each church and to indicate additions and those in need of attention or replacement, and to ensure that the church buildings were adequately repaired; their principal concern was to see that the services could be and were properly carried on, and though they sometimes, as in the Kent archidiaconal records, seem merely content to confine their attention to material rather than people, the Leicester records show a wider interest.[3] If rural deans ever carried out *ad hoc* commissions to visit the churches in their deanery, no trace of this activity remains. In areas exempt from episcopal and archidiaconal control, such as the peculiar of St. Albans or of Burton on Trent or of the dean and chapter and prebendal churches of a cathedral like Lichfield, the place and authority of the ordinary was occupied by the abbot in monastic, and by the dean and chapter in cathedral, peculiars, although the clergy of prebendal churches were immediately subject to the prebendary.[4] By presentment at these irregular and occasional visitations, and far more often by the remorseless and eager enquiry of apparitors into rumour and ill report, the offences of the clergy came to the notice of their superiors.

The sanctions available to the disciplinary authorities were

[1] G.L.C., MS. DL/C/330, and A. H. Thompson, *The English Clergy*, p. 48, n.

[2] *Reg. Mayew*, pp. 165–6; *Reg. Bothe*, pp. 65, 128; Lichfield MS. B/A/1/14, fo. 2r; M. Bowker, *Secular Clergy in Lincoln Diocese*, p. 17.

[3] Lyndwood, I.10.i, iii; C. E. Woodruff, 'An Archidiaconal Visitation in 1502', *Archaeologia Cantiana*, xlvii, 13–15; 'Leicester Archdeaconry Proceedings', *A.A.S.R.* xxviii, 117–220, 593–662. For Gloucestershire in 1498 see *Trans. Bristol and Glos. Arch. Soc.* xlviii, 276; for Norwich see *N.C.C.D.* No. 84, and *Inventory of Church Goods*, ed. A. Watkin (Norfolk Record Soc. 19), ii, p. xxii.

[4] *Reg. quorundam abbatum . . . S. Albani*, ii. 109–10; for the jurisdiction of Burton Abbey and Lichfield Dean and Chapter see the present writer's discussion of diocesan jurisdiction in the forthcoming volume of *V.C.H. Staffs.* which is devoted to ecclesiastical history.

all in danger of being self-defeating. A penance which would
not humiliate the offender might not intimidate, yet a severe
penance would jeopardize his authority among laymen and rather
embitter than reform him.[1] A solution to this, much favoured in
London and Canterbury dioceses, was to commute the penance
for a money fine, perhaps the most effective way of coercing the
recalcitrant and saving the dignity of the Church.[2] Excommunication of the clergy had the major disadvantage of drawing
everyone's attention to clerical misdemeanours. Deprivation
created a vacancy and converted an unruly incumbent into a
disgruntled stipendiary, and it was a grave step threatening the
patron's advowson and hence to be used sparingly and cauti-
ously; this it certainly was, being rare in any diocese on more
than one or two occasions a year, and then it was mainly
operated as a consequence of the legislation against pluralism or
incorrigible non-residence.[3] As for degradation, that was far too
solemn for frequent use and seems rarely to have been employed
at all; it would create almost as much scandal as the offence
which justified it. Undoubtedly the best weapon against offenders
was to suspend them from officiating and, when they were
incumbents, to sequestrate the fruits of their benefices, perhaps
confining them meanwhile to the bishop's prison; the most
eloquent testimony to the efficacy of this procedure is the
frequency of its occurrence in episcopal registers, visitation and
court books.

The working of this system is not easily judged, for of their
nature disciplinary cases leave less enduring records than instance litigation; apart from the great collection of London
commissary court books, which cover some half dozen years in
four huge volumes,[4] the disciplinary records of other courts are

[1] R. Hill, 'Public Penance', *History*, xxxvi, 216: penance had to be salutary,
deterrent and suitable; see also ibid., 223 for Bishop Sutton's care lest penances
imposed on the clergy should impair their authority among laymen.
[2] London Guildhall MS. 9064(i–iv), *passim*, and B. L. Woodcock, *Medieval
Ecclesiastical Courts in the Diocese of Canterbury*, pp. 98–99.
[3] One a year in Bath and Wells diocese under Bekynton (*Reg. Bekynton,
passim*). In Norwich diocese 1503–28, out of 1132 vacancies where the cause is
known, only 12 were by deprivation (Norwich Act Books XIII–XVI). Fox could
write almost at the end of his career 'I never pryved person in noo dyoces that I
have be in' (*Reg. Fox*, ed. M. P. Howden (Surtees Soc. 147), p. xliv), and his
episcopal career extended over 40 years and four dioceses.
[4] London Guildhall MS. 9064(i–iv).

usually too fragmentary or too discontinuous at this period to allow profitable analysis or generalization. One exception is a court book of the dean and chapter of York;[1] some fifty urban and rural parishes were constantly, and another thirty six occasionally, under the chapter's jurisdiction, so that over nearly half a century it affords a manageable unit for study, which is yet sufficiently extensive in time and area to be significant.[2] How far it reflects conditions elsewhere in England, except in so far as there is nothing patently untypical or special about the area (as there is, for example, about London), may only be judged as similar records from other courts are found and analysed. Four questions are to be asked of this material: how effectively did the system of purgation discover the truth; how wise and appropriate were the penalties; were the clergy more leniently treated than laymen; what state of clerical morale is revealed?

Purgation of a clerk ideally should have been in the deanery where the offence was committed and should have been by at least six clerks for fornication and twelve for adultery, though in necessity, if these were lacking, laymen could be employed.[3] Clearly this ideal was inappropriate where an isolated parish and not a deanery was the unit of jurisdiction and for the same reason sufficient numbers of clerks were rarely forthcoming. In the court book between 1453 and 1491 some ninety-three offences of fornication or adultery by clergy are recorded and the usual requirement was six or eight compurgators, combining clergy and some *meliores* of the parishioners; only on three occasions was a clerk allowed to purge himself and equally rare were those who had to purge themselves, as one did, with eight honest chaplains and five honest parishioners or, as in another case, with eight priests.[4] In some of the adultery cases the woman—and very seldom the clerk as well—was required to purge herself with four, six, seven or even eight women neigh-

---

[1] R.As.55, discussed by J. S. Purvis in *A Medieval Act Book* (privately printed, no date); it covers the period from the late fourteenth to the late fifteenth century, but attention in this chapter has been focussed on the years from 1453 to 1491, that is fos. 123v–233v, since the MS. is complete between these dates but not before or after them.

[2] The York dean and chapter visitation records cover ninety-two churches, but not all of these were parish churches; the prebendal churches only came within its jurisdiction during visitations or vacancies or by appeal.

[3] Lyndwood, V.14.iv, particulary note *g*.

[4] R.As.55, fos. 136r, 161v.

bours, a severe test of truth one might think.[1] Even when the
terms of purgation were less than the legal ideal, it was no empty
and futile procedure: of the ninety-three cases no information
about the result of forty-seven is known (which may indicate the
dropping or failure of the charges),[2] but of the other forty-six,
while purgation succeeded in twenty-five and failed in only five,
six offenders had confessed to the charge and ten had submitted
before purging was necessary; that almost a third were deterred from facing the process is surely a witness to its efficacy.
Typical of the submissions is that of a chaplain of St. John's
Hungate, York, who in 1463 was unable to find the necessary
three chaplains and three parishioners to purge himself, and of
the rector of Handsworth who two years later no doubt despaired
of finding a sufficient number of purgators from this parish un-
acquainted with some of his ten children by Joan Crookes.[3]
Occasionally, however, the difficulty was to get men away from
their fields, as when the vicar of Wetwang had his purgation
prorogued from harvest time in August until November so that
two neighbouring curates and four of his senior parishioners
could come to York and clear him.[4] A far greater weakness than
purgation was the geographically limited jurisdiction of the
chapter, which enabled a few to emulate a parish chaplain of
Drayton who in 1472 had fled with his miscreant spiritual
daughter out of their jurisdiction before the citations arrived.[5]
But this happened rarely in the York record and was far more
difficult for most subjects of a bishop.

The penance usually administered was to visit Beverley and
York minsters, sometimes Ripon as well, and to make an offering
of a quarter of a mark at their major shrines—the feretory of St.
John's at Beverley, the head of St. William and the *archam rubeam*
at York, and the shrine of St. Wilfrid at Ripon.[6] This might not
seem a crushing or reformative sentence, but it involved great

[1] Ibid., fos. 137r, 139r, 151r, 173v, 218v.

[2] Five of these inconclusive examples are explained by the non-appearance of
the defendant (ibid., fos. 161v, 184r, 202r(*bis*), 224r); about the others there is no
information in the MS. other than the charge, a fact which suggests that the
accusations were malicious and frivolous and the evidence patently inadequate—a
not uncommon feature of law-enforcement at that time.

[3] Ibid., fos. 167r, 175r.

[4] Ibid., fo. 153r.

[5] Ibid., fo. 202r.

[6] e.g. ibid., fos. 138r, 141r, 177r, 216r, 221r, 222r, 229v, 230r.

inconvenience and considerable expense in addition to the presented offerings, which were tantamount to a fine. More than this, the dignity of the cleric in his own parish was saved, if at the risk of concealing that justice was being done. Certificates were required, as of all penances, that these places were visited and the offerings made, but none are known to survive. Other penalties were sometimes added: John Skyrnes was suspended from celebrating divine service in the dean and chapter's jurisdiction and had to find at his own cost a chaplain to serve his cure within a week, and to pay 20s. to the chapter clerk before the next feast of St. Andrew.[1] He, like the vicar of Drayton and the rector of Handsworth, had submitted to correction and such men seem to have been dealt with more severely than other offenders: the vicar of Drayton was spared the pilgrimages but had to proceed on three holydays around the market and parish church of Retford, in bare feet and ankles, wearing merely a shirt, with his head bared; he was to carry through the market a candle of 1 lb. of wax and in the church he was to read devoutly from the psalter, bearing in his arms a cope worth 26s. 8d. which he was to donate to the use of that church; moreover, if before the feast of St. Mark next he had failed to exchange his vicarage or resign it and so remove himself from the dean and chapter's jurisdiction, he was to be deprived and his penance extended.[2] Public humiliation, coupled with a useful, expensive and apparently needed offering to the parish church, and finally removal from his cure, amounted to no light sentence. Thomas Tynley, the rector of Handsworth, whose fornication had produced ten children and whose negligence of repairs had reduced the rectory manse to the ground, in respect of his negligence was ordered to process before the cross around the parish church of Laughton en le Morthen on six Sundays, wearing only his cassock and surplice, and during High Mass kneeling at the font to read devout prayers; all the fruits, oblations and emoluments from Handsworth were assigned to the vicar of

---

[1] Ibid., fo. 154r.
[2] Ibid., fo. 187v. But compare More's anecdote, (*English Works*, ii, 216): 'it happed that a young priest devoutly in a procession bore a candle before the cross for lying with a wench, and bare it light all the long way. Wherein the people took such spiritual pleasure and inward solace that they laughed apace. And one merry merchant said unto the priest that followed him, *sic luceat lux vestra coram hominibus.* Thus let your light shine afore the people'.

Laughton en le Morthen, who was to allow Tynley 10 marks a year to support himself and his cure, while the residue was applied to the rectory repairs until they were complete.[1]

If the means of establishing or demolishing the charge were satisfactory, and the imposition of penances responsible and prudent, how did the clergy fare in these respects *vis-à-vis* the laity? In terms of purgation, except for the absence of clerics from lay trials, there was little to choose, though whereas six neighbours of the same sex was the usual requirement in the 1450s, by the 1490s the usual number was four or five;[2] though the numbers tended therefore to decline, the overall picture resembles that of clerical purgation: out of 284 cases, 154 lay offenders successfully purged, 26 failed and 104 confessed or submitted. As for penances the laity were usually spared journeys to Beverley and Ripon and were expected to process on six days in their parish church, usually dressed merely in a shirt and sometimes with a bandage tied round their head, and to offer there half a pound of wax; the pilgrimage to York Minster was for many a short walk from their urban or suburban parish. The lay penalties seem less severe in costs, though locally more humiliating, and the terms of clerical purgation are rather more rigorous.

Assuming, until new evidence arises, that only a small number of offenders eluded the vigilant detection processes of that age, the success of at least one ecclesiastical court in preserving clerical morale and discipline can be judged by its own statistics. In a period of some forty years and in over fifty parishes, ninety-three charges of fornication or adultery were made against eighty-two clergy; of the seven charged more than once, in none was there proof that both or all charges were justified and, in fact, only two were convicted at all and four were acquitted once, the other charges being inconclusive and perhaps dropped. Clearly no serious conclusion of recidivism can be entertained on such evidence, even if the rest of the charges had been proved; and if recidivism can be discounted, the efficacy of the machinery can be the more readily appreciated. As for the scale of clerical immorality, even adding the forty-seven inconclusive charges to

[1] R.As. 55, fo. 175r.
[2] Calculated from the following samples, ibid., fos. 123v–132r, 176r–180r, 226r–230r.

the twenty-one proved, the yearly average of 1.5 offenders from so many parishes corrects the impression of outrageous scandal which a rapid reading of the court book too soon suggests. That these ninety-three charges are shared among forty-four chaplains, thirty-one vicars and seven rectors is merely a reflection of the numerical preponderance of chaplains over vicars, and of vicars over rectors in these parishes. That the offences are limited to immorality, and other charges only introduced as an appendix to these, gives a somewhat distorted picture, and for neglect of services, illicit absence and dilapidations one must turn instead to the records of the dean and chapter's periodic visitations of these parishes;[1] but those were offences often with chronic causes, less susceptible of legal solution, and what the court book affords is a 'test-tube' study of the efficiency of ecclesiastical correction in an area of scandalous personal failure.

III: *Criminous Clerks*

For all other non-ecclesiastical offences the clergy were subject to the same courts as laymen. For manorial defaults they appeared before the manor court; in London they were subject to the City sheriffs; they are found as defendants in the court of Common Pleas; and for crimes they were called before the King's Bench.[2] Where the crime was more than a misdemeanour and less than treason, the offender could plead benefit of clergy.[3] What this meant in practice had changed considerably since the time of Becket when it first became the focus of controversy; relying on the developing definition of canon law and on the premiss that the clergy should be spared from the blood sentences on felonies, the Church had claimed since the twelfth century in England that any accused clerk should be handed over to the bishop to prove his clergy before indictment, trial

---

[1] York Visitations, which seem far from systematic in noting of these items, save for dilapidations. No picture of overwhelming and universal scandal leaps from the pages, except perhaps in the parish of St. Michael le Belfrey, York.

[2] H. G. Richardson, *T.R.H.S.* (3rd series) vi, 111; S. Thrupp, *The Merchant Class of Medieval London*, pp. 186–7; Col. Parker, 'Notes of Yorkshire Clerics', *Y.A.J.* xxii, 298–300.

[3] *Statutes of Realm*, 25 Edward III, 6, c. iv.

or conviction, and that if successful he should submit to trial and correction by the Courts Christian only, if unsuccessful he should be surrendered to lay jurisdiction.[1] This was far from being realized even in the twelfth century and by the fifteenth the indictment, trial and conviction were all conducted in the King's Bench, and the question of clergy only raised after conviction and only proved in the same court, surrender to the bishop following this.[2]

In 1462, however, this procedure suddenly appeared to be reversed, when by a charter of liberties to the Church, perhaps not unconnected with Cardinal Coppini's politically valuable friendship, Edward IV confirmed precisely what the Church had long been claiming.[3] It is a singular commentary upon the King and upon Church and State relations at the time that this solemn concession was wholly disregarded in practice, as the protests of Convocation against its violation in 1462, 1471, 1475, 1480 and 1483, as well as the evidence from York discussed below, demonstrate; even a papal bull of 1476 threatening excommunication to anyone indicting clerks or religious before secular justices made no difference in practice.[4] It only underlines the cynicism of kings and the weakness of the Church that in 1483 Richard III confirmed Edward's charter with equally negative results.[5] Two years later, although Henry VII was in need of papal reassurance for his title, Innocent VIII adopted a flattering and plaintive tone about the liberties of the Church, grieving to hear that some priests (*sacerdotes*) were still being examined by secular judges;[6] it was not a letter calculated to stir a king, preoccupied but vulnerable, into amendment. No further attempts were made to alter a procedure so resistant to interference; instead the privilege was modified in an area where both secular and ecclesiastical statesmen were nearer to agreement. The question of where the indictment, trial and proof of clergy took place, though of importance to legal theory and professional

[1] C. Duggan, 'The Becket Dispute and the Criminous Clerks', *B.I.H.R.* xxxv, 1–28, for the background.
[2] L. C. Gabel, *Benefit of Clergy*, caps. ii and iv; C. B. Firth, 'Benefit of Clergy in the Time of Edward IV', *E.H.R.* xxxii, 176, 185.
[3] C. B. Firth, *E.H.R.* xxxii, 179–80; *Reg. Bourgchier*, pp. 103–5.
[4] Firth, *E.H.R.* xxxii, 180; *Reg. Bourgchier*, p. xxxii; Wilkins, iii, 585, 609, 613.
[5] See the evidence from R.I.23 below.
[6] Wilkins, iii, 617.

pride, was a frivolous issue, for it in no way solved two major problems, how to identify clergy and how to reduce recidivism. The spectrum of clerical orders has already been described and the difficulties of establishing the clerkship of an erstwhile doorkeeper or exorcist noted. In the twelfth and thirteenth centuries it was sufficient to test them by their literacy and by their dress, which should be sober and clerical, but by the fifteenth, literacy—or the capacity to read a short specified passage —was an accomplishment ever more frequently displayed and clerical dress was merely a remote ideal, especially among minor clerics who had turned to other occupations.[1] Clothes were no longer the test, but what possible criterion could be substituted for the imprecise one of literacy? It was easy enough by consulting episcopal records or by scrutinizing his own letters of ordination to identify the man in holy orders, but the clerk in minor orders often defied confident recognition. In King's Bench the test continued to be by literacy. Unfortunately most offenders claiming benefit were of the kind, who, it was reported to Pope Leo X, 'sought minor orders, not in order to proceed to higher orders, but that they might be able to perpetrate freely crimes and excesses and evade the secular judges and enjoy impunity for their offences'.[2]

Such 'impunity' as they secured by establishing their clergy was that which resulted from the provisions of canon law. By this each bishop was to maintain a prison (or two if his diocese were especially large) where convicted criminous clerks were to be detained, perpetually if they were notorious offenders.[3] How many fell into this second category of notorious clerks, *clerici attincti*, condemned to perpetual imprisonment, it has not so far been possible to estimate; they are only mentioned in the bishop's registers in most exceptional circumstances[4] and the prison accounts of bishops for this period are exceedingly few and laconic.[5] Those who were not *clerici attincti* might in due

[1] L. C. Gabel, *Benefit of Clergy*, p. 81; C. R. Cheney, 'The Punishment of Felonous Clerks', *E.H.R.* li, 217–18.

[2] Rymer, *Foedera*, xiii, 532–3.

[3] Lyndwood, V.15.v., Firth, *E.H.R.* xxxii, 186, 187–8.

[4] *Reg. Mayew*, p. 101, where a royal pardon was granted to one in the bishop of Hereford's prison. Cf. the case of Christopher Ryder below, p. 121.

[5] The accounts of the bishop of London's receiver-general for the year 1518–19, and of the bishop of Lichfield's for 1464–5 and 1541–2 are not helpful on this point (London Guildhall MS. 10123/2; Staffs. County Record Office MSS. D 1734/

course be liberated by the process of compurgation. Before this could be admitted all persons who wished to oppose it had to be summoned by several public proclamations where the crime was committed and where the offender was well known, a procedure which could not be waived even with the agreement of interested parties. Those who responded were to come and prove their objections by the due process of canon law and if they failed to prove them, they were liable to face the consequences of perjury; this provision had the excellent intention of discouraging the medieval weakness for malicious accusation, but its unfortunate effect was to discourage objection; for while one objector, the victim of the crime, might willingly travel a short or long distance to the bishop's prison or see to prove an offence, perhaps committed some years before, it was understandably difficult for him to arouse the interest of other witnesses so far as to undertake the cost and inconvenience of a court appearance and deposition, and proof was by depositions; the solution of taking sworn depositions locally, normally adopted in other cases where a witness was ill or unable to travel, would have swollen the objector's expenses and seems not to have been considered by the Church. That when objectors did appear and prevail, the clerk was often given a second chance to proceed to purgation later is not borne out by the York records where this happened only once in nearly eighty cases. If no objectors appeared the clerk could be compurgated; that is to say usually twelve or more clerks would swear their belief in his innocence; Lyndwood makes it quite clear that they were not attesting his innocence, but simply *their belief in it*, credence which could well be mistaken.[1] Despite conviction of the clerk in the King's

[1] Lyndwood, V.14.iii, note *k*: not *'de veritate'* but *'de credulitate'*; *'id quod est verum, possum credere falsum'*.

J 1948, 1949). The London account merely records the cost of conveying four prisoners from Newgate (where they were convicted) to the bishop's prison at Stortford, namely 6s. 8d. for each of them; the bishop also had to pay 13s. 4d. to the Custodian of Newgate who kept the prisoners after conviction. From the earlier Lichfield account we learn that there were three criminous clerks in the episcopal prison at Eccleshall, two of them for the whole of the accounting year. The much later Lichfield account records the expense involved in releasing five convicted clerks, usually a penny to each of the compurgators and about 3s. to a smith to remove the shackles and chains in each instance—which suggests that they were of a formidable kind. From the same account we learn that those attending the Staffordshire assizes in order to claim convicted clerks were paid 8d. per day. Collecting and releasing these clerks was apparently far more costly than maintaining them.

Bench, the fallibility of all courts then and the fact that no 'ill fame' had barred his way to purgation and no objectors had appeared, allowed the compurgators to believe without cynicism in his innocence. It is these presumptions and this seemingly casuistical distinction of Lyndwood's which explain why often the same compurgators, drawn perhaps from the episcopal household, exonerated several clerks of several different crimes. It also explains why compurgation, once permitted, almost never fails.

The 'impunity', therefore, amounted for the attainted clerk to life imprisonment and for the rest to a period of incarceration varying from a few months to several years, usually shackled and on a meagre diet costing $\frac{1}{4}d$. a day per prisoner in Eccleshall in 1464 and even less in 1542, a time of much higher prices.[1] Although escapes from time to time abbreviated the sentence, they are not reported in surviving records with such frequency as to suggest that episcopal prisons were less secure than royal or secular ones (and in few ages has prison security been ideal).[2] Whatever the length of incarceration, the man successfully claiming benefit of clergy escaped the normal consequence of felony, execution.

Death is one certain way of eliminating recidivism, perpetual incarceration another. In parliament in 1449 a petition urged that a convicted felon who had once by benefit of clergy purged himself, should on a second offence be kept by the bishop in perpetual imprisonment or else the bishop should be liable to a £100 fine; the king merely ordered the bishops to do what they thought necessary and consistent with the Church's freedom.[3] It is possible that this happened already by virtue of the exclusion of notorious offenders from purgation. A petition of 1455 that the second offence, whatever its nature, should be deemed high treason and its perpetration therefore ineligible for benefit of clergy, received royal consent, but it seems to have remained a dead letter, merely signifying the reforming intentions and transitory influence of the Duke of York.[4] The

[1] Firth, *E.H.R.* xxxii, 187; *Reg. Stanbury*, pp. 35, 37; Staffordshire County Record Office MSS. D 1734/J 1948, 1949.
[2] A. F. Pollard, *Wolsey*, p. 30, speaks of frequent escapes, but offers no evidence; Firth, *E.H.R.* xxxii, 188–9, cites some examples, but makes no statistical evaluation.
[3] *Rotuli Parliamentorum*, v, 151b.   [4] Ibid., v, 333a–334b.

problem of second offenders was certainly not regarded as solved in 1489 when a statute provided that all clerks not in major orders who were convicted and claimed their clergy were, after first conviction, to be branded by the gaoler in open court on the 'brawne of the lefte thumbe' with M if murder were their crime, or T for other offences, and not admitted to such benefit again, unless in the meanwhile holy orders had been obtained; even in this case a certificate of ordination had to be produced within a day, if penalties appropriate to a layman were to be avoided.[1] Despite all this fuss about second offenders it is likely that they were in fact rare birds. No one in the York registers for the period was purged twice for successive offences and while this may mean the Church debarred them from a second release, the evidence of assize and eyre rolls scarcely justifies contemporary anxiety.[2] What is significant about the 1489 statute is the appreciation of the greater problem of minor orders, an acknowledgement that they were ambiguous and abused in a way major orders were not. The total removal of murder of a master from clergyable offences in 1497 may seem to deny this apprehension, but it is more probably a reflex action in the year of plots and rumours surrounding Perkin Warbeck.[3] The act of 1512 resumed the assault on minor orders, denying any benefit to such clerks convicted of murder.[4] This act only operated until the Lords in 1515 successfully resisted the Commons' pressure for renewal.[5] In the meanwhile a Lateran decree of 1514, that no layman had jurisdiction over the clergy, had hardened the Church position and made the definition of 'clergy' more urgent.[6] Wolsey was eager to include among his legatine and reforming acts the abolition of minor orders, but in 1516 Leo X

[1] *Statutes of Realm*, 4 Henry VII, c. xiii.

[2] After 1458 they are less specific about clerks and by the later part of our period they had been assimilated into the King's Bench plea rolls; the eyre and assize rolls have, therefore, been searched for the counties of Yorkshire (all ridings) and Nottinghamshire from 1439 to 1460, and no second offenders have been found (P.R.O., Just. Itin. 3/211, 213, and Just. Itin. 3/84/1–20). It is true that the search is geographically limited, but if recidivism were so rife as is often suggested one might expect some repetition within the boundaries of Yorkshire and Nottinghamshire over twenty years. Relevant Justice of the Peace rolls are lost, but their contents would be unlikely to qualify seriously the evidence of the eyre and assize rolls.

[3] *Statutes of Realm*, 12 Henry VIII, c. vii.

[4] Ibid., 4 Henry VIII, c. ii.

[5] A. F. Pollard, *Wolsey*, p. 45.   [6] Ibid., p. 31.

averted so radical a move by himself denying any clerical character for the next five years to those who either did not take all the minor orders and that of subdeacon at once (*simul*) or else did not obtain an ecclesiastical benefice.[1] The general burden of complaint had been against the equivocal clerkship of so many beneficiaries and not against the entitlement of professional clergy, so that Leo's solution has the obvious and simple character of genius. Unfortunately, it seems never to have been implemented. It did not, as Pollard states,[2] prohibit minor orders being taken singly and without major orders, but merely renounced on behalf of the Church the claims of those in minor orders to clerical status and privilege. If Pollard's statement were true a significant increase in ordinations of subdeacons could be expected between 1516 and 1521, but none is observable in episcopal registers.[3] If Leo's intentions were strictly noted by the king's judges one would expect to find no more clerks in minor orders being both convicted and surrendered to the bishop from that time until it lapsed in 1521, but strangely they are found.[4] For some unaccountable reason it appears to have been neglected during those five years and it was certainly not effective after them.

Wolsey attempted a more radical solution in 1528 when he obtained from Clement VII permission to have secular and regular priests who had committed crimes which merited it degraded with less formality than before and then surrendered to the secular court for punishment—a solution which was anathema to Becket in the twelfth century.[5] This could have nullified benefit altogether, but was probably only intended to deal with the minor clerks and the *clerici attincti*; as its operation depended upon Wolsey's power of licensing such degradations, it was a short lived practice. But further attempts at radical curtailment of the benefit were imminent.

By an act of 1531–2, to endure until the end of the next parliament, the privilege was wholly denied to those in minor

[1] Rymer, *Foedera*, xiii, 532–3.
[2] A. F. Pollard, *Wolsey*, p. 54.
[3] e.g. *Reg. Mayew*, pp. 237–72.
[4] At least, in 1533 in the diocese of Bath and Wells a miller and a yeoman were purged as criminous clerks for offences committed in 1516 and 1518 respectively, for which they were probably tried before 1522, *Regs. Wolsey and others*, pp. 73–74.
[5] Wilkins, iii, 713; Rymer, *Foedera*, xiv, 239, somewhat differently punctuated.

orders, while those in major orders were no longer to be purged
and released at the bishop's discretion, but in order to obtain
release had now to find two guarantors (of stated landed resources) who would give recognisances of £20 each, the
prisoner himself also finding £40, before two J.P.s in the shire
of the offence, and even this was denied to clergy who had
confessed their guilt or were outlawed; furthermore, if a bishop
wished to relieve himself of the responsibility and cost of keeping
such men in perpetual imprisonment, were recognisances not
open to the prisoner, the bishop could degrade the convicted
clerks and hand them over to the King's Bench for the prescribed
penalty of the crime.[1] This act was extended in 1536 and again
in 1540 when it was renewed in perpetuity.[2] By this last statute
those in major orders were to be branded on their first offence
and debarred from the privilege thereafter. As a consequence of
all this legislation we should expect to find no clerks in minor
orders successfully claiming their clergy after 1532, yet in Lincoln
diocese there is abundant evidence to confound these expectations. From 1533 to 1543 there are in Bishop Longland's register
seventy-four commissions to hear the purgations of named
criminous clerks, only four of whom were professional clergy,
the rest being from almost every conceivable lay occupation.[3]
Drawn from each year of the decade except 1535, almost all of
them had committed their offences no earlier than c. 1531–2,
and forty-two of them after 1532; their appearance, therefore,
was entirely unaffected by any of the three acts and is not to be
explained by the date of their crimes. No record is given of the
actual purgations and releases, but it cannot be assumed that the
bishop issued such commissions over ten years if they were
officially discouraged or ineffective. Moreover, the clerks who
sought purgation were evidently confident that they could
provide and secure the recognisances required by the statutes;
that these guarantees were exacted in practice is witnessed by
the only recorded instance, concerning a monk in 1538.[4] It is
certain, therefore, that the statutes did not prevent Pollard's so-

[1] *Statutes of Realm*, 23 Henry VIII, c. i.
[2] Ibid., 28 Henry VIII, c. i, and 32 Henry VIII, c. iii.
[3] Lincoln MS. Episcopal Reg. 26 (Longland), fos. 111v, 117v, 152r–153r, 161v,
164v, 171r, 187r, 205v, 206v–207v, 211r, 214v–215r, 230v–232r, 236r–v, 244v–
245r, 254r–v, 269r, 277r, 280r–v, 287r–288r, 291r–292r, 294v–295r, 296r.
[4] Ibid., fo. 273v.

called 'half-breeds' from successfully pleading their clergy in the royal courts and it appears probable that the conditions for release did little to reduce the exodus of criminous clerks from episcopal prisons. The explanation of this contradiction between practice and the law—extraordinary only in the context of Cromwellian administration, not in the history of benefit of clergy—is not readily apparent, and for the moment it must suffice to note that the years 1532, 1536 and 1540 did not mark the end of the privilege for minor clerks. The problem which these men created only vanished with the Edwardian ordinal of 1550 which abolished minor orders altogether. The privilege for those in holy orders continued in a vastly more restricted and highly technical form until 1827.[1]

For a study of the benefit of clergy before the 1530s the registers of the archbishops of York offer fuller information than can be found in most other episcopal archives of the time.[2] In York from 1452 to 1530 the records of purgations were systematically kept in five of the eight registers; for the tenures of George Neville and Lawrence Booth, from 1465 to 1479, and and of Wolsey, 1514–29, no records appear in the register or are extant elsewhere among York archives; the *sede vacante* register supplies some cases from the vacancies. The documents recorded are usually the mandate ordering proclamations to be called, the certificate that they have been called, and the memorandum from the dean of Christianity to the archbishop announcing the success of compurgation and the liberation of the clerk. Not all these documents are given for each clerk, but one of them frequently includes the text of its routine predecessors; moreover, in one or all of them the date and nature of the offence is given, and sometimes the date of indictment which may be as much as four years after the offence.[3] The compurgation of seventy-six clerks is recorded in these registers and these are the basis of what follows. None of the sporadic evidence in other registers or the facts assembled by Miss Gabel and Miss Firth allow us to claim a unique character for the York material; it is in fact its conventional quality which

---

[1] W. Holdsworth, *History of English Law*, iii (3rd edn. 1923), 300–2.
[2] See Appendix 4, below.
[3] e.g. R.I.20, fos. 301v–302r, where the offence occurred in November 1445 and the indictment in May 1449.

makes it a valuable illustration of, and buttress for, the general discussion above.

The first notable feature is that of the sixty-two offenders whose occupation is given, only six are what we could call professional clergy, incumbents, chaplains or religious; two more are parish clerks and seven more are described starkly as clerks without a hint at other occupations, though the one who murdered his wife by stabbing her in the heart might be safely discounted. As for the rest, twenty-eight fell within the rural categories of yeomen, gentlemen, husbandmen and labourers; five are from the textile trades—fuller, tailor, glover, vestment maker; a butcher, a chapman, a goldsmith, a wire-drawer and a minstrel appear among the remainder. Clearly the Church could only defend the benefit of those in minor orders for the advantage of clerks who were in effect laymen, and it was these privileged laymen, not the active—even nefariously active—clergy, who aroused the jealous and reforming zeal of the House of Commons, which was also aggravated by the swiftness with which purgation followed conviction.

We must remember that no figures survive of the *clerici attincti* doomed to perpetual imprisonment; these could have been calculated from the account rolls of St. Leonard's Hospital York, which provided the sustenance of the inmates of the bishop's prison, but for our period no accounts are extant. The only note of such a prisoner in the archbishop's registers is of Christopher Ryder, a labourer, indicted for, and convicted by confession of, murder in 1506; after successfully claiming benefit of clergy and being branded, according to the statute of 1489, with the letter M on his left thumb, he was handed over to Archbishop Savage to be kept in 'le convict house' at York and flogged for his offence; Archbishop Bainbridge visited the prison in 1509 and found Ryder held in irons as a *clericus attinctus* and detained him further. In June 1511, however, a royal writ ordered the gaoler to deliver Ryder and to reveal the cause of his detention to the king and to hear 'what shall be ordained concerning him'; in January 1512 Ryder received a royal pardon.[1] It is important to regard Ryder as the sole survivor of a vanished tribe, of unknown size, shackled and periodically flogged, with little hope of release in 'le convict house' at York.

[1] R.I.26, fos. 22r–v; *L. & P.* i(1), 1803(ii).

The other seventy-six named in the registers were released. Of these seventy-six the dates of purgation are unknown in three cases, and of indictment totally unindicated in three, leaving seventy. Of these seventy the date of indictment is known in twenty-nine and the resulting average period of imprisonment is 4.8 years. In forty-one cases the indictment can only be hazarded from the date of the crime; this is not always so misleading as suggested above when merely a year or two separate the crime from compurgation; but though somewhat optimistic, the resulting average is 3.6. A composite average of just under four years would be somewhere near the truth; or put another way, of the seventy, fifty-two spent five years or less in prison, and thirty-nine of these two years or less, for capital crimes.

When an attempt is made to collate offence and detention, it is discovered that while four men served only a year for homicide, other murderers spent four, seven, eight, ten and even seventeen years in prison. Equally no relation can be found between class and sentence, two labourers serving a year and one seventeen years for homicide, a vicar serving seven, an Austin canon one. Nor can it be shown that detention was progressively diminishing and release being accelerated as one moves towards and into the sixteenth century: true, William Booth in 1453–4 released three men detained from the 1430s and in 1461–2 freed six within a year of indictment, but although Rotherham liberated men in almost every year of the 1490s, no one indicted after 1493 was let out before the Archbishop's death in 1500 and three indicted in the early years of that decade were only released by Savage in 1501–2. At that time Savage allowed twelve to proceed to purgation, six indicted in 1500–1, but he released none during his next six years as archbishop. Nor can these discrepancies be explained by ecclesiastical prejudice against the violator of church goods, for the Lancashire yeoman who stole a silver gilt chalice from the vicar of Melling and Lonsdale and afterwards broke it up for easier disposal was allowed to purge himself within a year, as was a London mercer convicted of stealing a chalice, a portiforium and a manual from Edwinstowe church; another chalice thief, from Derbyshire, was only purged eight years after his offence, but the date of his indictment is not known.[1] A now inscrutable justice dictated the sentence endured

[1] R.I.20, fos. 314r–315r, 321r–v; R.I.23, fo. 316r.

129

by criminous clerks and it may not be too cynical to think that the fullness of the prison and the receiver-general's statement of account often influenced the ordinary to grant a prisoner's petition to proceed to purgation. In the documents discussed here it is related how the prisoner petitioned the Archbishop 'after a long time' (*post diutinam*) or 'after no short imprisonment' (*post non modicum incarceracionem*), but these formulae evoke surprise when referring to four years for burglary of goods worth £10, or to four years for murder, or even to two years for theft and assault,[1] though as we have seen there were some cases where they were perfectly appropriate; clearly it was an empty formula and no sign of the reasons which moved an archbishop to exercise his mercy.

The inescapable stage of proclamations is well illustrated in the registers. When the archbishop acceded to the petition of Richard Caterall on 3 August 1456 he ordered the dean of Pontefract to see that proclamations inviting opposers to purgation were made on Sundays and feast days in Halifax church during Mass and in the market there when most people were likely to be present, and in other neighbouring churches and markets where it seemed expedient; the opposers were to appear before the archbishop or his commissary in York Minster on 15 September to propound on oath whatever could be lawfully alleged against Caterall. The dean certified that this had been done on 12 September, three days before Caterall was in fact compurgated, no objectors appearing.[2] Similarly when a yeoman of Pontefract accused of murder sought purgation, proclamations were ordered in the churches of Pontefract and Tadcaster at Mass on Sundays, and in the public squares of Pontefract and other towns on market days.[3] And so it was in all the other documented cases. The prospect held out to objectors by these proclamations were of a costly journey and a solemn, if not intimidating, encounter, often after they had already spent money in the king's courts; it is not surprising, therefore, if this laudably intended procedure evoked such rare and vacillating response.

Robert Horsley, a shipman of Beverley, had been convicted in

[1] R.I.23, fos. 315v–316v.
[2] R.I.20, fos. 304r–v.
[3] R.I.23, fo. 313r.

1452 of breaking into the house of Stephen Reyner of Hull, armed with swords, bows and arrows, stealing bedding and cash, and murdering Stephen's son, Thomas. He had successfully claimed his clergy and five years later was seeking purgation; proclamations were ordered in the parish church and market of Hull and at other expedient places. At Hull certain aldermen and merchants avowed that Horsley was a known murderer and thief who before the mayor and aldermen sitting judicially in the Guildhall had confessed to the murder and there on his bended knees had sought forgiveness from Stephen Reyner. When the proclamation was made in the near-by parish church of Cottingham during Mass, Stephen Reyner and his neighbours proclaimed Horsley's guilt and declared their desire to affirm this according to law. As a consequence each of the opposers was cited by name, and others more generally, to appear at Cawood five days later, on Friday, 25 August, to accuse Horsley in court and on oath. On Friday none came.[1] What made these men change their minds, for they spoke with the vehemence of justified outrage and conviction? Had the Cottingham men hoped in vain for support at Cawood from Hull's aldermen? Were they deterred by the legal solemnities, by the bother and cost of the journey, by the weather, by farming priorities—for it was harvest time, by cajolery on someone's part, or by some awareness of opposers' fortunes elsewhere and at other times? Where opposers did appear some discouraging features are observable. When, for example, proclamations did call forth objectors to John Pierson's purgation in 1453, seven years after his offences of theft and murder, it is recorded that as a consequence he lacked sufficient compurgators; implying, unless it is a pompous circumlocution, that the process of purgation was still allowed to proceed, and fail. Moreover, he was admitted to purgation again in 1464, this time no objectors answering the proclamation. It should be noted that in the York registers this is the only instance of a man who failed purgation once being allowed a second opportunity, and Christian mercy may have governed the second chance which took place some seventeen years after his indictment.[2] Less susceptible of such charitable comments is the case of Thomas Meryn and Henry Loft whose

[1] R.I.20, fos. 316v–317v, 318r–v.
[2] R.I.20, fos. 308v–309v, 324v–326r.

opposers appeared on the due day, Friday 28 January 1508; for although they had been long awaited (*diutius expectatis*) the compurgation was postponed for a week and when that day came and John Johnson came from Askham Richard to object to Loft's purgation, the next day was assigned to him to put his objections on oath; understandably neither he nor anyone else came on that day or on the following Monday to which a further adjournment had removed purgation. On the Monday, Loft and Meryn were purged successfully by four chaplains and eight clerks.[1] Perhaps this next example should be ascribed to the Church's vocation to bring peace among men: Thomas Baildon, chaplain, had robbed William Walker of Esholt of wool worth 30s. and when objectors to Baildon's purgation were summoned, Walker was prominent among them; but his consent was sought and gained to postpone the purgation for a week in the hope of reconciling Baildon and himself. This was in fact achieved on the appointed day, when Walker withdrew his objections before the commissary in York Minster; compurgation proceeded successfully with two priests and ten clerks.[2] In these few isolated and not unequivocal examples the auspices were not calculated to encourage objectors; but they are too isolated and too ambiguous to bear the cynical conclusions which they tempt.

Scepticism has been more openly expressed by historians on the compurgations themselves. The duplication of lists of compurgators is at once apparent in the York registers and nowhere more vividly than where one entry announces the purgation by the same oath-helpers of several men convicted of diverse and unrelated crimes, scattered geographically and chronologically: on 25 August 1457 at Cawood, for example, the same twelve *clerici et literati* purged Robert Horsley of Beverley, guilty of burglary and murder, Christopher Bradshagh of Haigh, in Lancashire, convicted of murder, and John Croke of Ripon, guilty of theft;[3] similarly on 30 July 1530 thirteen clerks purged John Nevell and John Trapp of various thefts, John Symmes of assault and murder, John Watson of robbery, and John Cotes of cattle theft;[4] and where lists are not identical they

[1] R.I.5, fos. 532r–533v.
[2] R.I.20, fos. 324r–v.
[3] Ibid., fos. 315v–316v, 317v–318v.
[4] R.I.25, fos. 13v–14v.

often have common elements.[1] It has already been pointed out that compurgators swore *de credulitate* and not *de veritate*, and that where purgation had been allowed by the bishop and was unimpeded by objectors no cynicism or indifference to truth was necessary on their part. Though they received payment for their services,[2] it is unlikely that they were professional oath-helpers rather than the chaplains and clerks nearest to hand on the day, perhaps even members of the archbishop's household.

IV: *Conclusions*

The privilege accorded to criminous clergy, though it aroused passionate hostility in some quarters and among some writers, was less of a threat to social stability than was often alleged; in Lincoln diocese, where the figures of convicted clerks are most copious, the total of 148 in Longland's register is distributed over twenty years and eight counties, barely one a year in each shire; the hordes of incorrigible burglars and murderers which alarmed critics inhabited their imagination rather than reality. It is equally difficult to believe that such impetuous murderers and such desperate thieves as were the great majority of the beneficiaries would have been deterred by the death penalty or were encouraged to a life of crime by escaping it. That the Church, except under Wolsey's prodding, nevertheless shewed a marked reluctance to withdraw its protection from these minor clerks, could be reasonably explained by a fear of encouraging by such a concession a far more radical assault on the privilege. Whatever theology or canon law might suggest to the contrary, the Church was maintaining benefit of clergy very largely for the protection of men who were clergy only in name and were content to lead a life in no way distinguishable from that of laymen. It may well have been this thought which explains the eagerness of some bishops to empty their prisons and cut their costs. It was this thought too and the swift release, or the fact of release at all, which explain the violent passions provoked by the benefit in the unprivileged laity; the numbers of perpetually

[1] e.g. R.I.23, fos. 313v, 315v, 314r, 314v.
[2] See above, p. 121, n. 5.

imprisoned were not published, nor were any figures about the average terms of imprisonment, and no layman was likely then to be impressed by tales of the rigours of life in a bishop's gaol.

In ecclesiastical discipline perhaps the greatest defect was the extreme reluctance, except in cases of non-residence, to deprive offending incumbents, though clearly the technicalities of the parson's freehold and the reactions of the patrons must have been inhibiting thoughts in the mind of an ordinary who inclined to such action; indiscriminately employed, this measure was likely to remove the affair out of ecclesiastical jurisdiction entirely. With the unbeneficed a bolder resort to degradation might have been expected, but for the theological repugnance and difficulties which this undoubtedly aroused in those who contemplated the annulment of a sacrament, though more influential may have been the fear of public scandal which this step would entail: no church has been eager to expel or humiliate its clergy. Nevertheless, it is an importunate thought that such action more frequently or choicely taken would have had a widely stimulating and salutary effect, not only among the clergy but also among the affronted laity: justice must be seen to be done, and the Church was perhaps too afraid of impairing the clergy's authority. Short of these grave and difficult penalties, however, the Church showed a diligence in detection, a care in conviction, and an appropriateness in penalty for which it is seldom given credit, so much so that where the voluminous evidence can be subjected to careful analysis, the scale of disorder appears to be much less than that suggested by a mere impressionistic reading through the sources, and recidivism rare. Clerical disorder on a significant scale there certainly was, but short of abolishing minor orders and of adopting clerical marriage—both of them measures beyond a unilateral English decision, and short of uprooting the patronage system (protected by common law), little further improvement could be effected.

VIII

The Cost of Living

I: *The Problem*

F o r some incumbents their economic relation to their parishioners was the most important, if not the only, connection that
they had; the vocation which inspired them is plain enough
among the memoranda which a fifteenth-century vicar of
Lancaster wrote down with evident approval: ' "Love conquers
all" said a certain wise man; another retorted, "You lie; money
conquers all"; a third said, "Wisdom and money achieve most:
if you are rich you will always be reputed wise; if you are poor
you will be considered as simple as the next man" '[1] But before
this aspect of parish life is dismissed wholly in terms of clerical
avarice and lay resentment, some effort must be made to pene-
trate the enveloping clichés of historians and propagandists.
The stark valuations of livings in the 1535 *Valor Ecclesiasticus*[2]
must be converted into a fuller statement of account for the various types of benefices, and the economic facts which confronted
incumbents in the course of a year must be unveiled.

II: *Social Background and Attitudes*

Those victims of primogeniture, the younger sons, found in the
Church promise of a distinguished and lucrative career. George
Neville, whose father was Richard, Earl of Salisbury, in 1450

[1] F. R. Johnston, 'Richard Burton, Vicar of Lancaster 1466–84', *Trans. Historical
Soc. of Lancs. and Cheshire*, civ, 167.
[2] *Valor Ecclesiasticus*, ed. J. Caley and J. Hunter (Record Commission), 6 vols.

was vicar of Kirkby Kendal, and later archbishop of York.[1] From 1452 to 1463 a son of the second Lord Scrope of Masham was rector of Goldsborough.[2] Tavistock had for its rector in 1467 a man of royal lineage and nephew of a cardinal, John Bourgchier.[3] Several parishes in Northumberland between 1497 and 1546 were in the care of Cuthbert Ogle, a member of the lordly family of Ogle.[4] Other names might be cited, but the nobles never formed more than a small minority among the incumbents. Their influence in parishes, no doubt, was slight: Neville held Kirkby Kendal barely a year and probably never visited it; Scrope was archdeacon of Durham throughout his tenure of Goldsborough; Bourgchier was dispensed for pluralism; Ogle was a grand pluralist. The nobility were conspicuous by their absence and it is probable that their effect on clergy-laity relations was the less injurious for that: as remote and splendid names they might elicit respect; in person they were more likely to arouse resentment.

The knightly and gentry classes provided a much greater number of incumbents. Sir Ralph Verney, knight, was parson of Albury in 1509.[5] Gilbert Haydock, vicar of Rochdale, was the son of a family which flourished by marrying well, chiefly into the estates of old feudal families.[6] A priest kneels second among the sons on the brass of Nicholas Gaynesford, esquire, of Carshalton, c. 1490, and about the same time Henry Mountford, clerk, took up his place standing among the sons of Thomas and Agnes Mountford.[7] Henry Trafford, S.T.P., was presented to the rectory of Wilmslow by his elder brother Edmund; in the course of his career Henry became archdeacon of York (where his uncle, Booth, was archbishop), and parson of both Bolton Percy and Sigglesthorne; at Wilmslow he built the chancel.[8] Many of these men were absentees, but some of them neverthe-

---

[1] A. H. Thompson, 'Reg. Archdeacon of Richmond', *Y.A.J.* xxx, 97.

[2] Ibid., 106, 130.

[3] *C.P.L.* xii, 584.

[4] *History of Northumberland*, xiv (ed. M. H. Dodds), 263; the livings which he held were Ford (1497), Ilderton (1523–38), Stanhope (1526), Ingram (1533), Appleby (1537), and Bothel.

[5] *Letters and Papers of the Verney Family*, ed. J. Bruce (Camden Soc. o.s. 56), p. 40.

[6] F. R. Raines, *Vicars of Rochdale*, pp. 29–30.

[7] H. Druitt, *Costume in Monumental Brasses*, pp. 85, 105.

[8] J. P. Earwaker, *East Cheshire: Past and Present*, i, 88–89.

less exercised a beneficent rule over their parishioners. Ralph Lepton, for example, a scion of the Yorkshire family of that name and prebendary of Wells, rebuilt the rectory of Alresford and left a brass in St. Nicholas, Guildford—touches which suggest a man who had a sense of responsibility towards, and affection for, his parish livings.[1] Others, like Master George Brudenell, rector of Quinton in 1519 and a member of the Buckingham family of that name, showed only unwarrantable arrogance towards their flock: through his neglect the vestry roof was in need of repair; in his rectory Katherine Hows had conceived; he violated his parishioners' rights of common and seized many of their cattle; to the church, the record adds laconically, he owed 40s.[2] Lepton and Brudenell are both typical.

It is paradoxical that as a class is more numerously represented among the parish clergy, so it is more difficult to cite precise examples. An intimate knowledge of a village population is required to establish relationships; furthermore, the man of humble origin did not always obtain the living of his own parish. Thus while it is possible that William Grigg, rector of Compton in Surrey from 1452 to 1462, was related to William Grygge, a husbandman of Send, there is no proof of it.[3] For the majority of the clergy the clues are much more elusive, if they exist at all. An examination of manorial rolls may provide a few examples of villeins manumitted to take orders, but John Pyndere, a bondman at Terrington until 1456, when he was enfranchised for this purpose, appears to represent only a very small number from 1450 to 1530.[4]

Representatives of the merchant and trading classes among the parish clergy are more easily detectable. Master Roger Pysford, the absentee rector of Medbourne, and John Pysford, rector of Baginton, were both members of the well-known merchant family of Coventry.[5] They were also connected with William Wigston, the great Leicester merchant, whose brother,

[1] Manning and Bray, *History of Surrey*, i, 65.
[2] *Lincoln Visitations 1517–31*, i, 48.
[3] Manning and Bray, op. cit., ii, 14; *C.P.R. 1452–61*, p. 377. Few ordination lists record the ordinand's parish of origin; exceptions are the registers of the bishops of Lincoln during this period.
[4] Ely Diocesan Records MS. G/1/5 (Reg. Gray), fo. 16v.
[5] *Lincoln Visitations 1517–31*, i, p. xxx.

Master Thomas Wigston, was rector of Houghton-on-the-Hill. Thomas Rede, clerk and Doctor of Divinity, was rector of Beccles in Suffolk where his brother, William Rede, was a merchant.[1]

The proportions of town to country and of rich to poor men who entered the ranks of the beneficed clergy can scarcely be estimated without a searching examination of a restricted area; it is very probable that they will correspond to those of society itself. But whether the parson or vicar came with inherited social distinction or obscurity, he had prestige conferred upon him by freehold possession of a benefice and by the responsibility of the rule of souls (*regimen animarum*). By the former, for example, the rectors of East Mersea, Prescot and Wigan were lords of the manors appurtenant to their livings, and the parson of Aylesbury held views of frankpledge and assizes of bread and ale.[2] By the latter he was the spiritual ruler of his parishioners, their *medicus*—or mediator with God, as one writer expressed it:[3] to him they paid tithes and oblations; to him they confessed and from him they sought absolution; on him they called for the last rites. In virtue of both these aspects he was an employer of labour and a source of hospitality and alms; yet, as we have seen, in relation to some of his parishioners, particularly his patron, he was himself often an employee and social inferior. Nor were the social obligations which he incurred and the social expectations which his office aroused in others always equal to his economic state.

III : *Expenditure*

The status of the parson or vicar was manifested in his house. Not every incumbent was provided with one, as the vicars of Sandwich and Bringhurst well knew,[4] but in most parishes there

[1] *L. & P.* i(2), No. 2772(61).

[2] R. Newcourt, *Repertorium*, ii, 413; *Prescot Court Leet Records*, ed. F. A. Bailey (Lancs. and Cheshire Record Soc. 89), p. 1; G. T. O. Bridgeman, *History of Wigan*, i, 2; G. C. Homans, *English Villagers of the Thirteenth Century*, (Cambridge, Mass., 1942), p. 385.

[3] B. M. Burney MS. 356, fo. 113r.

[4] *C.P.R. 1452–61*, p. 283; 'Leicester Archdeaconry Proceedings', *A.A.S.R.* xxviii, 151; *V.C.H. Suffolk*, ii, 15, for an example from Sibton.

was a considerable building for the incumbent and his household. Their houses varied, of course, in size, but that this was related to the value of the living is doubtful, for whereas Winford rectory was worth nearly £22, its manse was 'of the smallest and simplest type'.[1] When King's College endowed the vicarage of Prescot in 1449, they promised to provide a house within two years; it was still unbuilt in 1458 when the college and vicar agreed that it should have chimneys and easements, two stairways, a louver for the hall, trapdoors and windows.[2] In 1453 the rectory of Clifton Campville in Staffordshire comprised a parlour, a principal chamber with two withdrawing rooms, a chamber over the parlour, a chimney, a priest's chamber and withdrawing room, a pantry and buttery with a chamber over, a larderhouse kitchen, bakery and brewhouse, kilnhouse, stable garner, and two stables and two other houses under one roof in the outer court, a long house next to the highway, a dovecote, and a garden surrounded by mud walls.[3] The rectory of Stapleford Tawney in the early sixteenth century contained a hall in which were a new staircase, a new fireback, and a door separating the hall from the entrance of the building; on the south end of the hall was a newly built parlour with two bay windows of glass and two fireplaces; to it was adjoined a store-room, and over it were two new chambers.[4] Small houses there certainly were, where the incumbent lived, like most of his parishioners, in the two rooms of hall and parlour, but there is plenty of evidence to support the conclusion of Pantin, that usually a medieval parsonage had two floors and as well as the hall five other rooms.[5] Indeed, the archaeological and record evidence suggests that the rectories and vicarages of late medieval England differed but slightly from those first systematically described in the glebe terriers of Elizabethan and Jacobean times;[6] some new rooms may have appeared, but no radical rearrangement or enlargement of the manse occurred in the interval.

[1] W. A. Pantin, 'Medieval Priests' Houses', *Medieval Archaeology*, i, 119, 138.

[2] *Prescot Court Leet Records*, p. 281.

[3] Lichfield MS. B/A/1/11, fos. 45r–46r.

[4] G.L.C., MS. DL/C/206, fos. 340r, 343r, 348r.

[5] W. G. Hoskins, 'The Leicester Country Parson in the Sixteenth Century', *Trans. Leics. Archaeological Soc.* xxi, 93; W. A. Pantin, *Medieval Archaeology*, i, 120, 126, 144.

[6] R. Newcourt, *Repertorium, passim*; especially, i, 64; ii, 15, 25, 73, 97, 115, 124, 193, 230, 248, 309, 343, 345, 452, 490, 546, 676.

The size and nature of the houses is clearly indicated by the expense necessary to maintain them. It was the responsibility of the incumbent to keep in good repair the parsonage or vicarage buildings, and usually the chancel as well,[1] but these obligations were not always, or punctually, met. The archdeacon on his annual visitation was to consider carefully the need of repairs to the fabric of the manse and the church and, if necessary, to fix a term within which they should be completed; if they were not done in that time, such of the income as was needed for them might be sequestrated.[2] Frequently, however, dilapidations awaited the new incumbent: when Richard Wheteley was appointed to the vicarage of Earlham on the death of Thomas Hall he found himself confronted by a vicarage house with no windows and needing repairs to the woodwork, the roof and the masonry which would cost some £10 or £12, and no account was taken here of the outbuildings which had all been destroyed.[3] In these circumstances an incumbent could sue his predecessor's executors for the cost; although it had long ago been decreed that such a part as was necessary of all the goods left by the deceased incumbent should be deducted by the bishop and set aside for the successor to make good the repairs within two years,[4] this never seems to have worked in practice. The suing of executors necessitated a formal inquisition into the extent and chronology of the decay and the executors would very often seek to prove the responsibility of an earlier incumbent and his executors, or else they would persistently fail to appear—stratagems which would lead frequently to costly inconclusion and to despairing abandonment by the plaintiff.[5] Against a predecessor who was still alive, remedy was no more certain, for the same methods of evasion were open to him. Yet the chief cause of decay, assisted no doubt at first by imprudent if venial neglect, was the sheer want of ready cash; without the modern aid of insurance policies, many incumbents must have found it extremely difficult to cope promptly with expensive repairs—estimated at £103. 10s. at Clifton Campville in 1453 and costing

---

[1] In many city churches of London and in some elsewhere the parishioners were responsible for the repair of the chancel (*V.C.H. London*, i, 224).

[2] Lyndwood, I.10.iv. See *Reg. Stanbury*, p. 99 for a bishop acting thus in 1464.

[3] *N.C.C.D.*, No. 405.

[4] Wilkins, iii, 722.

[5] J. S. Purvis, 'Dilapidations in Parsonage Property', *Y.A.J.* xxxvi, 318–24.

£16. 0s. 5d. at Hornsea and Riston 1487–90—yet delay merely increased the damage and the cost.[1] It was only in 1547 that injunctions required a reserve fund to be established and augmented each year for the purpose of repairs.[2]

Further evidence of the size of many manses is the number of people who were entertained or accommodated in them. About a third of a beneficed clerk's income was expected, ideally, to be disbursed on hospitality and alms.[3] How often this ideal was realized can never be known; who shall exclude from hospitality the accommodation and sustenance of elderly parents which brought tax relief for some?[4] Various church officers were entertained by the vicar of Mancetter, and at Riccal in Yorkshire it was customary for the vicar to give a dinner for the choir at Christmas, Easter and the Assumption of the Virgin,[5] but hospitality was primarily intended to benefit the needy of the parish. Some idea of the extent of this burden may be grasped from the plea of Hornsea's vicar that he did not reside there because the expense of hospitality would be more than he could afford.[6] It will, indeed, become clear below that in only a very small number of benefices could the ideal of a third be conscientiously met and that in most a far smaller proportion of the income than that was available for such disbursement.

Not merely were there parents and more casual guests to be accommodated, but often chaplains and almost invariably servants as well. Perpetual chantry chaplains usually had their own houses and lived after a style revealed in some recently published domestic accounts.[7] Other chaplains and stipendiary priests may have had their own house, or have shared one, but evidence of this is fugitive; some certainly dwelt in the parsonage (in the priest's chamber at Clifton Campville), though they

[1] Lichfield MS. B/A/1/11, fos. 45r–46r; *M.C.A.* pp. 53–54; we must suppose, however, that the estimate of Eastbourne's rectory buildings, burnt down *c.* 1491, at 600 marks (or £400), if not an error of transcription by the editor, was some form of extravagant concession by the tax authorities to its rector, then John Doget, royal diplomat (*C.F.R. 1485–1509*, No. 433, p. 172).

[2] J. S. Purvis, *Y.A.J.* xxxvi, 318.

[3] *Rotuli Parliamentorum*, iv, 290–1.

[4] F. R. H. Du Boulay, 'Charitable Subsidies granted to the Archbishop of Canterbury 1300–1489', *B.I.H.R.* xxiii, 158.

[5] P.R.O., E 101/519/31, fo. 10r; York Visitations, fo. 208v,—1519 when it was not given.

[6] *M.C.A.*, p. 11.

[7] K. L. Wood-Legh, *A Small Household of the Fifteenth Century*.

might be found in laymen's houses or even in taverns.[1] To an
even greater extent by their stipends chaplains constituted a
considerable, and largely inescapable, drain on the incumbent's
resources. The parson or vicar had to find lodging, too, for his
servants. Most incumbents had two or three of these; Thomas
Griffith, parson of Ilmington, in Worcester diocese, seems to
have had five at least—Owen, David, John, and 'moder hale',
who are described as servants, Richard 'my ladde', and 'two por
wenchis in my house'.[2] Servants were indispensible to clean the
house, to cope with the laundry, to bake and brew and cook, to
cultivate the garden and till the glebe, to groom the horses,
milk the cows and herd what other beasts the incumbent might
have, and perhaps above all to look after guests. How much was
expended on their wages is not easily known from surviving
records; the servant of two chantry priests in the 1450s received,
as we have seen above,[3] between a mark and 30s. a year; a
labourer engaged by the vicar of Easton in 1497 for the service
of husbandry for a whole year received 9s. and a garment; odd
shillings are paid to casual labourers for the collection of various
tithes, but we know no more than this.[4] There were often more
than one servant, yet even one was no small expense.

With all these denizens it is little wonder that the houses of
incumbents, like their wills, were crammed with beds, linen,
stools, tables, pots and pans. Simon Merflet, vicar of Wawne,
left eleven sheets, nine coverlets, eight blankets, three bolsters,
three featherbeds and two other beds, one mattress, five chairs
(a rare possession), ninety yards of cloth together with numerous and various kitchen utensils, ranging from seven brass pots
and six pans (which included one great frying pan) to a gilt
maser, a spit, two cobirons and two meat cloths.[5] The inventory
of the goods of Bernard Pope, who died parson of Faccombe in
1539, gives a similar picture: two beds, three pairs of sheets,
four coverlets (one of them with tapestry work), a pair of old
blankets, four pillows, one bolster, and a tester with a hanging;
one table, one form, two chairs, one towel, three napkins, three

---

[1] Reg. Warham, fo. 55v.
[2] P.C.C., Porch 32.
[3] See above p. 23.
[4] *Records of the City of Norwich*, ed. W. Hudson and J. C. Tingey, ii, 155;
M.C.A., pp. 27, 33.
[5] *Testamenta Eboracensia*, ed. J. Raine (Surtees Soc. 30), ii, 261–2.

tablecloths, three candlesticks; and in the kitchen, one washing basin, one old dripping pan, three kettles, a bread-bin and tub, a balance with weights, and a fire shovel.[1] And the contents would be much the same in any parsonage or vicarage in the country, a little poorer in some, a lot richer in others.[2] Most of these goods and chattels were left in their wills to parishioners and relatives and only very rarely to their successors, so that normally each incumbent had to furnish and equip the manse himself; Thomas Eland was exceptionally fortunate when he succeeded to the vicarage of Embleton in 1431 and inherited from his predecessor, as well as some farming equipment, a great variety of furniture and kitchen utensils.[3]

So much for the domestic expenses which confronted an incumbent; these did not exhaust his obligations, for there were in addition not only the annual costs of synodals and procurations and the purchase of such liturgical necessities as bread, wine and chrism oil, but also the irregular, yet not infrequent, demands of taxation, pensions and litigation.

Synodals and procurations were paid at very different rates in different parishes. Synodals, due to the bishop, cost the incumbents of Dagenham, Nazeing and Woodford a shilling each, but at Downham amounted to 1s. 6d. and at Kirkby Malham to 4s.[4] Procurations, much the heavier, were paid to the archdeacon or his official on visitation and had certain specified limitations. They could be paid only for that one day (of twenty-four hours, including supper and dinner) when the church was personally visited; when the archdeacon or his official descended on several churches in one day each church was to contribute proportionately, but parochial chapels were included in the procurations of the mother church. Furthermore, the train of the archdeacon was restricted, so far as the obligations of the incumbent were involved, to a horse for himself, four horsemen, two 'custodians', two more horses and at the most two more footmen; the incum-

---

[1] Hampshire County Record Office MS. inventory.

[2] e.g. George Percy, rector of Rothbury and of Caldbeck in 1474, and uncle of Lord Henry Percy, Earl of Northumberland, slept in a bed of arras work, the gift of his mother, Dame Eleanor (*Test. Ebor.* iii, 210–11); Roger Norton, parson of Streatham in Surrey in 1527, adorned his house with a coverlet of flowers, three others of tapestry work, and 'iii peces of paynted clothes' (P.C.C., Porch 27).

[3] *History of Northumberland*, ii (ed. E. Bateson), 66.

[4] London Guildhall MS 9531/12, fo. 48v; P.R.O., E 101/517/27, and B.M. Addit. Roll 32957, *passim.*

bent was under no obligation to support more, but he was free to invite others, 'lest the archdeacon should have to sit alone at table without the solace of congenial company'. Many archdeacons might nevertheless be inclined to exceed this train, for reasons of prerogative or dignity, but the incumbent's already considerable obligation could not be extended.[1] By law it had been established that the archdeacons visiting in person were to receive cash, their officials sustenance, but by the end of the Middle Ages, to judge from surviving records, custom had fixed the payment in cash and fixed the amount as well: at Kirkby Malham it was 7s. 6d., at Dagenham and Downham 6s. 8d., at Nazeing 5s. and at Woodford 3s.[2] At Hornsea the archdeacon's visit was a far more costly affair: in 1481–2 as well as 7s. 6d. for the archdeacon himself, 2s. 3d. was paid for the expenses of his official; in the next year in addition to the 7s. 6d. to the archdeacon, 8s. 4d. was expended on breakfast for him and his train; in 1483–4 these two items came to 15s; and in 1484–5 when the visit of the archdeacon was conducted in his own person 10s. procurations were augmented by 5s. for drinks; the following year he came again in person and again collected 10s., but breakfast this time amounted to 4s., a sum repeated in 1490–1.[3]

Other annually recurring expenses, of varying but limited magnitude, are most fully detailed in the Hornsea accounts. Each year at Michaelmas and Easter there were the general chapters mostly held in Hornsea and rarely costing more than 16d. each or 2s. 6d. in all;[4] these were assemblies of local incumbents (of the whole archdeaconry according to Lyndwood, but probably in fact just of the deanery) which dealt with various local business and problems.[5] In many years too, if not in all, the vicar of Hornsea had occasion to ride to York twice to attend synods of clergy there, a journey which cost him between 4s. and 6s.[6] A constant, though much less predictable, expense was the

[1] Lyndwood, III.22.i, v.

[2] See references above, p. 143, n. 4.

[3] *M.C.A.*, pp. 26, 34, 39, 47, 50, 56.

[4] Ibid., pp. 27, 33, 39, 46, 49, 56.

[5] Lyndwood, iii.22.i, note *t*; it is unfortunate that records of these assemblies and their activities are so hard to find in this period; they may be the subject of the depositions in *N.C.C.D.* No. 84, from 1508.

[6] M.C.A., pp. 34, 39, 46, 50, 56.

purchase of bread and wine for communion, which was usually around 2s., but which in 1485–8 rose to over 6s.[1] Lastly there was the cost of oil and chrism (from the archdeacon), rarely more than a shilling a year.[2] All of these expenses occur in other parishes, but only here do we have figures over several years.

The burden of taxation which fell upon incumbents became considerably more pressing towards the end of our period. Although papal attempts to levy tenths from the English clergy on twelve occasions between 1450 and 1530 were only twice successful, and then only by the grace of the king, in 1465 and 1502, archiepiscopal levies were now becoming a sinister feature of clerical life, since they afforded a model and a stimulus for a more efficient rearrangement of royal subsidy assessment.[3]

The earliest fifteenth-century example in Canterbury Province at present known occurred in 1454 when a shilling in the pound from all livings was conceded to the Archbishop by Convocation.[4] In 1463, 1473, 1475, 1481, 1485, 1487 and 1489 there were others where the levy was more closely graduated and though the records only speak of chaplains, the beneficed seem to be comprehended; those normally exempt from royal subsidies are not excused from this, though various mitigating reasons, such as the support of one (1481) or both parents (1473), do earn exemption. Incomes from £5 to 10 marks (£6.13s. 4d.) were to yield 6s. 8d., from 10 marks to £10, 13s. 4d., from £10, £1. The 1489 charitable subsidy, at more stringent rates still, coincided with a grant direct to the king by Convocation. Similar things, at present less well known, were happening in the Northern Province too. There an 'aid' or charitable subsidy of a tenth was granted from all benefices to the archbishop in 1453 and we find the living of Kirkby Malham yielding 15s. 4d. for the first half of this in 1454;[5] in 1481 a whole tenth from all benefices worth 10 marks or more was

[1] Ibid., pp. 26, 33, 35, 39, 46, 47, 49, 51, 52, 56. An entry on p. 59 suggests that it was provided by the abbey.

[2] Ibid., pp. 27, 33, 35, 39, 47, 50, 56.

[3] W. E. Lunt, *Financial Relations of England with the Papacy, 1327–1534*, pp. 141–68. What follows, except where otherwise indicated, is based upon F. R. H. Du Boulay, 'Charitable Subsidies granted to the Archbishop of Canterbury 1300–1489', *B.I.H.R.* xxiii, 147–64.

[4] Lichfield MS. B/A/1/11, fo. 52v.

[5] R.I.20, fo. 330v; B.M. Addit. Roll 32957.

granted to the archbishop to pay his debt and meet his burdens.[1] Alongside these levies royal taxation also had to be met. In the Southern Province this fell until Wolsey's day only on those livings valued at 12 marks, £8, or more in the 1291 *Taxatio*, a valuation notoriously incomplete and generous to the incumbent; and out of these, various exemptions were granted for various temporary reasons of necessity. In the fifty-five years from 1450 on average in two years out of every three the unlucky incumbents were dunned for their moiety; from 1512 to 1518 six-tenths were levied from the clergy there.[2] The same conditions obtained in the Northern Province (though only benefices under 10 marks were exempt) where twenty-four tenths were granted in sixty years from 1452, but there, with the Tudors and with Scottish threats, the incidence became remorseless: a whole tenth in 1496 was followed by grants of three-tenths in 1497, one in 1502 and again 1504 and 1509 and three in 1512.[3] It is against this background that in 1523 both Convocations were induced to grant a moiety of one year's revenue of all benefices in England, to be levied over five years, at the rate of one-fifteenth for those benefices worth less than, and a tenth for those more than, £8; the valuation was a new one and was to be freshly made each year, so that the exemptions of 1291 disappeared, although the revision made some allowances for building costs and for curates' stipends.[4] The beneficed clergy were, therefore, under considerable strain from taxation by the end of our period, though for some it had long been almost an annually recurring deduction from income.

Often crippling, though as often brief, were pensions. These were usually negotiated, by episcopal licence, between the incoming and retiring incumbents to provide for the latter a means of support in old age or ill health, though occasionally they were awarded to hale and prosperous celebrities, such as Erasmus.[5]

---

[1] R.I.23, fo. 294r.

[2] Calculated from *C.F.R.*; Wilkins, *Concilia; Reg. Bourgchier*; Lichfield MSS. B/A/1/11–14; M. Bowker, *Secular Clergy in Lincoln Diocese*, p. 12.

[3] *C.F.R.:* Wilkins, *Concilia; Records of Northern Convocation*, ed. G. W. Kitchin (Surtees Soc. 113); R.I.20–27.

[4] *Lincoln Subsidy 1526*, pp. v, ix.

[5] Out of 172 resignations in Lincoln diocese between 1504 and 1533, 52 were conditional upon receiving a pension (K. Major, 'Resignation Deeds in the Diocese of Lincoln', *B.I.H.R.* xix, 63). Erasmus was receiving a pension of £20 per annum from the rectory of Aldington (*L. & P.* i(2), No. 2424).

The scale of the burden, which very few churches escaped altogether, may be gauged from some typical cases. Wrentham, valued at £21, in 1526 yielded a pension of £9 to its retiring rector; a parson of Smallburgh had to survive on £2. 13s. 4d. instead of £8 13s. 4d.; and the vicar of Gayton in 1524 paid a pension of 3 marks from a living valued at 5.[1] The just claims of the pensioner often conflicted with the urgent needs of the incumbent, and the Church erred humanely, if sometimes extravagantly, in favour of the former.

Finally, the cost of litigation in lay and ecclesiastical courts, whither many clerics resorted and were summoned, could be particularly damaging. In 1499 the rector of Lydeard St. Lawrence, who was also vicar of Cheddar, obtained a licence to absent himself for two years while staying in London in order to conduct there a case against his parishioners who had refused to pay tithe on windfall wood.[2] Richard Knyght, parish priest of St. Andrew's in Eastcheap, was maliciously sued in the consistory court, the King's Bench, and the City court by Hugh Marshe, a brewer of the same parish; Knyght complained that Hugh 'Wyll not lette to sue one accion after a nother wyth oute ende to put your pore Oratour to endeles trowble and coste'.[3]

IV: *Income*

The resources from which the incumbent could meet these expenses varied in character as much as in value. Rectors drew in very different proportions upon tithes, mortuaries, fees and oblations, and upon the fruits of their glebe land. But in a third, by one estimate 37 per cent[4], of all the parish livings serious qualifications to this pattern obtained; these were the benefices appropriated to the use of religious houses or ecclesiastical corporations, in which livings a perpetual vicarage was usually, though not always, established and endowed with only a part

[1] Norwich Act Book XVI, fos. 91r–93r, 83r–86r, 81r–v, respectively.
[2] *Regs. King & Castello*, p. 25.
[3] P.R.O., C 1/329/19.
[4] D. Knowles, *The Religious Orders in England*, ii, 291. Compare the very much worse situation in Scotland, G. Donaldson, *The Scottish Reformation* (Cambridge 1960), p. 12.

of the original income: only some or certain kinds of the tithes, perhaps no mortuaries, no offerings where a cash stipend was received, and not always the whole glebe land. But just as vicars received only a part of the original rectorial income, so their burdens were variously defined: some had a house and had to maintain it, others with a house were excused maintenance; some were accommodated in the impropriating abbey, others— like the vicars of Barking[1]—merely fed there; some were to pay all expenses ordinary and extraordinary, others merely the normal ones; some were to find a chaplain, some not; some of those who received a cash stipend were only required to support themselves, all the usual 'beneficial' expenses being supported by the impropriator.[2] Behind the generalizations which follow, therefore, lurks great variety.

The most debated and contentious part of an incumbent's income was from tithes; chapters were written to advise on its tactful collection, fortunes were spent in litigation to extract or to evade its payment, yet the explanation of this is to be found far more often in the nature of the levy than in the malice of clergy or parishioners. The tithe was nominally[3] a tenth of each man's annual produce or profit from his labours. It could be levied in kind on his crops and animals, as it usually was, with cash adjustments when a tenth was exacted on fewer than ten animals.[4] Or it could be levied as a house rate, as at Mancetter, where each man paid 3d. for his house, or 2d. if it lacked a garden or was only a cottage; as the parishioners there paid tithes on animals as well, and as oblations were separately accounted for, this house rate appears to be a commutation of crop tithes, whereas in London all tithes were commuted to a tax levied on each householder.[5] Even the produce of gardens was not exempt; eggs, peas and onions all yielded their due. Where agriculture was not the occupation of the parishioner his profits, fees or wages were subject to tithing; in the commercial

---

[1] D. Lysons, *Environs of London* (London 1792–6), iv, 96–97.

[2] See below, p. 178.

[3] In practice allowances were made for certain expenses when calculating the rate, for example when fixing the fish tithes at Scarborough (see the present writer's forthcoming article, 'North Sea Fishing in the Fifteenth Century: the Scarborough Fleet', *Northern History*, iii, 1968).

[4] J. R. H. Moorman, *Church Life in England in the Thirteenth Century* (2nd edn.), pp. 118–19; *M.C.A.*, pp. 37, 43–44.

[5] P.R.O., E 101/519/31, *passim; V.C.H. London*, i, 248.

community of Scarborough, for example, such personal tithes were a large and important element of the church's income, though the accounts give no indication of the payers' occupations, except when they are servants.[1] At Mancetter the tithes levied from servants are listed; on wages of 16s., 2d. or 3d. was paid; on 6s. 8d. plus food (*cum panno*), 1d. or 2d; the variations imply some careful consideration of other, now inscrutable, factors.[2]

Since tithes were annual and affected the living standards of parishioners and clergy alike, conflict arose into which the acrimony of many personal and incalculable disputes and disappointments would be channelled. This conflict of necessity and reluctance was not the sort which would easily and suddenly abate, but more likely would it grow progressively worse unless charity and restraint were exercised on both sides. Between parishioner and incumbent there often existed a state of 'cold war', manifested by obstinacy and prevarication on the one part and by punctilious and zealous collection on the other. The clergy were not always distinguished by their tact. While some of the parishioners of Mancetter were excused all or part of their tithes on account of their poverty, Sir Christopher, the parish priest of St. Peter's in Nottingham, was presented by the constables there 'for ower sessyng of poor foulkes and menes servantes at Estur for theyr tyes and other duttes', and the parson of Swainsthorpe in Norfolk rode round the parish to collect tithes with his reputed mistress riding pillion on his horse.[3] There were, moreover, distinguished clerics to persuade the parishioner against tithes, or, indeed, oblations of any sort. Wycliffe and the Lollards agreed that if the clergy were vicious they should be dispossessed, if negligent their tithes lawfully withheld. In London itself, in 1464, the Carmelites proposed and disputed for, in public places and amid huge audiences, the poverty of all the clergy; a more egregious want of responsibility is hard to find in the late medieval English Church.[4]

[1] A. G. Little, 'Personal Tithes', *E.H.R.* lx, 67–68, for the subject in general; for Scarborough see P.R.O., E 101/514/31, 32, *passim*.

[2] P.R.O., E 101/519/31, fos. 11r, 12v.

[3] Ibid., fos. 3r, 7v; *Records of the Borough of Nottingham*, ed. W. H. Stevenson, iii, 364; *N.C.C.D.* No. 164.

[4] F. R. H. Du Boulay, 'The Quarrel between the Carmelite Friars and the Secular Clergy of London, 1464–8', *J.E.H.* vi, 156–74. See also the measures which Archbishop Morton took at Convocation in 1486 against those who criticized the Church in their sermons to laymen (Wilkins, iii, 618–19).

Against the reluctant tithe payer, as every reader of Chaucer knows, the incumbent could curse. This was pronounced in all parishes four times a year—on Sunday after Michaelmas, Sunday in mid-Lent, Holy Trinity and Sunday after the feast of St. Peter ad Vincula—and it was to be accompanied with lighted candles, ringing of bells, the display of the cross, and all appropriate solemnities 'in order to strike greater fear in the congregation';[1] it was, however, part of a general sentence which did not specify names, but enumerated offences, of which the non-payment of tithes was merely one, and for all of which the offenders were declared to be excommunicate *ipso facto*. The surviving texts of the general sentence reveal an incumbent or preacher embarrassed by it and careful to dissociate himself from any menacing tone and to emphasize its charitable, almost superfluous, function; perhaps tact prevailed over honesty in this.[2] Evidence that the clergy could excommunicate offenders *ad hoc* is hard to come by and in 1444 John Sothworth, vicar of Ilam, was alleged to have cursed a parishioner *without authority*, though the quarrel was not about tithes.[3] The clergy were empowered, though, to suspend defaulters who had ignored three warnings, after which those who were still recalcitrant could be compelled by ecclesiastical censure, if necessary,[4] but this probably implies action by or through a court and not by the *curatus* alone.

Certain tithe suits, those which involved more than a quarter of the parish's tithes and thus seriously threatened the value of the living and its advowson, came within the jurisdiction of the royal courts, and similarly with suits about the sale or lease of tithes, but these were disputes rather about the right to receive than about refusal to pay, and they were rarely between an incumbent and his parishioners.[5] Non-payment by parishioners might be due to two factors: firstly, a deliberate or accidental negligence; secondly, a serious doubt about the incumbent's entitlement, perhaps because of confusion, or because of novel or

---

[1] Lyndwood, V.17.viii, note *z*: *'ut maior auditoribus incutiatur timor'*.
[2] *Quatuor Sermones* (Roxburghe Club 111), pp. 56–60; *Instructions for Parish Priests by John Myrc*, pp. 60–67; *Jacob's Well*, ed. A. Brandeis (E.E.T.S. o.s. 115), pp. 8, 13–36,—on pp. 37–47, without cursing, the author is less apologetic for demanding tithes.
[3] B.M. Addit. Ch. 27343. The vicar here unwisely chose a knight for his victim.
[4] *Reg. Gray*, ed. J. Raine (Surtees Soc. 56), p. 220.
[5] N. Adams, 'The Judicial Conflict over Tithes', *E.H.R.* lii, 6, 11.

excessive demands by the priest. The first type were usually dealt with summarily by compurgation in the *ex officio* department of the bishops' courts and few extensive records of this branch are extant. The second type, about the obligation of the parishioner to pay the debated tithe, would probably be heard in the 'instance' division of the consistory court, where the solution was pronounced by a judge on the basis of sworn depositions. Some forty cases about tithe in the Norwich consistory court in the early sixteenth century have been published; a third of these are between ecclesiastics—incumbents and impropriators—disputing possession, and the remainder were brought by incumbents against parishioners.[1] All of these last are about obligation; some may be explained by the avarice of the parson or vicar, some by the parsimony or economy of the laity, others arise from intractable problems. The perplexity caused by pasturing animals of one parish in another and by rabbit warrens which ignored ecclesiastical topography had solutions in custom which were sometimes forgotten and challenged.[2] When a neighbouring incumbent was farmer of the tithes his abandonment of this office could result in confusion and in the continued payment to him of tithes which were now due to another.[3] The parishioner of Heydon who had paid no tithes on three tenements for sixteen years, whether rightly or wrongly, might well have been indignant when asked for them by his rector.[4] In Great Dunham two witnesses, one resident for fifteen years, the other for twenty-eight, were unable to recall whether tithes on a certain ten acres were due to the local rector or to the rector of West Lexham.[5] Frequently the parish boundaries, despite the annual beating of the bounds, were the subject of dispute, for a couple of new houses on the edge of the parish, or a new enclosure of fields, or the clearing of woodland there could all confuse ideas and knowledge of rights and limits.[6] Sometimes it was difficult to

---

[1] *N.C.C.D., passim.*
[2] Ibid., Nos. 53, 148, 149, 110.
[3] Ibid., No. 231.   [4] Ibid., No. 152.   [5] Ibid., No. 277.
[6] *Reg. Bothe*, pp. 76–77, for disputes over the boundaries of Dewchurch and Allensmore. For the thoroughness with which the bounds were sometimes beaten see *Select Cases before the King's Council in the Star Chamber 1477–1509*, ed. I. S. Leadam (Selden Soc. 16), pp. 164–8. Compare with that York Visitations, fo. 56r for the vigour of the parishioners of Preston, who were beating their bounds and their neighbours in Hedon.

know whether the owner or the lessee should pay the tithes, although usually a clause about charges is to be found in charters and leases; in 1522 the vicar of Cheshunt sued the prioress there for the tithes which the late Sir Thomas Lovell, lessee of her land, refused to pay.[1] Some of these disputed obligations, of course, were mere legal stratagems to conceal the parishioner's obstinate refusal to pay an undoubted debt, but some were the consequence of an incumbent seeking to augment his income by extending his demands, and since this certainly happened, some figures of instance cases brought by incumbents about tithes may be a useful index of its frequency. In Canterbury consistory court, the numbers of tithe cases of *all kinds* in any one year ranged from thirty-nine in 1397 to four in 1531; a sample of five separate years in the Lichfield consistory court ranges from eight tithes cases in 1472 or ten in 1525 to four in 1475 and again in 1530, each a very small proportion of the suits before the court in those years.[2] As these are total figures for all tithe suits, it is permissible to think that incumbents were only occasionally asserting new demands about the tithes due from their parishioners. The figures for 1525 and 1530 from so large a diocese at so critical a time are particularly noteworthy. The clergy would be most prone to make novel demands as prices rose and most of all in London; there predial (or agricultural) tithes had been commuted to a cash levy on rents fixed in 1457 and slightly amended in 1475, a rate which proved absurdly inadequate from a clerical point of view in the 1520s;[3] as personal tithes were by a mid-fifteenth century compromise a free-will offering, the London clergy lived on virtually a fixed income which must have been greatly reduced by the price rise of the sixteenth century. Elsewhere the rising prices were far more likely to provoke the wage earning laity to resist or resent the customary demands of the clergy than to drive the incumbent, whose income rose and fell with the market prices, to new claims; in the circumstances of the 1520s even the usual obligations, particularly in urban centres, were likely to seem extortionate.

[1] *L. & P.* iii(1), No. 1026, and iv(1), No. 368.
[2] B. L. Woodcock, *Medieval Ecclesiastical Courts*, p. 86; Lichfield MSS. B/C/1/1–2; B/C/2/1–3, for the 'test' years 1465, 1471/2, 1475, 1525, 1530.
[3] J. F. Thomson, 'Tithe Disputes in Late Medieval London', *E.H.R.* lxxviii, 2–3, 10, 15.

A closely related and equally vexatious source of clerical income was the mortuary, which some parishioners were bound by ancient custom to pay at their death to the rector or vicar. Lyndwood cites the decrees of Archbishops Winchelsey and Langham who clearly regarded mortuary as payment for tithes and oblations forgotten or inescapably miscalculated.[1] Yet this was not a view shared by the parishioners of Scarborough who, like some Lincolnshire testators noticed elsewhere, almost invariably left in their wills a gown for a mortuary and then a sum of money for tithes forgotten.[2]

What items were due as mortuaries varied with local custom: the best beast usually in country parishes, often the best gown in towns, but not infrequently a sum of money. Although mortuaries formed a small, if significant, proportion of the clergy's income, they were usually a substantial expense for the person concerned, as the accounts of incumbents show: in Scarborough in the early fifteenth century the best gown ranged in value from a shilling to a pound; at Kirkby Malham in mid-century the best animal ranged in value from 7s. to 26s; mortuaries collected in Riston each year, and there seem to have been only a few, totalled about 15s; in Downham in the early sixteenth century one mortuary was valued at 8d. but others were worth 5s. to 8s.[3] Perhaps the most considerable of all were collected not by a parish priest, but by the prior of Bridlington from gentlemen and ladies in the rural parts of Bridlington parish; by a compromise, devised in 1447 by Lord Falconbridge and confirmed in York consistory court, gentlemen owed for their mortuary their horse, saddle and armour, or, if they had none, their best possession, and gentlewomen similarly owed their horse, saddle and harness, the right of selection resting with the prior.[4] No wonder parishioners, to preserve family wealth from clerical depredations, sometimes sold the best beast or chattel just before death.[5] Trouble also arose when the incumbent preferred to take

---

[1] Lyndwood, I.3.i.

[2] Lincoln Wills, ii, p. xxiv; York Probate MS. Registers ii, fos. 366v–367r; iii, fos. 324r–325r, 329v–330r; iv, fos. 243v–244r; v, fos. 239r, 292v, 495r–v, for a random selection of the Scarborough evidence.

[3] P.R.O., E 101/514/31, 32, on fo. 1r or v of each booklet therein (Scarborough); B.M. Addit. Roll 32957 recto (Kirkby Malham); *M.C.A.*, pp. 40, 50, 52 (Riston); and P.R.O., E 101/517/27, fos. 4v, 6r (Downham).

[4] B.M. Addit. MS. 40008, fo. 12v (a Bridlington cartulary).

[5] *N.C.C.D.*, No. 396 (Beeston next Mileham).

a cow, albeit the best beast, when the deceased left abundant horses or sheep, but few cows.[1]

Payment was not to be evaded by moving from one parish to another, perhaps just before death. Who should receive the mortuary of one who had been living but a few days in the parish where he died was a problem partially solved in some places by the custom that a year and a day's residence was necessary in a parish before mortuaries were due there,[2] and definitively settled in 1529 when a statute decreed that mortuaries could only be paid once and only in one place, namely where the deceased had lived most.[3]

In practice, if not in law, almost everyone seems to have been liable for mortuaries: people who were not householders, sisters, brothers, wives, apprentices, poor women and scholars; even infants, it was claimed, were liable, and one, Hunne's, became the subject of a *cause célèbre*.[4] 'No man shall die in their debt; or if any man do, he shall pay it when he is dead', wrote Tyndale,[5] yet the surprising feature of the extant accounts is the fewness of mortuaries; even where frequent, as in Scarborough, their number is far smaller than the deaths indicated by funeral masses, and in Kirkby Malham, Riston and Downham—all of whose accounts should record the whole of the income—nowhere are more than five mortuaries recorded in a year.[6] It looks, therefore, as if some now indiscernible means test operated to the advantage of many parishioners and that the statute of 1529 in this feature was less radical than is often thought, exempting from payment, as it did, all persons with moveable goods worth less than 10 marks, all covert women, children and non-householders.[7] In its other provisions, however, it substantially reduced the burden of those who were liable: to 3s. 4d. cash

---

[1] Ibid., No. 352 (Little Snoring).

[2] Ibid., No. 127 (Bexwell).

[3] *Statutes of Realm*, 21 Henry VIII, c. vi.

[4] *Lincoln Diocesan Documents, 1450–1544*, ed. A. Clark (E.E.T.S. o.s. 149), p. 7. On Hunne, see A. G. Dickens, *The English Reformation*, pp. 90–95, and J. F. Thomson, *The Later Lollards*, pp. 162–70.

[5] 'The Obedience of the Christian Man', *Doctrinal Treatises by William Tyndale*, ed. H. Walter (Parker Soc.), p. 237.

[6] Riston is slightly suspect because in two of the three years the number of mortuaries is not given, but their totals fall below that of the third year which yielded only two (*M.C.A.*, pp. 40, 50).

[7] *Statutes of the Realm*, 21 Henry VIII, c. vi.

for those with chattels worth between 10 marks and £30; 6s. 8d. for chattels valued between £30 and £40; and a 10s. maximum for all with goods worth more than £40.

There is no denying that in some quarters mortuaries were particularly disputed and even where few records of contention survive, as in York diocese, there is little doubt that of all payments to the clergy this one rankled most. Nowhere was it more provocative of opposition than in London, and no case is better known than John Hunne's refusal to pay a mortuary for his dead infant, but outside London strife was not unknown. About 1509 the baillies and constables and over a hundred other inhabitants of Kingston on Thames drafted a strong protest against their absentee vicar, Nicholas West, later the bishop of Ely; the document was then sealed and entered in the town archives; it purports to have been drawn up with the assent of all the people of the town and parish, and continued: 'forasmuche as it is right merytorious, and a charytable dede and grete rewarde to mannys Soule to witnesse trouth, thereas lakke of knowledge thereof might ensue lamentable hurt, pite, or inconvenience, that God defende. We, therfor, for the very instruction of trowth, notifie and declare that Nicholas West, Doctour Dene of Wyndesour and vicar of Kyngeston aforesaid, wrongfully hath takyn and dayly taketh and witholde the old auncion custume with us in takyng of mortuarys otherwise than hath ben takyn and usyd tyme owte of mynde to ye grete hurte and harmys, and utterly undewing of the said towne and parishe in tyme to come, yf it be sufferyd, as God defende. In witness whereof we, the said parties, have sett oure sealys in evydence and fortefying of ye premisses'.[1] A few years later, in 1514, Edward Molyneux, the parson of Sefton in Lancashire, entered with force of arms some land in Little Crosby leased by Nicholas Blundell to John Cokeson of Warrington and had an ox belonging to Cokeson and worth 53s. 4d. killed. The following year the servants of Molyneux lay in wait by the king's highway and, as Cokeson was driving his beasts to Wigan market, captured thirty-eight animals and impounded them for a month, during which five died and the rest starved; by this means Molyneux extracted from Cokeson 40s. in cash and a bond that he would not sue at law under pain of another 20s. This wanton slaughter

[1] H.M.C. 3rd Report, Appendix, p. 333.

of Cokeson's ox and the rustling of his cattle was thus capped by a speciously legal agreement to deprive him of the right of complaint. Molyneux argued that Cokeson's wife and family had resort to the Sefton tenement and that when his wife died, seven years before, the ox was surrendered by some of her family as the mortuary; Cokeson, moreover, owed Molyneux and another as feoffees £3, but by the advice of the plaintiff's friends the rector had contented himself with 40s. The plaintiff argued that his wife did not die in Sefton but in Warrington, sixteen miles away and that in any case no mortuary was due for a covert woman in Sefton.[1] In these cases, as in Hunne's, clerical greed, rather than the institution of mortuary, was the cause of strife; such conflicts over mortuaries are relatively few, but they ignited resentment and polarized opposition with a speed which was symptomatic of an uneasy relationship.

Much more universal and rather less provocative than mortuaries were oblations. At four principal feasts in the year the incumbent or the curate, and no one else, could expect these from his parishioners, but they were not always the feasts traditionally designated;[2] Christmas and Easter certainly were observed, but in only one of the extant accounts, Downham, is the church's dedication feast a time for oblations, and again in only one, Kirkby Malham, is the patronal feast a time of gain for the incumbent. At Helmingham, Hornsea and Scarborough the Purification and Assumption of the Virgin supplant Pentecost and the dedication or patronal feasts.[3] In the 1470s the vicar of Rye had suffered some loss, because on 8 September, the feast of the Nativity of St. Mary, to whom the church was dedicated, the day on which oblations had long been paid, most of the parishioners were away from the parish, travelling abroad, attending fairs in neighbouring places, or herring fishing in remote waters; in 1476, as a consequence, Bishop John Arundel ordered that all parishioners of Rye of either sex who were admitted to Holy Communion, should henceforward make their offerings on 15 August, the Assumption of Mary, a copy of which command

[1] *Lancashire and Cheshire Cases in the Court of Star Chamber*, ed. R. Stewart-Brown (Lancs. and Cheshire Record Soc. 71), p. 75.

[2] For the traditional offering days see J. R. H. Moorman, *Church Life in England in the Thirteenth Century*, p. 126; and B.M. Addit. MS. 38112, fo. 10r, where John Beleth gives the following four times: Christmas, Easter, Pentecost and All Saints.

[3] *M.C.A.*, p. 22, n.

was duly kept among the town archives.[1] These donations were due, in theory, from all communicants over 18 years of age and of indepedent means. Throughout the year there were other occasions when the priestly income would be swollen by offerings: for weddings, churchings and funerals. At Hornsea a wedding was usually worth 4*d.*, at Downham 6*d.*, at Helmingham 6*d.* apart from 2*d.* for the banns and another 2*d.* for oblations (possibly in wax); at Kirkby Malham a wedding at the church door would cost 8*d.* but there would be in addition 2*d.* due to each priest, 2*d.* for candles at the altar, and a further 1*d.* if the woman was purified; at Scarborough, where the value of the wax offered is also recorded alongside the cash, the receipts from each wedding varied greatly from person to person, but whereas the average rate in the 1410s was 9*d.* and in the early 1430s nearly 2*s.*, in the 1440s it had fallen to 6*d.* and thus responds to and reflects the changing prosperity of the community itself. Churchings rarely brought in more than 3*d.* anywhere, though they could rise to 4*d.* at Downham and 8*d.* at Scarborough. Funerals yielded to the incumbent 4*d.* or 6*d.* on average, but in Kirkby Malham each adult communicant on his death owed 7*d.* which was called locally 'nythewax'.[2] The vicar of South Petherton in Somerset received a 1*d.* from each parishioner dying there.[3] These were in theory free-will offerings—no one was to deny to a parishioner burial, baptism, marriage or any of the sacraments of sacramentals for want of a sum of money[4]—but custom, tact and necessity, as well as the priest's monopoly, qualified this freedom. The Easter offerings probably include the 'confession pennies' and the 'secret tithes'; at Helmingham at Easter and Michaelmas several parishioners contributed a shilling each towards 'le certeyn', perhaps the Lenten veils; at Downham at Trinity 'sangrede' for masses for the dead was offered; on each Sunday at Kirkby Malham 1½*d.*, known as 'halybred sylver', was collected. No doubt incumbents also received a significant sum if they allowed a parishioner to be buried in the choir and in Herefordshire in the early sixteenth century the vicar of Clun received 7*s.* for every parishioner who was buried in the nave or

[1] *H.M.C. 5th Report*, Appendix, p. 496.
[2] *M.C.A.*, p. 22.
[3] *Regs. Stillington & Fox*, pp. 193–4.
[4] Lyndwood, V.2.i.

the chapels of the church.[1] The incumbent occasionally reaped further profit from an alms box, or a box placed before an image, or from collectors for extra-parochial institutions, or from bequests to the high altar.[2]

Of the three sources of income derived from the parishioners, oblations seem to have caused least trouble. The celebrated complaint of Londoners, at the time of the Hunne affair, that they had to pay exorbitant fees for marriages, burials and churchings, comes from a time when the City, with its lay tradition of corporate resistance to ecclesiastical dues, was particularly inflamed, and no satisfactory evidence in support of the complaint has so far been found.[3] Outside London complaints of this kind are rare indeed.

Quite different from the types of income surveyed above which emanate from parishioners, the glebe was the least controverted means of support. This freehold land, appurtenant to the benefice, varied in importance, for while it undoubtedly provided the major part of the income of Prescot, where it formed a rectory manor, one may suppose that tithes and oblations provided the incumbent of Boxley with a better living than his third of an acre of glebe.[4] Most incumbents, like those of Aston Tirrold and Castor, could rely on thirty or forty acres, sometimes all together and near the manse, as at Rothbury, sometimes widely dispersed, as at Wangford, an acre or two on the south-east, a few more on the south-west, several scattered through the open fields or in various meadows and pastures.[5] Equipment and labour, or else time, would be required by the glebe, which was therefore no unmixed blessing: ten or twenty acres might require more labourers and equipment than they could profitably support; a smaller area might absorb more of the incumbent's own time in weeding, digging, sowing and reaping than the cure

[1] *Reg. Mayew*, pp. 222–5.

[2] As at Helmingham (B.M. Addit. MS. 34786, fos. 5–6). In the thirteenth century the vicar of Peterborough was reckoned to derive 10*s.* a year from bequests (*Rotuli Hugonis de Welles*, ed. W. P. W. Phillimore (C. & Y. Soc.), ii, 127). For the levy from extra-parochial collectors see *M.C.A.*, pp. 28, 30, 35, 36, 42, 43.

[3] *L. & P.* i(2), No. 3602.

[4] *Prescot Court Leet Records*, p. 1; E. Hasted, *History of Kent* (Canterbury 1797–1801), iv, 351; for other large glebes see J. R. H. Moorman, op. cit., p. 113.

[5] *Domesday of Inclosures*, ed. I. S. Leadam, i, 145, 269–70; *History of Northumberland*, xv (ed. M. H. Dodds), 313; B.M. Addit. MS. 23962, fos. 7r–39r, an Elizabethan copy of an inquisition into the glebe lands of Wangford in April 1532.

of souls in fact permitted. Many, if not most, incumbents seem to have solved their difficulties by letting the glebe out to farm: a Thomas Skete leased some glebe houses, land and meadow at Downham for 13*s*. 4*d*. a year, and the priory of Ixworth farmed another glebe meadow for £2. 13*s*. 4*d*; the glebe land at Helmingham brought in 19*s*. 1*d*. a year, at Hornsea 31*s*. 6*d*, and at Riston at least £8.[1]

It often happened that glebe was not the only land an incumbent had. Many enjoyed what might be called a private income from land inherited or purchased or leased. In 1525 the vicar of Preston next Faversham, who was also the parson of Harrietsham, owned, as well as the lands in Sevenoaks bequeathed to him by his father, his own property in Middlesex, Northamptonshire and Oxfordshire.[2] He was ploughing back the fruits of his heritage and of his practice as an ecclesiastical lawyer into the land; many did the same on a smaller scale. The rector of Chilton in 1461 had two burgage tenements in Bridgwater; Thomas Coote, parson of Enmore, held freehold land in the city and suburbs of Exeter; a vicar of St. Nicholas in Leicester held a messuage from the Corpus Christi Guild there; a rector of St. Mary in the South, Gloucester, held two parcels of land from the mayor and burgesses.[3] Master Henry Caldey, vicar of Cuckfield, had lands in Ireland; Richard Purdy, parson of Icklingham, had a tenement called 'Frendis' with twenty-two acres of land in the town there, another tenement called 'biggyng', and others in Thurston and Holkham, as well as a close in Tostock.[4] It was sometimes known for incumbents like William Atkynns, parson of Little Oakley, to have two houses, or even like Thomas Sende, rector of Taynton, three.[5] The twenty-four year lease of 'William Hall' and its garden, next to Merton College, Oxford, which belonged to Richard Ruthyn, vicar of Iffley, though pro-

[1] P.R.O., E 101/517/27 *passim*; B.M. Addit. MS. 34786, fo. 1r; *M.C.A.*, pp. 34, 38, 46, 47, 50.

[2] P.C.C., Porch 2.

[3] *Bridgewater Borough Archives, 1445–1468* (Somerset Record Soc. 60), p. 114; *C.C.R. 1461–68*, p. 6; *Records of the Borough of Leicester*, ed. M. Bateson (1901), ii, 347; *Calendar of Records of Gloucester Corporation*, ed. W. H. Stevenson (1893), p. 418.

[4] *Munimenta Academica*, ed. H. Anstey (Rolls Series), pp. 608–9; Reg. Morton, fo. 11v.

[5] G.L.C., MS DL/C/354, fos. 9v–10r; *Some Oxford Wills, 1393–1510*, ed. J. R. H. Weaver and A. Beardwood (Oxfords. Record Soc.), pp. 22–23.

fitable, may not have been so lucrative as the lease of mills which John Russell, vicar of St. Andrew's of Pershore, had from the abbot of Worcester.[1] This investment or speculation has a wider significance than as an index of clerical prosperity, for by it the clergy became tenants and landlords of the laity, roles which cannot always have won them respect or affection.[2] The hostility it aroused in laymen is embodied in the statute of 1529 which prohibited any future farming and leasing of lands by any 'spiritual person' and enjoined him to dispose of any he was then holding before a stipulated date.[3] The Church feared this encumbrance of real estate as a distraction from the cure of souls and had long forbidden its clergy from farming secular lands—even while it had theoretically acknowledged patrimonial titles; in Lincoln diocese the bishop sought out the parson or vicar who was *firmarius temporalium firmarum*.[4] Yet the secular clergy were not sworn to poverty and there was no easy procedure for separating a man from his freehold. It was inescapable that some clergy would be landlords and tenants, but it was a fact which helped to blur the definition and spoil relations between clergy and laity.

Since it was from the fields about their parishes that they derived part, if not most, of their sustenance, parochial clergy, except in the towns and until quite recent times, have rarely been free from agricultural interests, whether they were sheep farmers as on the Yorkshire wolds, or arable farmers as in Holderness.[5] When they drew up their wills their minds turned instinctively to the combes of wheat, malt and barley, and to the sheep, horses, cows and bullocks, the plough cart and plough gear which they would leave. Could the parson of Cholderton walk far in the fields of his village without catching sight of some of his 184 sheep; or Richard Wolaston, rector of Aldwinkle, the cows and calves, heifers, ewes and lambs, the horses

---

[1] *Epistolae academicae Oxon*, ed. H. Anstey (Oxford Historical Soc. 36), ii, 600–1; *H.M.C. 2nd Report*, Appendix, p. 72.

[2] For an example of the clergy as landlords involved in litigation with the laity, see *Calendar of Plea and Memorandum Rolls of London, 1437–52*, ed. P. E. Jones, p. 63.

[3] *Statutes of Realm*, 21 Henry VIII, c. 13, i–iv.

[4] *Lincoln Visitations 1517–31*, i, 63–64, 88–89.

[5] J. S. Purvis, 'A Note on Sixteenth Century Farming in Yorkshire', *Y.A.J.* xxxvi, 435–54.

and the swarms of bees that were his?[1] The rector of North
Luffenham carefully noted in his will not only his animals and
carts and plough, but also his pitchfork, muckfork and shovel.[2]
The vicar of Woodhurst, John Farylton, left to his brother 'my
hole teame of oxen and sterys as they be with waynes and cartes
and almaner of harneys thereto belonging'.[3] How often had that
purposeful and slow procession moved about the fields of the
parish to collect his crops in the heat of a summer's day? How
often, we may wonder, did it arouse envy in the parishioner who
cultivated the plot next to the parson's and perhaps thought
indignantly of the tithe which he would have to surrender to his
neighbour; all the more bitter may his thoughts have been if he
knew that the parson had extensive lands elsewhere, another
benefice or private patrimony.

Incumbents sold the produce of their unleased glebe, together with a large proportion of their tithes, to, or in competition with, their neighbours and parishioners: grain to millers and
bakers, fleeces to woolmen, sheep, pigs and oxen to butchers, or
to the cellerer of a monastery. A parishioner of Helmingham purchased tithe corn and barley from the incumbent and a man from
Debenham bought the tithe cheese; the rector of Downham most
years had over a hundred sheep and between thirty and forty
stones of wool to dispose of, the sheep usually to the priory of
Ixworth, the wool to a layman seemingly.[4] About this time
William Howard, rector of Rayleigh in Essex, was cited in
Chancery by John Jamys, a London butcher.[5] Jamys complained
that he had made a bargain with Howard to buy from him 81
oxen at £14 a score and 200 wethers for £28; he duly took
the sheep and paid £20, the rest to be paid later; but meanwhile
Howard had sold the oxen at £17 the score to a butcher of
Stratford, and cited Jamys before the sheriff of London for
the outstanding £8 for the sheep. Jamys was now seeking
writs of *Corpus cum causa*, to obtain release from prison, and
sub pena in order to sue Howard for breach of contract. Howard
for his part tells quite a different story. Jamys first visited him

[1] P.C.C., Porch 1 and 23.
[2] Ibid., Porch 33.
[3] Ibid., Porch 22.
[4] B.M. Addit. MS. 34786, fos. 4r, 11r–v; P.R.O., E 101/517/27, fos. 1r, 3r, 4r, 5r.
[5] P.R.O., C 1/242/14, 15.

and offered £14 a score for his oxen, but having heard that Jamys 'was noted but an easy keper of his days of payement', Howard declined to bargain; when Jamys next appeared, the oxen had been sold (for £14 to the butcher of Stratford) and Jamys bought 120 sheep for £14, £6 of which he paid and £8 subsequently refused. Howard sued him in the Queen's court at Romford in the manor of Havering at Bower and was awarded £8 with 10s. costs; when for the sake of delay Jamys removed the matter by a writ of error to the King's Bench, Howard again won the case; he denied any such bargain as Jamys had declared. Whatever may have been the truth, we have here a vivid picture of clergy doing business in a shrewd and resolute manner, and on a large scale; 81 oxen and 200 (or was it 120?) sheep, a turnover according to Jamys of £96, or even by Howard's claim £70. Trading of this sort, of not always on this scale, must have been common and goes far to explain the large sums of ready cash which many incumbents left at their death.

Disputes such as these, tried as they often were before Chancellors and Lord Keepers who were prelates, induced the bishops and their deputies to take a severe view of clerical trading. Robert Downes, who had the cure of souls in Clavering in 1528, was warned in the London consistory court under pain of excommunication to abstain from the buying and selling of grain.[1] James Even, vicar of Latton, and Dominus Morecroft, who incidentally boasted a variety of other vices as well, were accused of selling wine in the vicarage to persons gathering there —an offence of ambiguous significance for clergy-laity relations.[2] A year later a statute prohibited the clergy from selling anywhere for profit any manner of produce or chattels; they could buy only animals and goods and chattels necessary for the maintenance of their household and lands, and they could sell them again only if they were found unsuitable.[3] Those alone who had insufficient glebe to support their unavoidable expenses could farm other land and trade in corn and cattle, so long as the profits were used only for the expenses of household and hospitality. It is indicative of the prosperity and commercial activity of many clergy that they should have aroused such enmity or jealousy.

[1] G.L.C., MS. DL/C/330, fo. 104v.
[2] Ibid., fos. 160v, 168v.
[3] *Statutes of Realm*, 21 Henry VIII, c. 13. v, vi, viii.

The parson of St. Nicholas, Guildford, enjoyed from the reign of
Edward II onwards the right to hold a yearly fair at the chapel
of St. Katherine in his parish for five days from the feast of St.
Matthew the Apostle and Evangelist.[1] Robert Cowhull, vicar
of Preston, appears with two chaplains, Richard York and John
Hirdson, on the roll of the gild merchant of Preston in 1459;[2]
whatever the explanation of their membership, as a sign of their
identity with, and prestige among, the trading classes it is noteworthy. Similar testimony comes from Southampton during
Henry VIII's reign when, at different times, the vicars of St.
Michael Holy Rood and of St. Mary the Virgin were enfranchised and admitted to the register of burgesses.[3]

In view of all this, and recalling the often remote and elevated
employment of some incumbents, the riches which a number of
them list in their wills should cause no surprise. Robert Somerby,
vicar of Kingston on Thames, left over £100, John Cammell,
rector of Ditcheat, over £50; John Sparhawke left three silver
cups, John Dier many silver spoons, a silver and gilt salt, a silver
cup and cover, and a silver bowl and cover; and John Clyfton,
parson of Barwick in Elmet, left to a friend 'my biggest Turkes
sett in a Ryng of golde and my finall emerode sett in a Ringe
of golde'.[4] Not all incumbents were so affluent.

V: *Poverty and its Remedies*

Where all these sources of income failed to meet the charges
upon a benefice, various causes might be operating. A rectory,
depending for its income upon the local harvests, markets and
conditions, shared equally in the rising prosperity of the parish
and in its declining fortunes; nowhere is this clearer than in the
accounts of Scarborough parish church in the early fifteenth century, where the rector, in fact the priory of Bridlington, bene-
fited like the parishioners in the 1410s from the sudden boom in
Iceland fishing, but where in the depressed 1430s not only the

[1] *H.M.C. 7th Report*, Appendix, p. 600.
[2] *Rolls of Burgesses at the Gilds Merchant of the Borough of Preston, 1397–1682*,
ed. W. A. Abram (Lancs. and Cheshire Record Soc. 9), p. 12.
[3] *H.M.C. 11th Report*, Appendix, part iii, p. 19.
[4] P.C.C., Blamyr 15; *Somerset Medieval Wills, 1383–1500*, ed. F. W. Weaver
(Somerset Record Soc. 16), pp. 175–6, 222–5, 382–3; P.C.C., Porch 33.

tithes but also the oblations were significantly lower in yield.[1] The fishing boom of the East Anglian fleet must have transformed the economic condition of the incumbents of Wells next the Sea, Blakeney and Yarmouth during the fifteenth century. Elsewhere a bad harvest, murrain among the sheep, inundation, erosion or the visit of some pestilence, even the occurrence of a battle, could reduce the often narrow margin of a rector's profit, perhaps just at a time when extensive building repairs became urgent.

Vicarages were similarly responsive to the local economy, but there were some interesting variations in this time. Where they had no or few grain tithes, the current trend to convert from arable to sheep farming must often have been to their advantage, rather than the impropriator's, so long as the conversion stopped short of complete depopulation which would eliminate the need of a curate at all and end in a deserted village, an empty unserved church and the annexation of its sheep tithes by the impropriator.[2] *Per contra* in one parish a change from pastoral to arable farming was blamed for the vicar's poverty.[3] Otherwise the same factors which governed the fortunes of rectors operated upon vicars; the differences appear in the remedies available to each.

There was no way permanently to augment the income of a rectory except by uniting two rectories. But for this there were a number of conditions to be fulfilled: the churches had to be close enough for them both to be conveniently served; the patrons of each had to agree to some arrangement, which was not always easily achieved, to compensate each other for loss of patronage, in effect usually done by granting each the right of alternate presentation; thirdly, either one of the benefices had to be vacant, or one incumbent induced to resign. Such an instance occurred in the Norwich diocese in 1505 when Framingham Pigot, worth 7 marks, was united to Framingham Earl nearby, worth only 5 or 6 marks; henceforth, the rector was to pay the usual charges for both churches and keep both chancels in repair, but he would have only one house and household to maintain,

[1] P. Heath, 'North Sea Fishing in the Fifteenth Century: the Scarborough Fleet', *Northern History*, iii, 1968.

[2] K. J. Allison, M. W. Beresford, J. G. Hurst and others, *The Deserted Villages of Oxfordshire* and *The Deserted Villages of Northamptonshire*.

[3] *M.C.A.*, p. 10.

THE COST OF LIVING

and have a larger glebe.[1] Although it is by no means difficult
to find other instances where these conditions obtained and the
opportunity for permanent union was seized,[2] they were
markedly few when the number of penurious rectories is counted.

Not all unions, however, were of a permanent kind: Richard
Nikke, bishop of Norwich in the early sixteenth century, united
merely for the life of the incumbent, usually by collating one
living to the rector of another, some sixty rectories, on two
occasions linking Panxworth with a vicarage.[3] If temporary
union of this kind were impossible there were other transient
solutions available. Like John Harlow, rector of Marksbury in
1458, the impoverished incumbent could be licensed to supplement his income by singing masses for the dead, which could
even be done in his own church; or like Robert Fabel, rector of
Beckington in 1463, he might be licensed to absent himself and
keep a grammar school for a limited number of years in order to
raise enough money to meet his creditors or to execute repairs.[4]

Two vicarages like two rectories could be united permanently,
but only if they had the same impropriator or rector. There are,
however, from the episcopate of Nikke at Norwich examples of
eleven vicarages being united for the life of a common incumbent and even of some being thus united with rectories. For a
permanent augmentation of a vicarage, however, where a plea
to the rector had proved unavailing, the procedure was by litigation, initiated by an appeal to the bishop, which since 1439
could be heard *in forma pauperis*.[5] In the early part of the fifteenth
century, oaths were sometimes extorted from vicars not to sue
for augmentation of their incomes, but no case of this form of
'wage restraint' has been found after 1450.[6] In any event records
of such litigation as we have offer little encouragement to the
vicar. Other palliatives were open to him, a lease of tithes and
oblations or the farming of the appropriated rectory, which was
a frequent solution according to the Canterbury Convocation of
1530.[7] The poverty of vicarages should have been easier to deal

[1] *N.C.C.D.*, No. 57.
[2] e.g. *Reg. Myllyng*, pp. 39–41, 63–66; *Reg. Bothe*, pp. 192, 200.
[3] Norwich Act Books XIII–XVI.
[4] *Reg. Bekynton*, pp. 302, 400–1.
[5] *Reg. Chichele*, iii, 286–7.
[6] R. R. Hartridge, *Medieval Vicarages*, pp. 193–4.
[7] Ibid., p. 201.

with than that of rectories, for augmentation, short or long term, was much more often possible; we should expect, therefore, greater fluctuations in the lists of impoverished vicarages. Yet perhaps the real reason for the chronic nature of the poverty of many livings is that their incumbents often enlarged their income in the simplest way of all, by holding two benefices; this alone will explain how some penurious rectors and vicars survived.

VI: *Close-up: Hornsea*

The circumstances which provoked a lawsuit for augmentation are nowhere more clearly illustrated than in the parish of Hornsea in East Yorkshire, for which alone before the mid-sixteenth century we have a series of the incumbents' accounts of income and expenditure over several years.[1] These were kept by the vicars of Hornsea and their assistants between 1481 and 1493. In this latter year Master William Otway, vicar there, began a suit in the York consistory court, after the abbey of St. Mary's, York, the impropriator, had spurned his petition for augmentation; it was in the course of this suit that the accounts discussed below were exhibited as evidence.[2]

This parish, situated on the East Yorkshire coast, some twenty miles from Beverley and Hull, included the then extensive town of Hornsea and the chapel and surrounding manors of Riston, extending south-westward some five miles and containing— according to contemporary estimates—somewhere between 900

---

[1] *M.C.A.* where six of the accounts of beneficed clergy are described and analysed, and one—discussed here—printed in full. Since then my attention has been drawn, by the kindness of Dr. Robert Dunning, to memoranda detailing the income of Angmering (P.R.O., E 135/3/12(1)) and Stogursey 1454–63 (*Stogursey Charters*, ed. T. D. Tremlett and N. Blakiston (Somerset Record Soc. 61), p. 91, No. 262); a rental of Isleworth rectory for 1439 is noted in *Calendar of Longdon, Lichfield, and other Staffordshire Charters*, by I. H. Jeayes (Staffordshire Record Soc. 63), No. 1980.

[2] Now preserved among York cause papers, R.VII.F.306, R.VII.F.102, and R.As.16/18. All the information which follows in this section has been extracted, except where otherwise stated, either from the text or from the introduction of *M.C.A.* and since the accounts are there printed in chronological order further references have not seemed necessary here. Where there are several accounts for one year I have preferred those with the fullest totals, and I have corrected here, though not in the printed text of *M.C.A.*, the scribe's arithmetic.

and 2,500 souls. The rectory, which had long been in the gift of St. Mary's abbey, York, was appropriated by the abbey in 1423 and a vicarage ordained. By the terms of this the vicarage was endowed with two bovates of glebe land or of the abbey's demesne in Hornsea and two more bovates in Riston. In Hornsea it appears to have been none too productive demesne land on which there was one tenant house, if not more; the whole two bovates the vicars in the 1480s let out to farm each year for a rent of around 30s.,[1] and this included 10s. for the house. At Riston by contrast, while just over half the glebe was let out in 1483–4 for 18s. 6d., the rest yielded grain and vegetables worth £6. 14s. 8d; in 1486–7 glebe at Arnold, Riston and Woodhouse was farmed out for £9. 13s. 4d. and various houses and their crofts were let for 18s., a total of £10. 11s. 4d.; in 1487–8 when the houses and crofts were let for 16s. the produce of the remaining glebe at Riston brought in £9. 10s. 10d., and this was the largest item in his income from either Hornsea or Riston.

So far as tithes were concerned the vicar received all the tithes of wool, sheep, flax, hemp, pigs, geese, chickens, eggs, doves, onions, leeks and garden fruits but none of grain or fish in Hornsea; from Riston and from the vill of Arnold he was to receive all the grain tithes and tithes of wool, sheep, calves and foals. Grain tithes at Riston brought in about 24s. a year; sheep tithes usually amounted to between 13s. and 16s. in Hornsea and between 7s. and 12s. in Riston; wool tithes were similar in both places, the remaining tithes yielding only very small amounts. Oblations, with which the vicarage was also endowed, rarely exceeded 13s. in a year in Hornsea and in Riston averaged about double that sum. The vicar was entitled to mortuaries only in Riston where, seldom more than two a year, their annual value ranged from 15s. to 20s.

Out of this income, estimated in 1423 at £26. 13s. 4d., the vicar had to find a chaplain for Riston and, though he was freed from paying tithes himself in the parish, to support all the other ordinary and extraordinary charges. These ironically included two of his assets; the abbey built for him a manse adjacent to Hornsea cemetary, with a hall, chamber, kitchen, stable, garden and sufficient close, and provided another manse at Riston;

---

[1] Never lower than 28s. 8d. or higher than 31s. 6d.

these, together with the two chancels and the tenanted houses on the glebe, required considerable upkeep: the purchase and transport of sand, nails, straw, lathes, spurs and timber, and the employment of carpenters, glaziers, thatchers and labourers were to reduce substantially the income of successive incumbents. In 1487—though this was not the first time in these accounts—extensive repairs were necessary at Hornsea: spars had to be bought at Hull Brig, timber from the wood of 'Lord Fithow' lathes from John Gamyll, lyme from Richard Clarke of Beverley and tiles from Anthony Thomson; the carpenters, Richard Hewitson and John Waltham were engaged for 12s; Robert Marshall busied himself with 'le erth worke'—the foundations or drains perhaps—at a cost of 3s; Richard Kirkham and his servant worked seven days at 10d. per day—5s. 10d. A total of £4. 6s. 8d. resulted. The next year, however, Hewitson and Waltham were again at work there, repairing the south hall, the wainscot of the window, the doors, and the threshold (perhaps the porch), at a cost of 7s. 5d., and two years later the repair of the walls and of a glazed window cost 9s. 3d.

Riston meanwhile had also required attention. In 1488, with timber obtained from Rise Wood and spars from William Gamyll, a Beverley merchant, a carpenter from Beverley and three servants worked ten days at 2s. a day repairing one house and its doors, at a total cost of £1. 6s. 8d. The next year William Gamyll supplied 'le thake burde' at 5s. and Robert Wright of Beverley repaired the chapel and the roofs of the houses for 7s. 4d. In 1491 and 1492 repairs to the same chapel and houses amounted to £9. 10s. Over five years, therefore, repairs at Hornsea and Riston had totalled £16. 14s. 4d., an average of £3. 7s. a year, enough to consume almost all the normal profit, as a year by year analysis will show.

In 1481–2 the vicar, Dominus Proktour, let Riston to farm to Robert Neville for £8. 10s. We know from later accounts in this series that Riston's total income averaged about £15 and we know that later the vicar found Riston's chaplain at a cost of £4 or £4. 13s. 4d. per annum. If we assume these things in 1481–2 and also that the farmer paid the annual pension of £3. 6s. 8d. to the precentor of Beverley, he would stand to make a sizeable profit, whereas the vicar would have £3 or £4 clear, out of which he might have to provide, as he certainly did later,

hospitality at Riston and pay a proctor. This is the most favourable interpretation of the ambiguous figures of the accounts. If
we proceed along these lines and reckon that each year the vicar
derived a gross profit from Riston of some £4 to £6 and add
to this his income from Hornsea, a highly optimistic picture of
his finances will emerge. Hornsea's income in 1481-2 fell short
of its expenditure (including the stipend of the chaplain) by
£1. 15s. 5d., so that the vicar's overall profit could have been
no more than £2. 5s. at best. His situation was aggravated by
the absence of sheep tithes (which usually amounted to some
14s), but this was balanced by the absence also of any repair
bills, unless he had merely deferred needed repairs. The next
year he increased the farm of Riston by 30s. and, therefore, his
clear profit there would be at most £6. But Hornsea showed a
loss of 14s. 7½d. this year, and at Riston £3. 14s. 11d. was spent
on repairs, leaving again very little clear profit.

In 1483-4 Riston was still let to farm at £10 although the
total income was £15. 18s. 1d; since expenditure exceeded
income in Hornsea that year by £1. 3s. 8½d., and £6 at the
most was cleared from the £10 farm of Riston, the vicar's total
profit was between £4 or £5. But from this estimated annual
surplus must be deducted the wages of servants and proctors,
unrecorded in the accounts, though in 1525 the proctor at
Riston was paid £4;[1] for food the vicar could, and did probably,
live off his glebe and tithes, and for clothing, mortuaries in
Riston (if they were customarily a garment) or bequests might
suffice; there was probably little inducement to think about
hospitality and alms! If we have misinterpreted the accounts and
the vicar was in fact paying the Beverley pension as well, his
financial state would have been dire indeed. Whatever the
arrangements, it may well have been these circumstances which
prompted Proktour to exchange Hornsea with William Otway
for Handsworth in August 1486. A sixteenth-century valuation
reckons Handsworth about 7s. a year poorer,[2] but no evidence
on this point from 1486 is extant nor is there any reference to a
pension, in one direction or the other, between Proktour and
Otway.

We cannot precisely date the accounts which survive for the

---

[1] 'The East Riding Clergy in 1525-26', *T.A.J.* xxiv, 77.
[2] *Valor Ecclesiasticus*, v, 61, 116.

years 1484 to 1487, nor in any of these years are there any complete accounts for both Hornsea and Riston, but what do survive shew that the same conditions still obtained: Hornsea would normally lose 20s. or 30s., Riston produce a surplus of about £5, so that Otway, in normal years, could expect much the same sort of overall profit as his predecessor had received, if there were no accumulated debts. But in 1485–6 over £2 was spent on thatching at Hornsea and in the years 1487–90 inclusive repairs at Hornsea and Riston totalled £6. 4s. 4d.; subsequent evidence shows that extensive as these costs were they coped with only the most essential items. It may have been anticipation of greater expenses to come that induced Otway to rearrange his income.

In 1490 he let out to farm his vicarage of Hornsea and all its fruits, saving to himself the manse and stables; the farmer, William Hubbylday, who had been the steward of the abbey's fish pond, the mere, in Hornsea, and since 1486 the vicar's proctor, agreed to pay for the lease all the ordinary and extraordinary expenses, estimated for this year at £6. 8s. 8d. Since the income rarely passed £5, and he must have known it, Hubbylday was confronted with a loss and Otway relieved of it. The following year, however, the lease was renewed on different terms, Hubbylday paying £6 and Otway finding the parish priest at a cost of £5. 6s. 8d.[1] Even by this arrangement Hubbylday would be astonishingly fortunate to make a profit and since he was presumably not a fool and certainly employed for his acumen, we must suppose that he perhaps received such perquisites as food and accommodation in the vicarage, though they are not mentioned; it may even be possible that he was undertaking this loss with the assurance of repayment and profit in the future; on this point speculation can be endless. What is sure is that Otway was deriving a very slight profit from Hornsea.

In Riston, meanwhile, the vicar's proctor there, Thomas Bransby, had been induced to take the farm of the chapel and its fruits and to bear all the charges, for a rent of £8 to the vicar. It seems clear from the testimony of some witnesses that Bransby supported the Beverley pension of £3. 6s. 8d. and Otway the chaplain at 6 or 7 marks, in which case as in Proktour's time both

[1] Or £5 13s. 4d. if 6s. 8d. for his chamber in the vicarage is not included—the MS. is ambiguous on this point.

farmer and vicar would have some few pounds profit from Riston, but now the vicar had in addition a slight surplus from Hornsea. In 1492, however, he was asked by Bransby for £9. 10s. towards repairs at Riston in the previous two years; no doubt it was this which prompted Otway's suit for augmentation. Until this demand, it is just possible that Otway was breaking even. We know nothing of his personal expenses or of his private income; no will has been traced (he died late in 1499) and though he may have had another benefice, for which he received a papal licence in 1474, none is known, let alone whether it was more or less profitable than Hornsea. It may have been knowledge of these personal facts which induced the judge to reject Otway's petition, but such facts were hardly relevant to future incumbents who had to live on the income of Hornsea and Riston.

At best they would be lucky to have £4 or £5 a year from which to meet personal needs and the requirements of alms and hospitality; what, if any, could be saved out of this might soon be swallowed up by the costs of maintaining the houses and chancels. In 1423 the income had been estimated at £26. 13s. 4d.; in 1483–4 by these accounts the overall income was £21. 1s. 3d. and the expenditure £17. 3s. 3½d.; collation of the income of Hornsea in 1485–6 and of Riston 1487–8 (£18. 19s. 1d.) and of the usual joint expenditure c. 1490 (£14. 13s. 4d.) shews a similar picture. In 1535 its income was given as £17. 2s. 4d., which, after deducting procurations, sinodals and the pension to Beverley's precentor, left £13. 3s. 2d.;[1] deducting from this the stipends of chaplains at Hornsea and Riston, a surplus of some £3 or £4 would be left, much as in the 1480s and 1490s, to cope with the unrecorded and the unforeseen dilapidations, among other things. Before drawing any conclusions from this we should enquire whether the vicars of Hornsea in the 1480s and 1490s were exploiting their resources efficiently and economically.

So far as the farming of Riston was concerned, provided we are correct in our assumption that for the early years as well as in the later the farmer supported the Beverley pension, the vicar could certainly, after raising the farm to £10, have lost little and may have gained slightly. As for the farming of Hornsea we have seen that it converted a loss for the vicar into a slight

[1] *Valor Ecclesiasticus*, v, 116.

profit. There is more doubt about the necessity for a chaplain in Hornsea (the one in Riston was envisaged by the ordination deed), for the abbey's lawyers argued that such a chaplain, in in receipt of £4 or £5 p.a. would not have been needed if Otway had chosen to reside. Otway argued that by absenting himself he was excused the costs of residence and hospitality, presumably the costs of servants and food for guests, which might conceivably have exceeded the stipend of a chaplain.[1] Apart from this consideration, a population breakdown of the parish of Hornsea and Riston, made c. 1490 probably by Hubblyday and listing the souls in each township or vill, concludes that Hornsea's inhabitants totalled at least 674, whereas Riston's numbered 250; medieval figures evoke the readiest suspicion, but these, in contrast with the other rough and rash estimates of the same period, ranging from 1,400 to 2,500, by their topographical precision are more persuasive and likely to under- rather than over-estimate the cure. Nearly 700 souls is not a large parish by modern standards, but a chaplain might reasonably be deemed necessary to assist even a resident incumbent.

Less comprehensible was the necessity of separate proctors in Riston and Hornsea; not only might one have sufficed, but he might have been one of the chaplains; thus instead of maintaining two chaplains and two proctors, the latter could have been eliminated. But parochial proctors are an obscure race and an absentee (or resident) incumbent might well pick men whose business ability he respected and whose integrity he trusted. Parochial chaplains were not always able administrators and they should have been busy about the cure of souls. The exact responsibilities of these proctors in Hornsea is not easily discerned, and their somewhat superfluous functions are only hinted at, in the muddle of account manuscripts which survive.

On the whole, therefore, the vicars of Hornsea cannot be convicted of extravagance or carelessness and one may legitimately offset the cost of a chaplain at Hornsea against the saving on the vicar's residence and hospitality, though even if he had been resident he would probably have needed an assistant there.

---

[1] On the basis of the accounts of Munden's chantry at Bridport (see above pp. 22–23) and bearing in mind that the 1480s and '90s were years when prices had risen briefly but considerably (E. H. Phelps Brown and S. V. Hopkins, *Essays in Economic History*, ed. E. M. Carus-Wilson, ii, 179–96).

It would appear, therefore, that a benefice estimated in the *Valor Ecclesiasticus* at a clear value of £13 was barely adequate to support its incumbent and his necessary expenses.

VII: *The National Scene*

After payment of a chaplain, of occasional stipendiaries, and of occasional pensions, to meet the small and regular expenses, to support the incumbent and his household, and to pay for the costly repairs, frequently needed, medieval building being what it was, an income of £15 would seem desirable and reasonable, or where there was no chaplain £10. But only a small minority of England's incumbents enjoyed even this modest affluence; independent surveys of benefices in midland England, valued in the *Valor Ecclesiasticus*, suggest that three-quarters of all the parochial livings in England were worth less than £15, and that a half of all the livings were not worth £10, and many less than £7.[1] We have seen that pluralism and private lands qualify any conclusions drawn from their benefices about the wealth of individual incumbents,[2] but one may not assume that each successive incumbent of a poor benefice had this private fortune, and many parsons and vicars lived a life, if not of penury, of considerable hardship and strain. Undoubtedly there were examples of incumbents or their deputies being ruthless or extravagantly zealous in the collections of tithes and mortuaries, but it has to be remembered that while such men were reprehensible and dangerous to clergy-laity relations, there was often little room for charity. If cupidity or sheer necessity did not impel incumbents to insist on tithes and other legal dues, then practical wisdom should have done so. A lapsed right in medieval society, where memory was often the stuff of proof, was usually a lost right; an interval of forebearance by one incumbent, regardless of his private means, could mean a lifetime

[1] *M.C.A.*, p. 24, n.
[2] Compare the words of J. S. Purvis, *T.A.J.* xxxvi, 435, where he notes how some holders of very poor benefices leave large amounts of stock and farming gear and employed several servants. See also F. W. Brooks, 'The Social Position of the Parson in the Sixteenth Century', *Journal of British Archaeological Soc.* (3rd series) x, 28.

of bickering, litigation and hardship for his successors. Apart from these legalistic and clerical considerations, it must be remembered that the price rise of the 1520s was such as to make even the most customary and lawful demands seem to the laity extortionate, when to the clergy they were most vital.

IX

The Religious Orders and Parish Churches

Not all parish clergy were in fact seculars. Apart from the monks and friars who were sometimes to be found serving chantries, there is plenty of evidence to suggest that they also came into possession of parish livings. Between 1447 and 1492 413 religious were papally dispensed to hold secular benefices.[1] This stark figure needs some qualification. First of all, the average number of these licences each year was nine, and this average was fairly consistently maintained over the whole period, so that a sensational, even a detectable, increase is sought in vain. Secondly, secular benefices included some of the administrative offices about the monastery.[2] Then again a third of the licences, 144, were to Austin canons whose *raison d'être* was pastoral rather than meditative; with them too should be considered the seventy-five friars whose work lay rather in the parishes, if not canonically in benefices. Little can be said in mitigation for the 177 Black Monks who constituted most of the remainder, but the reasons which prompted the majority of the 413 licences were generally far from scandalous. Some of these religious were either heads of houses too poor to support the usual burdens of office or were about to retire and were seeking some form of pension which the house could not afford; there were fifty-three of these, and William Burton, who resigned from the abbacy of Alcester and sought dispensation for a secular benefice to maintain his dignity in retirement, is typical.[3] If this concern

---

[1] *C.P.L.* x–xiv, *passim*. The argument in this chapter is well illustrated by M. Bowker, *Secular Clergy in Lincoln Diocese*, pp. 67, 77–78, 100, 130, 134–5, 190–2.

[2] A. H. Sweet, 'Papal Privileges granted to Individual Religious', *Speculum*, xxxi, 603.

[3] *C.P.L.* xi, 538.

for dignity seems inappropriate in a monk and an abbot, it was not remarkable in an age when monastic superiors increasingly lived apart from the community in their own houses.[1] Then there were religious, mainly friars, who were chaplains and confessors to the royal family, to the nobles or to prelates.[2] Others were scholars, who after laudable service to the Church, required help: Thomas Derby, O.F.M., in 1452, was broken with age; he had taught theology for two years and preached for thirty, and he sought dispensation for a secular benefice to enable him more conveniently to devote himself to study and preaching.[3] For some a secular benefice was a concealment of apostasy, a remedy for the inmate who found the Rule too demanding or too lax: Thomas Cowper, an Austin canon of Ashridge, in 1462 was suffering from a disease which made it impossible for him to observe the usual religious austerities and he was dispensed to receive a secular benefice;[4] William Strod, a Cistercian of Lettley, sought a secular benefice that he might more readily preach to the people as he desired to.[5] The reasons, therefore, were not all unworthy, even if we assume, as we should, that petitions for dispensations were thoughtfully composed.[6]

Nevertheless, while pastoral enthusiasm motivated men like the Cistercian Strod, sick or senile abbots were likely to have little connection with their parish church beyond the receipt of its fruits, and it is doubtful if more than a small minority of those religious who obtained parish benefices by virtue of dispensations in fact resided and served in them. There were few licences

[1] The ideal of poverty for heads of houses, as for the other inmates, had by the late fifteenth century suffered the erosion of successive relaxations (see especially D. Knowles, *The Religious Orders in England*, ii).

[2] e.g. *C.P.L.* x, 48, 68, 119, 122, 148.

[3] *C.P.L.* x, 109.

[4] *C.P.L.* xi, 639.

[5] *C.P.L.* x, 139.

[6] A closer analysis of religious who *obtained* parochial livings in Norwich diocese over a quarter of a century shows that there just over one a year and just under one in thirty presentees instituted were religious (34 out of 1187). Eleven of the thirty-four were heads of houses; religious houses and bishops presented thirteen and nine respectively; lay patrons accounted for seven, though at least two of these patrons had been granted the advowson *hac vice* by the abbey itself (Norwich Act Book XVI, fos. 47r, 99r; see too fo. 148r). Two of the episcopal collations were to livings in his gift *iure devoluto* (Norwich Act Book XIV, fos. 99r, 102r). So far as their order is indicated in the registers, of the twenty-three who were not heads of houses, the great majority were canons regular.

quite so specific about non-residence as that granted to John Tumbrigge, a monk of Canterbury in 1454, to allow him, afflicted with palsy and fearing long torment in the future, to obtain a secular benefice and have its cure served by another, and to farm out its fruits even to a layman.[1] There were more dispensations, though still few, like that to the Cluniac John Carter of Wenlock who was dispensed for a secular benefice and explicitly granted permission to dwell therein and serve the cure, provided he sought, even if he failed to obtain, his superior's assent.[2] The clause about whether or not the superior assented occurs in other licences and hints at the influential sponsors of the petitioner or at his firm intent to apostasy.[3] Residence is clearly implied in other licences which mention permission or record the fact of wearing the regular habit *under* an honest priestly dress; so John Winton, a canon of St. Osyth, and vicar of Rickmansworth attired himself in 1452.[4] Though a recent scholar has laid stress upon this licence to dress as seculars 'without any apostasy',[5] it cannot be maintained that such licences were frequent.

Of all the religious resident in the parishes the overwhelming majority were doubtless the Premonstratensian canons, for the cure of souls was regarded as part of their vocation and from the twelfth century they could present their own colleagues to be vicars of their churches.[6] One should not expect such canons, therefore, to seek papal licences, yet seventeen did so between 1447 and 1492; these seem, however, to have sought dispensation not in order to serve a cure, but, for example, to enlarge their income by pluralism,[7] or to support an indigent prior by holding a benefice *in commendam*,[8] or to allow an inmate of the coastal house of Torre (Exeter Diocese) to escape future recourse to arms, often necessary there—his petition is in 1455—to ward off invasions from pirates and Frenchmen.[9] Mostly, Premonstratensians could act without such licences and beyond

[1] *C.P.L.* x, 164.
[2] *C.P.L.* xii, 542.
[3] *C.P.L.* xi, 537.
[4] *C.P.L.* x, 240.
[5] A. H. Sweet, *Speculum*, xxxi, 608.
[6] D. Knowles, op. cit., ii, 139–40; A. H. Thompson, *The English Clergy*, p. 120.
[7] *C.P.L.* xi, 594.
[8] Ibid., 527.
[9] Ibid., 93.

the 413 religious noted above we must bear in mind these unrecorded canons resident and active in the parishes; all the vicars of Sheffield, for example, from 1307 to 1540, except one, were canons of Worksop.[1] In one respect, in the necessity for a *socius* or companion from the house to reside with them, the order, for want of numbers, had fallen away from the rule,[2] and the accounts of John Dytton, vicar of Kirkby Malham in 1454, shew clearly that no other canon was employed there.[3]

The Austin canons, by contrast, seem to have required papal licence to serve the cure of souls in parishes, and they form a large proportion of the 413 recipients mentioned above. Evidence of their residence is hard to find, but that they commonly served the livings they acquired seems probable from the nature of their order. They too can seldom, towards the end of the Middle Ages, have been accompanied by another canon.

One problem created by these religious was discipline, for the Premonstratensians and friars only came under the jurisdiction of their order and were exempt from the bishop's control,[4] yet it would be hard to prove, and unwise to argue, that they were better or worse than the secular clergy as a consequence of this.

As for economics, the religious where they occupied a vicarage ordained and endowed by their mother house enjoyed its full fruits, so that we find John Dytton receiving the full vicarage stipend of £6. 13s. 4d. cash from Kirkby Malham;[5] it was no mean stipend, for all the normal expenses, such as repairs, taxation, procurations and even the hire of a *locum tenens* and of the cost of twice yearly journeys to the mother house in Norfolk were borne out of the rectorial income, a fact worth remembering before these low value cash vicarages are everywhere written off as clerical slums; the vicar of Kirkby Malham was a good deal better off even in the 1520s, though his affluence was diminished, than the vicar of Hornsea who nominally had far more valuable receipts.[6]

Nevertheless, religious exploitation was more apparent to

[1] A. H. Thompson, op. cit., p. 120.
[2] D. Knowles, op. cit., 139–40; H. M. Colvin, *The White Canons in England*, pp. 278–80.
[3] B.M. Addit. Roll 32957 dorse.
[4] H. M. Colvin, op. cit., pp. 285–6.
[5] B.M. Addit. Roll 32957 recto.
[6] See above p. 171.

the secular vicars and to none more vividly than to the vicar of Stalisfield who tried in vain to survive on and meet the benefice burdens from an income which was not worth 8 marks, while the impropriator, the priory of St. Gregory's, Canterbury, drew £8.13s. 4d. from the farm of the parsonage.[1] Even where appropriation had not taken place, as at St. Nicholas Dover in the gift of Dover priory, the parson was often obliged to pay, as here, a critical portion of his meagre income—11s. out of £3. 6s. 8d.—to the religious house or to its superior.[2] A suit for augmentation was sometimes begun by the incumbent, but even when the judgement was more favourable than Otway's in 1493[3] the long term result for the mortal vicar (as distinct from the undying rector) was often no more encouraging: the vicar of Sibertswold won his suit in the archbishop of Canterbury's court of audience against the abbot of St. Radegund's, but the abbot and convent appealed to the Court of Arches and threatened their readiness to go to Rome, which appeal, unless he could call on considerable money—an unlikely facility in a plaintiff for augmentation—the incumbent could well lose by contumacy; but it was reported that the abbot was not content with this foolproof stratagem, but 'sent oon of his chanons into the said churche atte divine service troblyng the same' and abusing the vicar with 'many obprobryous and contumelyous wordes openly there and said "Thou preest what doeth thou here in our church; gett the hens or we shall pluke the owte by the hed, how be it thou berith the bold and was institutid by my lord of Canterbury, he hath nought to doo here for we are exempte from hym and soo tell hym" '.[4] It is, therefore, among the vicarages which are endowed in kind rather than with a fixed cash stipend that hardship is especially to be sought, for though fixed stipends suffered with rising prices, they seem to have been less burdened with the expenses of the benefice, and they were easier to estimate accurately at ordination, and free from the calamities which could afflict and radically change the value of other vicarages; in the latter a change from arable to pastoral farming could transform, often to his great advantage, the fortunes of an incumbent, though if it led to serious depopulation it could terminate his cure of souls altogether: tithes which

[1] Reg. Warham, fo. 54v.   [2] Ibid., fos. 50v, 49v, 52r.
[3] See above p. 171.   [4] Reg. Warham, fo. 48v.

beareth a man up also casteth him down, according to the local economy and market. But of the 392 York diocese livings which were appropriated, 100 were served by curates receiving a cash stipend,[1] small but doubtless free—like Dytton's vicarage—of the burdens which normally bore upon the instituted incumbent; their stipends, however, were not on Dytton's scale but on those of normal parish chaplains whose fate they shared. Among such curates were the Austin canons serving the churches belonging to their houses, as they served ten or eleven of those belonging to Guisborough.[2] In Stafford archdeaconry in 1531 alongside forty-one rectories and thirty-eight vicarages, there were in addition some eighteen churches which were served by stipendiary curates; nine of these were appropriated to houses of Austin canons, one to Wolsey's college at Oxford (formerly to the Benedictine priory of Sandwell), one to Stafford royal free chapel, one to the Cistercian house of Bordesley, and six to Lichfield cathedral. Most of the curates in these eighteen churches received four marks (£2. 13s. 4d.) yearly for their labours.[3]

While the fact and scale of appropriation is frequently and justly the subject of disapproving comments, it is doubtful if the money thus diverted would have served better ends; St. Mary's York, for example, appropriated Hornsea rectory, said to be worth £100, and endowed a vicarage estimated at £26, though nearer £20 by our time,[4] yet had it been untouched by St. Mary's (whose expenses were certainly enormous) the rectory would most probably have fallen into the hands of an influential, absentee pluralist who could advance St. Mary's interests at London, York or Rome; the cure of souls was very little affected if at all by such appropriations. What one could have expected was more generous endowment or more ready augmentation—until one recalls the economic difficulties of the religious house itself, often only aggravated by the considerable legal costs of appropriation.[5]

1 A. H. Thompson, op. cit., pp. 115–16.
2 Ibid., p. 116.
3 Lichfield MS. B/A/17/1(2).
4 See above p. 171.
5 Meaux Abbey paid dearly for the right to appropriate Easington in the fourteenth century—*Chronica Monasterii de Melsa*, ed. E. A. Bond (Rolls Series), iii, 6–7, 11 particularly. I owe this point and reference to Mr. F. W. Brooks.

Any estimate of the contribution of the religious to parochial life would need to consider their service to preaching not merely personally and verbally but by such collections of sermons as the *Festial*, ascribed to an Austin canon. The same canon put the parish clergy further in his debt by his guide to the priestly vocation, the *Manuale Sacerdotum*. Whether Myrc was quite such a solitary eminence as he at present seems is a question which must await a much more systematic study of fifteenth-century remains. Nor should the religious orders be forgotten among the teachers and patrons of young scholars, some of whom found their way into the parish clergy. Least of all should we forget that monk of Evesham, Robert Joseph, who wrote words of encouragement and learning to neighbouring clergy.[1] Indeed, the influence of the monasteries on some seculars was so immediate as to lure them into enclosure: Syon in the early sixteenth century especially appealed to the beneficed in search of a stricter life;[2] the Carmelites secured John Bouge, whose piety and courage as well as his learning in the 1530s may not have been uninfluenced by contact with an earlier parishioner of his, Thomas More;[3] and John Houghton, perhaps the most distinguished prior of the London Charterhouse, had spent his earlier years among the secular—if not parish—clergy.[4] There were seculars no doubt who chose not to cross this Rubicon, but were yet moved and encouraged by the monastic ideal and acquaintances. There were others, and perhaps they were many, whose acquaintance with monastic reality could only embitter and dishearten—the vicars of Hornsea and Sibertswold, for example, vainly seeking alleviation of their poverty, or the vicars of Stalisfield who saw their parish exploited and neglected by a house too lax, too ill administered or itself too poor to do better. The religious perhaps redeemed their orders where they directly served the parishes; accounts are not always reliable windows into the past, but the brief, comprehensive manuscript from Kirkby Malham seems to tell of a well-ordered parish. While not denying, therefore, the pernicious

[1] *The Letter Book of Robert Joseph*, ed. H. Aveling and W. A. Pantin (Oxford Historical Soc. n.s. 19), Nos. 27, 40, 77, 150.
[2] D. Knowles, op. cit., iii, 213.
[3] F. S. Boas, 'Chronicles and Histories', *The Thought and Culture of the English Renaissance*, ed. E. M. Nugent, pp. 547–9.
[4] D. Knowles, op. cit., iii, 225.

and deplorable influence of the religious orders on some areas and aspects of English parish life, the present writer would stress that there were some positive—and as yet hardly explored—influences, that the evils have often been carelessly and wrongly located, that extenuating circumstances—though doubtless these can be exaggerated—have been ignored.

X

Old Age

WHEN an incumbent became too old or too feeble to fulfil his duties adequately he could resign on a pension. Although these were extremely common by the end of the Middle Ages they were by no means obligatory, being a matter of mutual arrangement between the retiring incumbent and his successor. The only guarantee of a pension was to negotiate for one before resigning, but as this was suspiciously like simony an episcopal licence was first necessary.[1] The bishop or his deputy could obviously refuse to allow negotiation if he thought there was little cause for resignation and still less for the support of the retiring rector or vicar. If the pension that was settled on looked suspiciously large, however, he could only intervene in certain cases; in a few licences to treat for pensions the parties are empowered to conduct and to conclude arrangements; but in others the clause to conclude is either omitted altogether or the power is specifically reserved to the bishop.[2] Yet some licences from London and Hereford dioceses suggest that a process very like simony often did take place. If the aspirant to a living would not spare the six marks or whatever the incumbent was asking as a pension, another more accommodating candidate, provided he had the favour of the patron, would secure the benefice. This is

---

[1] K. Major, 'Resignation Deeds in the Diocese of Lincoln', *B.I.H.R.* xix, 63, and see above p. 46.

[2] G.L.C., MS DL/C/330: for examples of the first kind see fos. 7v, 94r, 145r; for instances where the clause is omitted altogether, fos. 14v, 20r, 40r, 58r, 59r, 65r, 130r; for the third and by far the most common type, where the final approval is reserved to the bishop, fos. 3r(3), 8r(4), 14r(2), 15r, 33v, 48r, 81r, 95v, 96v(2), 110r, 123v, 152r, 153r, 155v, 156v, 157r, 169r, 171v, 172r, 176v, 179r, 180r, 180v, 196r(3), 199r.

confirmed by the fact that many parties named in the licences did not subsequently obtain the living. Master Walter Blount, rector of Ribbesford, is typical; in March 1517 he was licensed to treat and settle with David Coupar, vicar of Caynham, for a pension from Ribbesford if Coupar succeeded him there; in 1519 Coupar is still at Caynham and in May 1520 Blount, still rector of Ribbesford, has another licence, this time to treat with Thomas Parker for a pension if Parker succeeds him.[1] To avoid all suspicion of simony it would have been necessary to leave all negotiations until after resignation and the induction of a successor, upon whom no legal, and very little moral, pressure could then be exerted to produce a pension. Some sanguine incumbents did just this. Geoffrey ap Howell resigned the vicarage of Lugwardine on account of his old age and infirmity and 'in the hope' that a pension would be provided for him till the end of his life by his successor; the bishop duly licensed him to treat with the new vicar, Thomas Wilmott.[2] Master John Yngham, S.T.B., on resigning because of infirmity the rectory of Teversham in Ely diocese appealed to the bishop for a suitable pension, and with the assent of the then rector the bishop granted him ten marks a year and free access to one room in the rectory to be assigned by the rector.[3] Yngham did not petition, as Howell did, for a licence to treat, but for a pension, and one worthy of his status; seemingly Yngham could not, or would not, prolong his incumbency in order to negotiate for a pension. It is noteworthy that the bishop sought the assent of the rector here, and it is likely that he also consulted the patron. Whether a patron's concurrence was always necessary for a pension cannot be said; his right after all was in the advowson and not in the fruits of the benefice, but a diminution of these would undoubtedly impair the value of the advowson; nothing is heard of a patron refusing consent.[4]

Those ageing incumbents who did not resign could seek a licence for absence, leaving the administration of the cure to a parish priest. This allowed the incumbent to live out his last days either in the manse and among his familiar parishioners or else-

[1] *Reg. Bothe*, pp. 23, 68, 77. Parker did eventually succeed him there, (ibid., p. 278).

[2] *Reg. Mayew*, p. 192.

[3] Ely Diocesan Records MS. G/1/4 (Reg, Bourgchier), fo. 33r–v.

[4] *Reg. Bothe*, p. 118.

where among friends, and many an incumbent remembered in his will the servant who nursed him in his last illness.[1] William Bassett, rector of Bennington in Lincoln diocese, was in his eighties in 1475 when he was papally dispensed to take the fruits for life and not reside.[2] Such licences, in reality less for absence than for enforced inactivity, are not uncommon in the papal registers, which no doubt explains why co-adjutors were so rarely appointed.

For the incumbent who resigned without a pension and for the unbeneficed a post as chaplain in a private household might prove a convenient, though probably a rare, solution. A chantry too was much less arduous than a parochial benefice or cure and possibly some of those exchanges, which look so sinister, of a rectory or a vicarage for a chantry, may be accounted for by old age on the part of the incumbent. But for the infirm or unwell the problem of old age could best be solved by seeking a corrody in an abbey, though these were now an uncommon feature and beyond the means of many clergy.[3] An alternative was to purchase what was in effect a corrody from a layman: Master John Carpenter, late the parson of Compton Bassett, contracted to hand over to William White of that parish all his moveable goods, valued at twenty marks, on condition that White 'shold honestly fynd hym mete and drynke duryng his life for that the same M. Carpenter was of so grete age and feblenes that he cowde not that tyme nor yet can not helpe hym self'; but White defaulted on this agreement and Carpenter's piteous appeal to Chancery is the result.[4] This practice was clearly perilous and probably rare, though the vicar of Ash in Kent in 1519 provided in his will 'That mine ooste William Wren and his wife be contented for all my costs laid out for me in the time of my sickness'.[5] Where friends or relatives, or even strangers, were unable or unwilling to sustain and comfort the ageing cleric, resort might be made to one of the numerous hospitals of medieval England, all of which employed a chaplain or two for the restricted religious needs of the community, and a few of which were specifically endowed to accommodate the sick and indigent

[1] e.g. G.L.C., MS. DL/C/354, fos. 19v–20r.
[2] *C.P.L.* xiii, 426.
[3] D. Knowles, *Religious Orders in England*, iii, 267.
[4] P.R.O., C 1/299/43.
[5] *Archaeologia Cantiana*, xxxiv, 51.

clerk. Since 1415 the hospital of St. John the Baptist at Cricklade had been a retreat for poor priests disabled by age and infirmity; St. Giles, in Norwich, offered refuge to the chaplains of Norwich diocese in a like condition; in London the hospital of St. Augustine Pappey gave food and shelter particularly to poor priests, while St. Mary within Cripplegate received blind and paralysed clergy.[1] The state of most hospitals at this time, however, was parlous and whether in fact these four, let alone others, adequately fulfilled their intended role is open to grave doubt.[2]

The old age of the clergy was in terms of privation no worse —and for many incumbents much better—than that of their lay contemporaries, but in terms of isolation, removed as they often were by the nature and course of their career far from their family, it may well have been a lonelier experience.

[1] *V.C.H. Wiltshire*, iii, 336; *V.C.H. Norfolk*, ii, 443; *V.C.H. London*, i, 550, 535.
[2] Ibid.

Conclusions

A T first sight the state of the clergy appears less alarming than the anxiety of Colet and the vituperation of Tyndale would suggest. Far from perfection though most of the parish clergy undoubtedly were, their ignorance, negligence, indiscipline and avarice have been crudely magnified by commentators; to a large degree the Church seemed to be keeping the distance which separated the clergy from the ideal as narrow as society and history would permit.

Such an optimistic estimate might seem at once contradicted by Melton's review of ordination examinations, but in view of the great number of clergy needed in early Tudor England the examiners who were contented with a minimum competence in grammar and a *prima facie* suitability, rather than with fluent Latin and a sense of vocation, were making a necessary compromise with reality; there was, after all, no guarantee that the literate and earnest, once ordained, would find their way into parochial service, and Melton's criteria presupposed more systematic educational opportunities and training than then obtained. Cynicism and carelessness were not imputed by Melton to the examiners, but rather to the candidates eager to obtain ordination by any deceit. Though he and More describe the tricks of the unscrupulous they give no reliable clue to scale and indicate no way in which the examiners could extinguish such frauds as were practised upon them. At the level of admissions to benefices bishops and their officers resisted the ruthless disregard shown by patrons for canonical and pastoral requirements by firmly rejecting the unfit; but where the letter of the law was met, and where the inadequately ordained or the incompatibly beneficed were armed, as they so often were, with papal dispensations, the ordinaries stifled any deeper curiosity and jettisoned any pastoral considerations, admitting men blatantly indifferent to the cure of souls. To do otherwise where the presentee either met the legal requirements or was papally dispensed from doing so, was not possible without provoking a legal conflict which would almost certainly have proved futile. The closely allied problem of absenteeism was similarly controlled with vigilance so far as the law and the needs, or habits, of the Church and society allowed; so much was it a social institution and not just an ecclesiastical abuse that the Reformation Parliament itself endorsed and protected a wide range of non-residence and it endured into the nineteenth century. Non-residence was nothing new in the English or European Church in the early sixteenth century and it had, indeed, been pruned of the greater scandals which had characterized it earlier,[1] but it is particularly unfortunate at this time that it created a shortage of the better educated, the graduates, among the active parish clergy. In the parishes men competent within the requirements of the law were far more numerous and sermons far more frequent and somewhat more functional than is often acknowledged, but the abler clergy were syphoned off to more remunerative, if not more demanding, roles around bishops, cathedrals, courts and palaces. This state of affairs was only likely to change in response to stimuli outside ecclesiastical control: as the opportunities for lay education changed and grew in Renaissance England, fewer clergy would be needed as diplomats, administrators and counsellors and more would be available for episcopal and capitular employment than could be usefully absorbed; in this way, perhaps, graduates would percolate into the parishes. The men who did serve in the parishes, men perhaps of limited education and narrow capacities, were no doubt vulnerable to temptations, but chronic and universal indiscipline among the clergy was not the result. There certainly was more clerical disorder and vice than our society would deem appropriate, but its magnitude has been enlarged by careless reading of the sources and by neglect of the strains placed upon the clergy by their social context and by celibacy. In fact recidivism was infrequent and the judicial machinery of the Church was as effective as any other law courts of the time. Even in the vexed question of criminous clerks, few of these were clergy in any

---

[1] W. A. Pantin, *The English Church in the Fourteenth Century*, p. 41.

serious or active form, few were second offenders, and many—
perhaps very many if the unlisted *clerici attincti* could be counted
—suffered painful spells of incarceration. Clerical discipline, or
its statistics, would have been enormously improved by the
abolition of minor orders, but this was something which the
English Church could not attempt alone; a theological revolution was necessary for that. Meanwhile minor orders remained
a sanctuary for the criminally minded which provoked the layman's envy and hatred of the whole clergy. Perhaps an even
more critical area of clergy-laity relations was the system whereby a crucial part of the beneficial income was levied from
parishioners. No significant change to this was conceivable in
Tudor England and in fact none was made until the commutation
of tithes in the nineteenth century. If it proved difficult to reduce
the parishioners' obligation (except for a far from radical
reassessment of mortuaries), it was no less difficult to reduce the
clergy's need of such dues: monastic dissolution did not bring,
as Sir Francis Bigod had urged,[1] the disappropriation of parochial
livings or the redeployment of monastic wealth to assist the cure
of souls; clerical marriage brought some relief later in the
century, though how much, how often and precisely why are as
yet uncertain; some deliberate mitigation of clerical poverty
only came in the eighteenth century with Queen Anne's Bounty.

In all these areas the Church had to content itself with the art
of the possible, but not in all did it gauge accurately what was
possible. In two directions, education and discipline, intrinsic
improvement and the amelioration of clergy-laity relations might
have been achieved by the exercise of courage and imagination:
the establishment of professional training, the adoption of
vernacular texts (particularly of the Bible), a more frequent,
though judicious, resort to degradation and deprivation, and the
abandonment of benefit of clergy for those in minor orders should
not have been beyond accomplishment. Yet no one, not even the
most forceful and able critics, advocated such measures. Colet
and More argued, and their contemporaries implicitly agreed,
that the strict enforcement of old laws, rather than the adoption
of new ones, was all that was needed. There were, indeed,
throughout this period hardly any new laws: Wolsey's reform-

---

[1] *Tudor Treatises*, ed. A. G. Dickens (Yorkshire Archaeological Soc. 125), pp.
41–58.

ing legislation of 1518 made no serious advance beyond earlier provincial decrees; and even the laws of the 1529 Parliament— on absence, ordination, trading, farming and mortuaries—were far less novel than is often thought. Old laws, however, were being as diligently enforced as circumstances allowed; in very few areas, and those not of central importance, was a more vigorous application possible. It was a failure of perception and nerve on the part of the legislators, rather than any lack of diligence in the administrators, which accounts for the state of the parish clergy at this time.

The legislators, who were in fact the bishops, could have contributed to a notable improvement among the clergy without legislating at all, simply by setting an example. But although there were on the episcopal bench men who strove by their writings, by their sermons, by their visitations, by their foundations, or by their persecution of heresy to protect and kindle the faith of their Church, there were few, if any apart from Fisher, who might conceivably inspire by their private and public integrity, and Fisher lacked the extrovert qualities of a charismatic leader. The rest were possessed by a vision of goodness which was bounded by the already obsolescent conventions of their age; they took their stand on the legislation of past centuries, however inappropriate or ineffective it had already proved, and they allowed no searching revaluations to grip or guide them. Their failure here might be explained by the circumstances in which they themselves had prospered: in a land where the right of ecclesiastical patronage was construed at law as a lay fee and where royal priorities usually prevailed in episcopal elections, ecclesiastical incomes and offices were distributed with only the minimum regard to their appurtenant responsibilities and at every level clergy were induced to contend for preferment and promotion rather by neglecting than by fulfilling their pastoral obligations. It was difficult for men to condemn or to escape a system which had produced them and harder still for bishops who rarely, if at all, had experience of parish work to understand the hardships and psychology of the parish clergy. Difficult, yet not impossible: in the kingdom of Francis I where, by the Concordat of 1516, royal control of episcopal appointments was greater even than in England, Bishop Guillaume Briçonnet of Meaux was merely the most outstanding of several reforming prelates; in Italy Bishop Giberti of Verona led a reform movement among bishops which by implication condemned and sought to extinguish the conditions which had assisted their elevation to sees. It did not require a reforming monarch to appoint reforming bishops, it merely needed bishops who thought more deeply and carefully about the spiritual implications of their office: all of Henry VII's and Henry VIII's bishops would have been thoroughly familiar with the example and paradox of Becket.

But on several counts the need either of example or of legislation might have seemed to the bishops somewhat less than urgent. In the first place, as we have tried to show, the condition of the clergy was no worse, and probably much better, than it had been; secondly, prelates could see—or so their decrees and actions suggest—few means of improving it further; then, too, they were probably aware that there was nothing peculiarly vicious about the English parish clergy, for all over Europe—to judge by the testimony of satirists, reformers and legislators— the picture was at least as bad and probably—as in Scotland, Wales and Ireland—much worse; finally, there was the myopic tendency of bishops to regard as heretical any anti-clericalism, however justified its provocation. Unfortunately for the bishops Lollardy was about to be supplanted by a far more dynamic challenge and the clergy were to be embarrassed by new circumstances and judged by more exacting standards.

No more delicate relationship existed than that between a priest and his flock. He had to be at once their counsellor and friend, their example and corrector; too much familiarity, too much relaxation, too much diffidence, too much isolation—all equally could impede or ruin harmony; a prudent and loving blend of intimacy and detachment was required. So precarious a balance, however, was threatened by many obstacles. Though for some part of each day the clergy were exclusively clergy, for much of it they were, like their parishioners, farmers and traders, and while this could strengthen their ties it could also conceal their differences—in the minds both of the priests and of the laity. This blurring of the distinction might be exaggerated where the clergy lacked the ability and reading habits commended by Melton and sought recreation with the villagers in various bucolic and unseemly pastimes. How far it helped or hindered a priest to be a native of his cure would depend, of course, on his own personality. Perhaps what in the eyes of most men separated the clergy from themselves was the obligation to celibacy, the breach of which, in a society so full of bastards as early Tudor England, could be as easily imagined as achieved. Yet there is little evidence, apart from Kent in 1450, to suggest that this seriously alarmed or outraged the laity, and Luther soon made it fashionable among the Church's fiercest critics to argue that the clergy should be allowed to marry anyway. Far more common and serious a threat to amicable relations was the economic bond between the clergy and the laity, for very often the priest competed in the market place with the laymen by means of the latter's tithe contribution. The needy collector of tithes, mortuaries and dues, however just his demand, could soon be mistaken for an extortionist and bitter passions and fierce resistance were aroused by these matters. How often they were aroused by greed and excess on the part of the clergy is concealed both by the natural tendency of evaders to denounce all resented claims as novel and by the fragmentary nature of individual records, which too often prevent objective, let alone statistical, conclusions by the historian; all that can be asserted on the basis of a few celebrated and well documented cases and from our knowledge of the economic difficulties facing many incumbents and their parishioners is that some new claims were undoubtedly attempted by the clergy, and equally some old dues were challenged by the laity. From the extant records no precise dimensions can be given to this problem, but it would probably grow as the cost of living increased. Whatever its extent we may conclude that economics became a critical factor in clergy-laity relations of the early sixteenth century, reaching a crescendo in the 1520s on the very eve of England's severance from Rome. In this decade the tension between clergy and laity, to which their relationship inescapably gave rise, was screwed tighter by the price rise, and minor irritations and individual discontents were transformed into a chronic and nationwide crisis. The crude, abusive attempt of Simon Fish in his *Supplication for the Beggars* (1528–9) to explain the poverty of England by ecclesiastical rapacity marks this transition.

The next factor which imperilled old standards and old sufficiencies was printing:

hereby tongues are known, knowledge groweth, judgement increaseth, books are dispersed, the Scripture is seen, times compared, truth discerned, falsehood detected . . . through printing the world beginneth now to have eyes to see and hearts to judge . . . By this printing, as by the gift of tongues, and as by the singular organ of the Holy Ghost, the doctrine of the gospel soundeth to all nations and countries under heaven; and what God revealeth to one man, is dispersed to many, and what is known in one nation is opened to all.[1]

In these words the martyrologist, John Foxe, assessed the significance of this technological revolution. There had been anti-clericalism as long as there had been vices—and indeed virtues—in the Church, but in the past, except for some popular movements such as Lollardy, and except in London, it had been an ephemeral and local affair, an oral, invisible, intangible matter; what the printing press brought was a sense not only of a national but also of an international movement. The crude resentment of the people was now nourished, stimulated, transformed by the works of English and European writers. The anti-clericals found themselves confirmed by the abler and more learned, and recognized themselves as part of a movement which was entertaining, eloquent and fashionable; their passions feasted on the words and ideas of more articulate men; and no doubt the wit as well as the *visible* success of ideas circulating from book-seller to book-buyer and from reader to reader encouraged and strengthened discontent. It was not merely in England that the clergy provoked amusement, contempt and hatred; if anything, the clergy of Europe were a degree worse and as the satires which they aroused came into England the nuances which distinguished national Churches were quickly overlooked. Sebastian Brant's *Narrenschiff* was translated into English as the *Ship of Fools* twice before 1509, and though it was not principally concerned with the parish clergy, it made some bitter observations upon them. Far more brilliantly and corrosively witty was Erasmus's *Praise of Folly* and this book was a well established favourite by 1520. It had of course been written for a man and a circle of unquestionable orthodoxy, where nonetheless the clergy were objects of derision; printing

[1] *The Acts and Monuments of John Foxe*, ed. G. Townsend (London 1844), iii, 720. Foxe has many more stirring things to say about printing on pp. 718–22.

(but not yet translation) transformed a private joke among devout and understanding men into a public scandal among all men. Yet it was not only the scale of anti-clericalism which was changing; Foxe realized that ideas deepened and sharpened with the exchange of knowledge facilitated by the press and it is to new ideas that we must now turn.

European religious thought at the end of the fifteenth century was marked by four influences. The mystical tradition which had characterized the *devotio moderna* and was most potently epitomized by Thomas à Kempis' classic work, the *Imitatio Christi*, stressed the humanity of Our Lord and the essentially ethical character of the Christian life as a first step to divine union. Neo-Platonism, which in an earlier form was the basis of most medieval mystical writing, had enjoyed a revival among the humanists, for whom it echoed and illuminated many Christian tenets; it drew attention to some neglected facets of Christian truths about the nature of the worlds of the flesh and the spirit. Philology, a principal source of humanism, led scholars to textual criticism of the *Vulgate* and to a fresh reading and a new understanding of the Greek gospels and epistles, and indeed to an enthusiasm for Biblical translation (which was stifled in England). Finally, these three factors combined to promote the rediscovery of St. Paul and of his emphasis upon the Christian life.

These influences had seeped into England by various channels, but only with the visit of Erasmus did they gain momentum here. No man, indeed, better represents all these influences than he does, and none of his works better than the *Enchiridion Militis Christiani*, written in 1503 and translated into English, perhaps by Tyndale, *c.* 1522 as *The Handbook of the Militant Christian*.[1] Some idea of its circulation can be gained from the sale of at least fourteen copies of the Latin version by an Oxford bookseller in 1520.[2] As the title suggests, it is a guide for the Christian who is battling with his sins; it discusses the need to fight, the weapons appropriate, the battleground of self, some rules for a Christian life and some special remedies for particular vices. The *devotio moderna* is apparent when Erasmus writes of

[1] The most accessible version of the *Enchiridion* in translation is in *The Essential Erasmus*, ed. J. P. Dolan (Mentor-Omega paperback edn. 1964), cited here.
[2] *The Daily Ledger of John Dorne, 1520*, ed. F. Malden (in Oxford Historical Soc. vols. 5 and 16), *passim*.

'our determination to imitate Christ', a sentiment which reverberates through the whole book; neo-Platonism is the basis of his description of the inner and outer man, the soul aspiring upwards to celestial heights and struggling against the body which sinks and presses downwards to temporal things. Throughout the work there are constant appeals at critical points to the authority of St. Paul, 'the standard-bearer of Christian warfare'; Erasmus advises his reader to make himself 'completely familiar with Paul', to 'keep him in his heart at all times', to 'memorize what he has to say'.

Under these influences and in pursuit of the imitation of Christ Erasmus sees the key not in the sacraments, though these he does not deny (or mention), but in the Bible: 'If you approach the Scriptures in all humility and with regulated caution, you will perceive that you have been breathed upon by the Holy Will. It will bring about a transformation that is impossible to describe'. Could any thought be more devastating in a land where laymen were suspected of heresy for reading the Bible, where vernacular translations were in effect proscribed, where the parish clergy themselves were so ill acquainted with Holy Writ, and where salvation was taught to be by way of the sacraments? Yet this was only the threshold of new ideas: the Bible had to be properly understood, its meaning plucked from its words and phrases, and Christ thought of not as an abstraction but as an historic person exemplifying the virtues of 'charity, simplicity, patience and purity'. It was not sufficient to admire 'the tunic that reputedly belonged to Christ' and yet to 'read the wonderful sayings of that same Christ half asleep'. No matter how much people might read or hear of the Passion of Christ and adore and display the image of the Cross, no matter what agonies and tears they might suffer meditating on His Passion, 'the true value of the Cross is in profiting from its many examples' and 'you cannot say that a person loves Christ if he does not follow His example'. Though these words were directed at the reader, any application of them to the clergy would quickly prove disturbing. The emphasis throughout the work is upon conforming to Christ's example, not the world's conventions; Erasmus—like St. Paul—set out 'to stress the difference between the visible and invisible because I find so many Christians, either out of neglect or sheer ignorance, are as superstitious as the pagans'. Readers who became familiar with these ideas and with assaults on the virtual polytheism and the devotional malpractices of the time would hear the sermons of John Myrc and his fellows with little patience or respect. It was even more devastating that Erasmus was able to write a guide to salvation (though he did not express it so) without mentioning the clergy in their confessional and sacramental role; they have slipped entirely from view. It may well be that Erasmus had no doubts about this role, or refused to express any, but in the setting of this work the silence was indeed pregnant.

Anti-clerical feeling in England towards 1530 was thus transformed in scale, temper and conviction: economic factors sharpened and with printing diffused and strengthened it, Pauline and humanist ideas informed and enlarged it. The critics of the early sixteenth century clergy now had an imaginative explanation of the moral failings of the Church and a dynamic solution for them. They had a new and energizing view of Christ and Christianity and new texts from which to gain understanding. What made the movement more penetrating than any which preceded it was that it began with a reappraisal of self; the reader of the *Enchiridion* and kindred works was taught first to see himself with new eyes, and then, inescapably, all men. The days of the sterile indignation and resentment which had characterized traditional anti-clericalism were passed; an age of constructive, revolutionary, criticism was at hand. It was in this context that the English clergy and their superiors proved inadequate and it is against this background that the impact of Luther's ideas must be reckoned.

Appendix 1

The Registers of Bishop Nikke;
Norwich Episcopal Act Books XIII–XVI

THE way in which the Norwich statistics given in the text have been calculated requires a brief discussion of the complex sources from which they are drawn.

Act Book XIII falls into three sections. The first part which occupies 17 numbered folios contains institutions, admissions and collations from March 1501 to December 1503 and all its information is repeated (in slightly different order) in the second part. This second section occupies folios numbered from 1 to 85 and is a register, arranged chronologically, of institutions, etc., by the bishop or his deputies from March 1501 to September 1507; most of its entries after September 1503 are included also in Act Book XIV. The third section, from fo. 86r to 107r, similarly contains institutions and admissions, but arranged under, and only for, the two archdeaconries of Norwich (fos. 86r–95r) and Norfolk (fos. 97r–107r), from October 1507 to October 1510, and from March 1508 to November 1511 respectively; all its information is to be found in the first part of Act Book XV. The volume concludes on fo. 108v with some ordination lists. For statistical purposes, therefore, this register can be disregarded except for the entries from March 1501 to October 1503 in part two.

Act Book XIV begins abruptly on fo. 1r with an entry for 1 October 1503 and thereafter it is arranged chronologically up to 1528 on fo. 228r; to that point it is a register of institutions, collations, sequestrations, mandates, probate administration, fees and first fruits. Between fos. 60v and 61r, however, is a fragment of an unfoliated 'office' and memorandum book, introduced by an eighteenth-century note to that effect. Folios 228v–229r contain an entry for 1536. After that follows a section for

197

the years 1529–38 and separately foliated 1r–33v; this has a title paper, much used, upon which the headings 'from 1529 to 1534' and 'from 1529 to 1538' are legible. For our statistical purposes everything after fo. 228r has been disregarded.

A heading on the first folio of Act Book XV proclaims it to be a register of admissions to benefices with notes on the first fruits and the guarantors, kept from 1 October 1507 by Thomas Godsalf, who that day was appointed to the office of registrar by the bishop. (Despite this the text shows quite another hand at work for a while. *c.* 1512–14). It is arranged by archdeaconries and under them chronologically, and it finishes in 1516 on fo. 98, fos. 91–97 being lost. It includes all the information in part three of Act Book XIII, but none which appears in XIV.

On fo. 100r of this same volume a new heading declares that there follows a record of the bishop's receipts from institutions, collations, first fruits, testaments and fees, from 1 October 1507 till the same day each following year. This section, arranged chronologically by years (and within these by archdeaconries) covers fos. 100 to 168 and the period October 1507 to August 1513. Some of its folios are misplaced and others for the period October 1510 to October 1511 missing. It shares no common entries with the first part of this register, but all its information appears in Act Book XIV and can be safely ignored therefore.

Act Book XVI begins with two unnumbered folios containing full transcripts of memoranda for 1507, 1516 and 1534. These precede fo. 1r on which appears a heading to the effect that this is a register of institutions and collations in the time of Bishop Richard from 28 April 1535. This register ceases on fo. 36r with an entry concerning November 1535, a month before Nikke died. Folio 37 is missing and fo. 38r when the text resumes has no heading except a date, November 1516. What follows is clearly a register of institutions, collations, resignations and pensions, executed by or before Nicholas Carr, the vicar-general, though the bishop appears in August 1526. It is arranged chronologically by years and continues until 1527 on fo. 106r. There follows immediately, in a later hand, an inserted document of 1541, and thereafter, until fo. 129v, the texts of several dispensations and mandates issued by Wolsey, Leo X, Peter Vannes and even Warham, the dates ranging through the 1520s and 1530s. That completes the volume. The second section of institutions, etc., from 1516 to 1527 is entirely independent of Act Book XIV, whose information for those years it supplements.

The statistics cited in the text are, therefore, extracted from these four registers as follows:–

1501–1503	Act Book XIII (ii)	fos. 1–25v
1503–1528	Act Book XIV (i)	fos. 1–228r
1507–1516	Act Book XV (i)	fos. 1–98r
1516–1527	Act Book XVI (ii)	fos. 38r–106r

Although grossly inaccurate and inflated totals are thus avoided, complete accuracy is precluded by the illegibility, as well as by the loss, of certain folios.

The reasons for all this duplication and its implications for the organization of the episcopal secretariat and exchequer must await fuller discussion of Nikke's episcopate and its records elsewhere.

Appendix 2

Extracts from two cases which came into the consistory court of London early in the sixteenth century follow. They are recorded in the Deposition Book for the years 1510–16, G.L.C., MS. DL/C/206. These depositions were made in answer to questions based upon the libel (made by the plaintiff), or upon the replication (made by the defendant), or upon subsequent interrogatories (which either party might make upon the answers to the libel or replication); none of these questions, usually called articles, are preserved for the London courts for our period. One result of this procedure was that many deponents repeat, with minor variations, the same information, so that heavy editing is necessary to eliminate needless, though colourful, reiteration and much common form.

Almost all, except matrimonial, causes afford vivid and useful information to support and illustrate this study; from an abundance of material the two following cases have been selected because of their wide relevance. The first illustrates absenteeism, but contains as well what is virtually a clerical autobiography in Civi's own testimony, and concludes with some telling evidence of lay or patronal irresponsibility. The second case contains a long and informative account, by a parishioner, of the vicars of Braughing and their assistants, and shows one court case that was a rare and unhappy event in a parish.

APPENDIX 2(a)

Dominic Civi, though still only in his twenty-third year, on 10 June 1503 was granted a papal licence to receive priest's orders and a benefice despite his age (London Guildhall MS. 9531/9, fo.

200

37r–v). Seven days later he was admitted to the rectory of Gressenhall in Norfolk (Norwich Episcopal Act Book XIII, fo. 23r). Over a year later on 26 August 1504 he was admitted to the rectory of South Ockendon in Essex, on the presentation of the Earl of Oxford (Guildhall MS. 9531/9, fo. 36r), and barely a fortnight after that the fruits of Gressenhall were sequestrated (Act Book XIII, fo. 17v). The explanation for this action emerges from a papal dispensation issued to Civi on 8 October 1504, dispensing him again for age and now for two incompatible benefices (Guildhall MS. 9531/9, fo. 36v). He seems to have recovered Gressenhall, for nothing more is heard of it until Henry Glover is instituted rector there on 10 December 1514, when no explanation of the vacancy and no mention of the name of the last incumbent are offered (Act Book, XV, fo. 24r). Some time before 1 September 1515 Civi was deprived of South Ockendon, and the bishop collated it, by failure of the patrons to present within the legal term of six months, to John Aleyn (Guildhall MS. 9531/9, fo. 63r). His deprivation occurred probably as a result of the lawsuit begun in the London consistory court in 1511. It was in the course of this litigation that the following testimony was offered; apart from Civi's own inaccurately recollected autobiography and the consequences of absence, this is chiefly remarkable for the account of a most unusual induction ceremony. The customary mandate for the induction was addressed to the archdeacon or his official on the day of the institution of Civi, 26 August 1504 (Ibid., fo. 36r). Two days later the archdeacon, pleading excessive and arduous business and making no mention of his official, commissioned all and each incumbent *in literis* in Chafford deanery to execute the induction (Ibid., fo. 36r–v). Unusual though this was, its strangeness was far exceeded by the testimony that the Earl of Oxford, a great magnate in Essex and patron of the living *pro hac vice*, had sent a mandate of his own to Sir Thomas Tirell, knight, to induct Civi. (See Civi's own deposition below; though he was remote at the time, the evidence of others makes it clear that Tirell was the one who inducted Civi's proctor into the living.) Surely no more eloquent commentary on the attitude of patrons to their responsibilities at that time survives.

John Cobdow, aged 26, who had lived in South Ockendon for nine years, is the first witness who interests us :–

[fo. 50r] Dicit quod licet ipse Dominicus fuerit et steterit Rector dicte ecclesie per quinque annos tamen iste iuratus numquam eum vidit ibidem nec novit ut dicit.

He went on to describe how this had come about and what its consequences were:–

[fo. 50r] dicit iste iuratus in vim sui prestiti iurati quod chorus sive chancellus dicte ecclesie est in tectura plumbea defectivus et eget reparacionibus adeo quod aqua pluvialis intrat et inficit ac corrumpit et putrifacit tigna et meremium eiusdem adeo eciam quod, ut dicit, ipsa aqua pluvialis descendit deorsum in chorum et cadit super lectrina, anglice le deskes, ibidem in tantum quod libri dicte ecclesie ibidem dimissi sunt pluries inadefacti et cum stillis aque huiusmodi deteriorati. Dicit insuper iste iuratus quod tempore quo dictus dominus Dominicus Civi erat per patrem suum Johannem Andream Civi in possessionem dicte Ecclesie inductus, et hostia ecclesie predicte erant tunc clausa et obserata, eo quod dictus dominus dominicus obtinuit dictam ecclesiam contra voluntatem Magistri Willielmi Terell armigeri dicte ecclesie patroni, prefatus Johannes Andreas Civi cum auctoritate Magistri Thome Tirell, tunc iusticiarii domini Regis, rupit et fregit hostia tam dicte Ecclesie quam eciam unum hostium quod ducit in campanile ibidem ut ingrederetur et nancisceretur possessionem [fo. 50v) dicte ecclesie nomine eiusdem domini Dominici filii sui et pulsaret campanas ibidem ad eundem effectum. Et dicit iste iuratus quod licet dictus Johannes Andreas Civi per eundem Magistrum Thomam Tirell iusticiarium memoratum monitus et iussus tunc fuit ut reficeret et repararet ipsa hostia sic per eum rupta et fracta, tamen citra illud tempus, videlicet per quinque vel sex annos ultimos iam elapsos, illud facere non curavit, sed adhuc remanent non sufficienter reparata nec emendata, ut dicit.

Ulterius Examinatus iste iuratus dicit quod mansus et Rectoria eiusdem beneficii et alia edificia eidem pertinencia sunt in tegulis et muris et le grouncellis tam in opere ligneo, lapideo et luteo, ruinosa et multum defectiva adeo quod nisi celerius subveniantur et provideantur in hac parte infra breve verisimiliter pacientur ruinam et iacturam non modicam. Et deponit de visu et sciencia suis adeo quod isti defectus et alii qui oculis intuencium clare possunt apparere vix possunt reparari et emendari minori summa quam summa xxti. librarum et iste iuratus, ut dicit, non subiret onus refeccionis et reparacionis defectuum huiusmodi minori summa quam summa xxxti. librarum. Dicit tamen iste iuratus quod horrea et columbarium eiusdem Rectorie sunt sufficienter reparata et dicit quod audivit dici a patre dicti Rectoris et domino Thoma Goodwyn capellano quod xxiiii^{or} libre fuerunt ibi circa reparaciones exposite sed omnia alia edificia sunt ruinosa et defectiva, ut predeposuit. Ulterius quo illam particulam materie, Que sic incipit Que omnia et singula et cetera, Dicit quod per eum predeposita sunt vera publica notoria manifesta et famosa, dicit quod de et super eisdem in eadem parochia laborant publica vox et fama. Et aliter de contentis in ipsa materia nescit deponere, ut dicit, Excepto quod dictus dominus Dominicus Rector antedictus non residet super beneficio huiusmodi nec umquam personaliter resedit ibidem in quantum iste iuratus umquam novit, ut dicit, et ubi degit et an insistit studio literarum in aliqua universitate vel non nescit deponere, ut dicit. Sed dicit quod communiter dicitur ibidem quod est mortuus. Dicit tamen quod sufficienter deservitur dicte ecclesie in divinis et cure ibidem per quendam capellanum qui vocatur dominus Philipp, qui est presbiter parochialis ibidem, [fo. 51r] excepto quod non habent servicium divinum cum nota et cantu sicut posset habere si curatus ad hoc esset dispositus et vellet adiuvare, quia sunt ibi diversi parochiani dicte parochie qui sciunt et vellent cantare si ipse curatus vellet, sed non vult ut dicit.

Other witnesses came forward to support Cobdow's testimony, with minor variations in the estimated costs of repairs needed. Then came a particularly interesting witness, Dominus Thomas Goodwyn, vicar of West Thurrock, farmer of the church of South Ockendon:-

[fo. 53v.] Dicit quod dominum Dominicum Civi Rectorem predictum numquam novit, quia ipsum numquam vidit, ut dicit, nec residet ipse Rector super beneficio suo predicto nec residebat ibidem per quinque annos ut dicit iste iuratus.

He did not know whether Civi had an apostolic licence for absence or whether he was at a university.

[ibid.] nisi ex relacione patris dicti domini Dominici et aliorum amicorum suorum qui sic dicunt.

Referring to the repairs of the choir, which he estimated at four shillings,

[Ibid.] dicit quod onus incumbit Rectori predicto, ut dicit iste iuratus, ex speciali pacto, licet ipse habeat eandem ecclesiam sive beneficium predictum ad firmam.

He stated too that the services were adequate,

[fo. 54r.] tamen parochiani non habent servicium cum nota et cantu sed submissa voce dicitur, quia non sunt ibidem coadjutores pro cantu dicit.

A husbandman called John Prowde agreed with his fellow witnesses but added a little more to the story.

[fo. 55r.] Et de aliis contentis in huiusmodi materia nescit deponere, ut dicit, nisi ex relacione Johannis Andree Civi patris dicti Rectoris qui dicit et refert parochianis et inhabitantibus ville predicte quod idem dominus Dominicus, filius suus et Rector memoratus, Degit in studio generali ubi vacat literis in partibus transmarinis et quod est secum dispensatum pro non residencia ut dicit, et quod parochiani videbunt eum tali die et tali die et sic dixit et multos dies prefixit per biennium iam elpasum ad introducendum eum coram eisdem, sed nihil in hoc fecit cum effectu, ex quo presumunt et coniecturant dicti parochiani et inhabitantes quod Rector eorum antedictus est mortuus.

In January 1512 Master Dominic Civi himself appeared in the consistory court to reply to charges laid against him by William Tirell. In the course of his replies he gives some interesting biographical details, interesting because they are fairly typical.

[fo. 99r.] Et ubi in eadem posicione continetur et ponitur quod tunc esset Laicus ad hoc Respondet negative, quia, ut dicit, tunc temporis erat in sacris subdiaconatus et diaconatus ordinibus constitutus, quos ordines et alios minores recepit Veneciis a quodam Episcopo ibidem de cuius nomine et titulo iam non recordatur absque inspeccione litterarum ordinum suorum predictorum, ut dicit. Et dicit quod complevit xxx^{um} annum etatis sue in festo omnium sanctorum ultimo iam preterito, Et credit quod in xxiii^o anno completo etatis sue obtinuit ecclesiam de Southwokyngdon predictam. Et dicit quod antequam obtinuit aliquod beneficium ecclesiasticum recepit ordines omnes supradictos (in xix^o anno etatis fuit incepto et non completo). Et dicit quod obtinuit ecclesiam parochialem de Gressenhall Norvicensis diocesis per iiii^{or}. annos antequam erat provectus ad sacerdocium Et, ut credit, tunc non habuit aliquam dispensacionem, apostolicam vel Episcopalem, ad obtinendum illam ecclesiam absque ordine presbiteratus per quadriennium, quia toto illo tempore stetit in studio et ideo non credit quod opus erat aliqua dispensacione, ut dicit. Ulterius dicit quod habuit literas dimissorias a domino Episcopo Londoniensis tunc existenti ad recipiendum omnes ordines a quocumque Episcopo Catholico quia oriundus fuit, ut dicit, in parochia Sancti Andree Undershaft Civitatis et

APPENDICES

diocesis Londoniensis. Dicit ulterius quod eo tempore quo obtinuit ecclesiam de Southwokyngdon erat presbiter. Ad quartam posicionem dicit et fatetur quod vigore presentacionis predicti fuit institutus Rector in dicta Ecclesia de SouthWokyngdon per dictum Magistrum Willielmum LichFeld xxvi^{to} die mensis Augusti Anno in eadem posicione specificato in persona Johannis Andree Civi, patris sui laici, prout in litteris institucionis sue exinde confectis ad quas se refert plenius continetur. Et, ut credit, dictus Willielmus Tirell ad illam institucionem non fuit vocatus, licet ad presentacionem suam, ut premittitur, erat requisitus et renuit consentire, ut prefertur. Et dicit quod ratum habuit et habet totum et quicquid per patrem suum, suum in hac parte procuratorem, erat actum et factum in hac parte.

The penultimate statement refers to an arrangement between Tirell and the Earl of Oxford, disputing patrons. The advowson of the church, one witness states on fo. 101r., had descended from Maurice Bynne, lord of the manor of South Ockendon, to his eldest son Henry, and from him to his two daughters, mothers respectively of William Tirell and Clement Harleston, who were now the patrons. Harleston confirmed this on fo. 104v. Civi on fo. 98v. stated that John de Vere, Earl of Oxford, had Clement Harleston, then about 13 years of age, in wardship (by purchase from the king); Oxford in his own and Harleston's name presented Civi to the living of South Ockendon.

[fo. 98v.] ad instanciam et requisicionem Magistri Benedicti Civi patrui istius iurati,

and sent letters to Magister William Tirell

[Ibid.] ad effectum obtinendi eius consensum et bonam voluntatem ut consentiret huiusmodi presentacioni.

When Tirell refused his consent de Vere went ahead and after Civi's institution wrote this time to Magister Thomas Tirell, knight,

[Ibid.] ad inducendum istum iuratum in possessionem eiusdem beneficii ex illa sola presentacione sic ut premittitur per ipsum facta.

Civi stated his belief that he was peacefully inducted, and so he may have believed for he was nowhere near. In fact there were several witnesses willing to swear the contrary. John Abraham, a husbandman, formerly of South Ockendon, stated [fo. 101v.] quod quodam die contingenti circiter festum sancti Bartholomei erunt octo anni, ut recolit, in festo sancti Bartholomei proxime futuro quem diem nescit aliter specificare, ut dicit, quidam dominus Thomas Tirell miles venit ad villam de Southwokyngdon predicte et ad ecclesiam ibidem cum nonnullis aliis personis ad numerum Centum personarum, ut firmiter credit, ad inducendum dictum Dominicum Civi in possessionem dicte ecclesie in persona patris sui mandato praenobilis dicti domini Johannis Veer comitis Oxonis. Et quia dictus dominus Thomas Tirell non potuit tunc habere clavem hostii dicte ecclesie ideo misit pro fabro ad aperiendum seram dicti hostii qui cum venisset et hostium aperire nequivisset, Tunc servientes dicti domini Thome Tirell militis et alii secum venientes et sibi adherentes cum ferramento, anglice a barr of Iryn, cum magno impetu et violencia ruperunt unum de le Stapilles dicti hostii, quo facto ipsis adhuc ingredi nequentibus tunc tot persone quot potuerunt manum apponere et attingere apprehenderunt quoddam tignum ligneum longum iuxta murum ecclesie iacens et consimili violencia et impetu currentes percusserunt hostium ecclesie predicte, quo ex violencia et impetu predictis tandem quassato fracto et rupto, tunc in eandem ecclesiam unacum Johanne Andrea Civi patre dicti Dominici intrarunt, quibus sic ingressis tamen campanas pulsare nequiverunt pro eo quod funes et corde campanarum erant in cameram campanilis ab area ecclesia sursum tracti, quod cum perciperent hostium campanilis tunc clausum infra ecclesiam erumpere fortiter enitebantur, quibus in hoc non prevalentibus, tandem fregerunt et eruperunt cum le pollis et tunsionibus quoddam hostium camere campanilis predicti supra capita eorum per quod solent campane sublevari et sursum trahi atque a campanili deponi quando opus est supra quod hostium extranumsale anglice a Flate dore corde et Funes campanarum remanebant, quo hostio sic fracto, funes et corde predicte in area ecclesie ceciderunt et sic campanas pulserunt. Et sub istis modo et forma dictus Dominicus Civi in persona patris sui ut premittitur per memoratum dominum Thomam Tirell erat inductus in possessionem dicte ecclesie. Et deponit de visu et sciencia suis quia tunc interfuit, ut dicit.

Other witnesses generally confirm this, though it is suggested on fo. 102v. that the crowd was only thirty or forty in number. This witness, Thomas Freman, states that the crowd with Thomas Tirell

[fo. 102v.] non effregit hostium ecclesie predicte nec anglice aliquod le Stapill eiusdem cum ferramento nec hoc temptabant, ut

APPENDICES

dicit in quantum ipse recordatur, Sed cum ferramento ipso, de quo
dictus Johannes Abraham precontestes suus deposuit, opus ferreum
et barras cuiusdam fenestre vitree aggressi sunt, sed ipsam fene-
stram vel barras ferreas eiusdem erumpere et effringere non vale-
bant et ideo ad hostium cum tigno accedentes et concurrentes Illud
effregerunt et sic in ecclesiam ingressi sunt, ut dicit. Bene recordatur
et scit, ut dicit, quod rumpebant hostium extranumsale in area
campanilis factum, vocatum a lope hole, per quod campane erant
sursum erecte et assumpte et deposite cum scala et anglice le pollis,
sive Banershaftis, et sic apprehenderunt cordas campanarum quas
in signum apprehense possessionis huiusmodi tunc pulsabant.

John Prowde, although not present at the induction, saw the
damage the next morning:

[fo. 103v.] et postea erat unus illorum qui equitabant ad dictum
dominum Thomam Tirell, pro huiusmodi hostio reficiendo et emen-
dando eo quod mediis suis erat fractum, qui mandavit ipsis, ad se
hac occasione venientibus, quod irent Magistrum Willielmum
Tirell et requirent ab eo claves ecclesie et quod facerent hostium
predictum emendari, promittens idem dominus Thomas Tirell quod
pro huiusmodi emendacione satisfaceret, qui tamen pro emendacione
huiusmodi usque in hodiernum diem non satisfecit ut dicit.

APPENDIX 2(b)

The following extract from a case in the consistory court of
the bishop of London in 1514 illustrates much more than the
negligence which had provoked the parishioners' complaint
against Robert Philipson, vicar of Braughing. The deponent is
John Broke, a maltman of Braughing, and he is replying to
articles of the libel:

[fo. 304r.] Ad primum articulum dicti libelli dicit et deponit quod a
tempore quo discrecionem cepit habere, videlicet a quinquaginta
annis citra, vicarius dicte vicarie tenebatur residere ibidem una cum
alio capellano suis sumptibus exhibendo ad finem et effectum in hoc
articulo specificatos.
  Ad secundum articulum dicit iste iuratus quod ipse tempore suo
ad quinquaginta annos elapsos et ultra novit quendam vicarium
dicte vicarie, cuius nomen iam nescit specificare ut dicit, qui postea
erat Rector ecclesie parochialis de Fancherche londoniensis; sed

207

quanto tempore stetit vicarium ecclesie de Brawghyng ignorat, ut dicit. Sed dicit quod ipse vicarius residebat personaliter ibidem una cum capellano suo suis sumptibus exhibito, cuius tamen capellani nomen nescit modo exprimere, ut dicit, sed dicit quod cum eodem presbitero primo literas didicit. Et deinde post dictum vicarium successit quidam vicarius ibidem vocatus Magister Sowthwell, qui similiter residebat ibidem cum suo capellano similiter per eum exhibito. Sed quanto tempore ipse stetit ibi vicarius nescit iam exprimere, ut dicit. Cui Magistro Sowthwell successit dominus Thomas Miton vicarius dicte vicarie, qui similiter cum suo capellano suis sumptibus exhibito residebat ibidem. Sed quanto tempore stetit et continuavit vicarius iam ignorat, ut dicit. Post quem quidam dominus Hugo Ysaac, oriundus in dicte villa, successit et stetit ibidem vicarius per sex vel septem annos, ut recordatur, et cum capellano suo residebat similiter ibidem, qui capellanus dominus Johannes vocabatur, in partibus borialibus natus, cum quo iste iuratus partem gramatice eciam addidicit et bene cum eo et sub eo proficiebat, ut dicit. Post quem successit quidam dominus Willielmus Sawge qui, ut recordatur, fuit et stetit ibi vicarius per xx^{ti} annos. Et parimodo residebat cum suo capellano aliquo tempore sue incumbencie. Et tandem exhibicionem capellani huiusmodi subtraxit unde parochiani ibidem querelam contra eum fecerunt pro non exhibicione huiusmodi capellani [fo. 304v.] penes Reverendum patrem dominum Kempe tunc Episcopum londoniensis. Et deinde racione ipsius querele idem dominus Willielmus Sawge, ex mandato dicti Reverendi patris, denuo cepit huiusmodi capellanum exhibere et invenire. Et deinde post eum successit in dicta vicaria quidam dominus Johannes Kent qui fuit ibi vicarius, ut credit et recordatur, per septem vel octos annos qui secum dum presens ibi erat sumptibus suis exhibebat unum capellanum, suum socium sive coadiutorem adiunctum. Et dicit quod dictus dominus Johannes Kent romam profectus cum Magistro David Williams tunc magistro rotulorum; interim dimisit duos capellanos ibidem in divinis deservituros suis sumptibus et expensis exhibitos et inventos. Cuius in locum surrogatus fuit quidam Dominus Ricardus Tailliour qui fuit ibi vicarius per circiter octo annos, qui pari modo capellanum secum habuit tunc ibidem ipsemet eciam personaliter ibidem residente et ibidem moriente. Et ulterius dicit quod post dictum dominum Ricardum Tailliour quidam consanguineus Magistri Yarford, civitatis Londoniensis, erat eciam vicarius ibidem per dimedium anni, Sed eius nomen nescit specificare, ut dicit, cuius tempore in studio apud Oxoniam degentis presbiter parochialis tantum residebat et deserviebat cure ibidem. Post quem supervenit Magister Bulgen,

capellanus Reverendi patris domini Ricardi FitzJames londoniensis
Episcopi moderni, qui stetit et continuavit ibi vicarius per annum
cum dimedio, ut recolitur, et communiter dum ibidem residebat
suum capellanum secum pari modo exhibebat et inveniebat, sed pro
maiore parte erat in familia dicti Reverendi patris moram faciens, ut
dicit. Et deinde post eum dictam vicariam resignantem, dominus
Thomas Percy, tunc prior Monasterii sancte Trinitatis Londoniensis, eandem vicariam obtinebat et occupabat, qui cum ibidem
personaliter residebat, capellanum parochialem secum eciam cum
uno canonico capellano suo ibidem exhibuit et sumptibus suis
invenit. Et ipso absente habuit ibidem presbiterum parochialem et
unum canonicum residentes ibidem. Deinde quidam Magister
Oressell erat ibi vicarius vix per annum, qui postnactam possessionem non residebat personaliter ibidem, Sed dumtaxat exhibebat
presbiterum parochialem, ut dicit. Et demum institutus fuit in eadem
vicaria dominus Robertus Philippson vicarius ibi modernus qui citra
tempus prime incumbencie sue in eadem vicaria certo tempore personaliter residebat ibidem, capellanum suum pari modo suis sumptibus
secum exhibens. Et premissa deponit de visu et auditu et sciencia suis,
ut dicit. Praeterea dicit et deponit quod a senioribus et a maioribus
suis ibidem, quibus fidem adhibuit, audivit dici quod quondam erat
quidam vicarius ibidem, vir bonus, quem parochiani ibidem propter
eius virtutem et bonitatem adeo diligebant quod per primum annum
incumbencie non requirebant ab eo [fo. 305r.] Exhibicione huiusmodi capellani sui, Sed lapso anno retulerunt ei quod tenebatur ad
exhibicionem unius capellani eciam propter seipsum ibidem
personaliter residentem, prout ex hoc habuerant evidencias scrip-
turas et munimenta, qui hoc audiens referebat eis gracias de
humanitate, et bona voluntate eorum erga eum, sed si hoc onus sibi
incumberet, non erat contentus quod eum de hoc prius non certiora-
verant, unde postea satisfaccionem inveniebat et exhibebat duos
capellanos ibidem suis propriis expensis tanto tempore quanto hoc
non fecerat ante ipsemet eciam personaliter ibidem residente, ut
dicit ut audivit dici ut supra. Ulterius dicit quod parochiani de
Brawghyng moderni habent evidencias sive munimenta sub Sigillo
quibus patet quod vicarius pro tempore existens ad exhibicionem
capellani huiusmodi modo in primo et ii° articulis libelli specificato est
astrictus, de visu et sciencia suis ut dicit.

Appendix 3

Letters dimissory in the York registers

THE following figures because of scribal negligence or caprice (especially, it would seem, in Lawrence Booth's register) may well give a misleadingly low proportion of scholars.

Archbishop: Dates: Registers:	Wm. Booth (1452–64) R.I.20	Neville (1465–76) R.I.21, 22	L. Booth (1476–80) R.I.22	Rotherham (1480–1500) R.I.23, 24	Savage (1501–07) R.I.25	Bainbridge (1508–14) R.I.26	Wolsey (1514–30) R.I.27	Sede Vacante (1452–1530) R.I.5	Totals
Recipients									
Scholars	45	58	1	341	106	147	364	9	1071
Graduates	20	9	5	31	3	1	8	6	83
Already Acolytes	17	48	7	209	92	101	624	17	1,115
Already in Holy Orders	12	4	0	41	6	6	35	4	108
Remainder	198	28	46	259	28	28	34	96	717
Total	292	147	59	881	235	283	1,065	132	3,094

Appendix 4

Criminous Clerks

I N most episcopal registers of this time records can be found of the bishop empowering clergy to receive convicted clerks from the royal courts, but these are prospective commissions and give no guide to how many clerks, if any at all, were received. Records concerning the individual purgations, which tell us about the crime of the offender and the date of his release, are much more capriciously registered: four dioceses, or some eight counties, yield only fifty-four examples between 1450 and 1530; out of twenty-four registers eleven have no such entries. It might be inferred that these eleven simply reveal the reluctance on the part of the eleven prelates to release criminous clerks, but the hazards of such an argument from silence are underlined by the Lincoln records: whereas the registers there allude to only six purgations between 1452 and 1524, 148 are listed between 1525 and 1543, far too large an increase to be explained away as a crime wave. (Unfortunately, all but one of these 148 are merely commissions to hear purgations, allowing, therefore, little useful insight into the use or abuse of the privilege.) Listed below, against the names of each bishop are the numbers of purgations recorded in his register.

Bath and Wells

Bekynton	(1443–65)	8
Stillington	(1466–91)	1
Fox	(1492–4)	0
King	(1495–1503)	7
De Castello	(1504–18)	5
Wolsey	(1518–23)	0
Clerke	(1523–41)	8 (all in 1533)

Canterbury

Stafford	(1443–52)	0
Kempe	(1452–4)	0
Bourgchier	(1454–86)	0
Morton	(1486–1500)	6 (1 Bath and Wells and 5 Sarum sede vacante)
Deane	(1501–3)	0
Warham	(1503–32)	2

Hereford

Beauchamp	(1449–50)	0
Boulers	(1450–3)	1
Stanbury	(1453–74)	5
Myllyng	(1474–92)	9
Audley	(1492–1502)	} not consulted, still in MS.
De Castello	(1502–4)	
Mayew	(1504–16)	3
Bothe	(1516–35)	1 (1529)

London

Kempe	(1448–89)	3
Hill	(1489–96)	0
Savage	(1496–1501)	0
Warham	(1501–3)	0
Barons	(1504–5)	0
Fitzjames	(1506–22)	0
Tunstall	(1522–30)	0
Stokesley	(1530–9)	0

Bibliography

I: *Manuscript Sources*

(i) *British Museum*
Additional MS. 34786: Compotus of Helmingham rectory, 1510.
Additional Roll 32957: Account of Kirkby Malham vicarage, 1454–5.
Cotton MS. Cleopatra F.VI, fo. 342: Letter concerning the 'Amicable Grant' in Kent.
Cotton MS. Tiberius B.I., fos. 271–2: Letter concerning the 'Amicable Grant' in Ely and Cambridgeshire.
Burney MS. 356: Theological miscellany.

(ii) *Public Record Office*
C.1.: Early Chancery Proceedings.
E. 36/58: A taxation of ecclesiastical benefices in the diocese of Coventry and Lichfield, temp., Henry VII.
E. 36/60: The same for the diocese of Rochester, temp., Henry VII.
E. 36/61: The same for the archdeaconry of Richmond, temp., Henry VIII.
E. 36/62: The same for the diocese of Lincoln, temp., Henry VI.
E. 36/149: The same for the archdeaconry of Richmond, 14 Henry VIII.
Just. Itin. 3/211,213; 3/84/1–20: Eyre and Assize Rolls, 1439–60.
E. 135/8/31: Account Book of the Archdeacon of Wiltshire, 1497–1501.
E. 101/514/31, 32: Accounts of proctor of Scarborough church 1414–42
E. 101/517/27: Compotus of Downham rectory, 1513–20.
E. 101/519/31: Account of Mancetter vicarage mid-fifteenth century.

(iii) *Somerset House*
Prerogative Court of Canterbury, Registers of Wills, 'Doggett', 'Blamyr', 'Porch'.

(iv) *Lambeth Palace Library*
Register of Archbishop Stafford, 1443–52.
Register of Archbishop Kemp, 1452–4.

Register of Archbishop Morton, 1486–1501.
Register of Archbishop Deane, 1501–4.
Register of Archbishop Warham, 1504–33.
Cartae Miscellanae.

(v) *London Guildhall Library*

MS. 9531/7: Register of Bishop Kempe, 1449–89.
MS. 9531/8: Registers, bound together, of Bishops Hill, Savage, Warham and Barons, 1489–1506.
MS. 9531/9: Register of Bishop Fitzjames, 1506–22.
MS. 9531/10: Register of Bishop Tunstall, 1522–30.
MS. 9531/11: Register of Bishop Stokesley, 1530–9.
MS. 9531/12: Register of Bishop Bonner, 1540–9.
MS. 9064 (i): Acta quoad correctionem delinquentium, 1470–3.
MS. 9064 (ii): Acta quoad correctionem delinquentium, 1489–91.
MS. 9064 (iii): Acta quoad correctionem delinquentium, 1492–3.
MS. 9064 (iv): Acta quoad correctionem delinquentium, 1494–5.
MS. 9065: Liber examinationum, 1489–1516.
MS. 9071 (v)–(x): Commissary Court Registers of wills, 1449–1539.
MS. 10123/2: Accounts of Bishop's Receiver-General, 1517–18.

(vi) *Greater London Council Record Office*

DL/C/205: Consistory Court Deposition Book, 1467–76.
DL/C/206: Consistory Court Deposition Book, 1510–16.
DL/C/207: Consistory Court Deposition Book, 1521–4.
DL/C/208: Consistory Court Deposition Book, 1529–33.
DL/C/1: Consistory Court Act Book, 1496–1505.
DL/C/330: Act Book of the Vicar-General, 1521–39.
DL/C/354: Register of wills, mostly clerical, proved before the Vicar-General, 1514–20.
DL/C/418: Original wills proved before the Vicar-General, 1508–56.

(vii) *Borthwick Institute of Historical Research, York*

R.I.5: Sede Vacante Register.
R.I.19: Register of Archbishop Kempe, 1426–52.
R.I.20: Register of Archbishop William Booth, 1452–64.
R.I.21, 22: Register of Archbishop George Neville, 1465–76.
R.I.22: Register of Archbishop Laurence Booth, 1476–80.
R.I.23, 24: Register of Archbishop Rotherham, 1480–1500.
R.I.25: Register of Archbishop Savage, 1501–7.
R.I.26: Register of Archbishop Bainbridge, 1508–14.
R.I.27: Register of Archbishop Wolsey, 1514–30.
R.I.28: Register of Archbishop Lee, 1531–44.
R.As.55: Dean and Chapter Court Book.

R.VII.F.102, 306
R.As.16/18 } Accounts of Hornsea vicarage.

(viii) *York Dean and Chapter Library*
L.2(3)c: Visitation Book 1472–1550.
XVI.o.11: John Myrc's 'Manuale Sacerdotis'.

(ix) *Lincoln Diocesan Record Office*
R.19: Sede Vacante Register.
R.20: Register of Bishop Chedworth, 1452–71.
R.21: Register of Bishop Rotherham, 1472–80.
R.22: Register of Bishop Russell, 1480–94.
R.23, 24: Register of Bishop Smith, 1496–1514.
R.25: { Register of Bishop Wolsey, 1514.
       { Register of Bishop Atwater, 1514–21.
R.26: Register of Bishop Longland, 1521–45.

(x) *Lichfield Diocesan Record Office*
B/A/1/10: Register of William Booth, 1447–52.
B/A/1/11: Register of Reginald Boulers, 1453–9.
B/A/1/12: Register of John Hales, 1459–90.
B/A/1/13: { Register of Willam Smith, 1493–6.
          { Register of John Arundel, 1496–1502.
B/A/1/14: { Register of Geoffrey Blythe, 1503–31.
          { Register of Rowland Lee, 1534–43.
B/A/17/1(2): A tax list for Stafford Archdeaconry, 1531.

(xi) *The William Salt Library, Stafford*
Salt MS. D 1734/J 1948: Account Roll of spiritual and temporal income of Bishopric of Lichfield, 1464–5.
Salt MS. D 1734/J 1949: The same for 1541–2.

(xii) *Norwich County Record Office*
Act Book XIII
Act Book XIV } Registers of Bishop Richard Nikke and his Vicars-
Act Book XV } General, described in full in Appendix 1 above.
Act Book XVI
Consistory Court Will Registers 24–57 (1500–50).

II: *Printed Sources*

(i) *Canon Law*
Corpus Iuris Canonici, 2 vols. ed. E. Friedberg, Leipzig 1879–81.
Provinciale seu Constitutiones Angliae. W. Lyndwood, Oxford 1679.

Concilia Magnae Brittaniae et Hiberniae . . . 446–1718, 4 vols. D. Wilkins, London 1737.
Councils & Synods with other documents relating to the English Church, vol. ii, ed. F. M. Powicke and C. R. Cheney, Oxford 1964.
The Records of the Northern Convocation (Surtees Soc. 113), ed. G. W. Kitchin, 1907.

(ii) *Bishops' Registers*
Register of Henry Chichele, archbishop of Canterbury, 1414–43 (C. & Y. Soc. 45), 4 vols. ed. E. F. Jacob, 1937–47.
Registrum Thome Bourgchier, Cantuariensis archiepiscopi, 1454–1486 (C. & Y. Soc. 54), ed. F. R. H. Du Boulay, 1956.
Register of Thomas Bekynton, bishop of Bath and Wells 1443–65 (Somerset Record Soc. 49, 50), 2 vols. ed. H. C. Maxwell-Lyte, 1934–5.
Registers of Robert Stillington, bishop of Bath and Wells 1466–91, and Richard Fox, bishop etc. 1492–94 (Somerset Rec. Soc. 52), ed. H. C. Maxwell-Lyte, 1937.
Registers of Oliver King, bishop of Bath and Wells 1496–1503, and Hadrian de Castello, bishop etc. 1503–18 (Somerset Rec. Soc. 54), ed. H. C. Maxwell-Lyte, 1939.
Registers of Thomas Wolsey, bishop of Bath and Wells 1518–23, John Clerke, bishop etc. 1523–41, William Knyght, bishop etc. 1541–47 and Gilbert Bourne, bishop etc. 1554–59 (Somerset Rec. Soc. 55), ed. H. C. Maxwell-Lyte, 1940.
Register of Richard Fox, bishop of Durham 1494–1501 (Surtees Soc. 147), ed. M. P. Howden, 1932.
Registrum Ricardi Beauchamp, episcopi Herefordensis 1449–50; Registrum Reginaldi Boulers, episc. Hereford., 1450–53; Registrum Johannis Stanbury, episc. Hereford., 1453–74 (C. & Y. Soc. 25), ed. A. T. Bannister, 1919.
Registrum Thome Myllyng, episc. Hereford., 1474–92 (C. & Y. Soc. 26), ed. A. T. Bannister, 1920.
Registrum Ricardi Mayew, episc. Hereford., 1504–16 (C. & Y. Soc. 27), ed. A. T. Bannister, 1921.
Registrum Caroli Bothe, episc. Hereford., 1516–35 (C. & Y. Soc. 28), ed. A. T. Bannister, 1921.
'Registers of the Archdeacon of Richmond 1442–77' (*Y.A.J.*, xxx, 1931, pp. 1–132; xxxii, 1936, pp. 111–46), ed. A. H. Thompson.

(iii) *Ecclesiastical Court Records*
Act Book of the Ecclesiastical Court of Whalley 1510–38 (Chetham Soc. n.s. 44), ed. A. M. Cooke, 1901.
'An Archidiaconal Visitation of 1502' (*Archaeologia Cantiana*, xlvii, 1935, pp. 13–54).

Dean Cosyn and Wells Cathedral Miscellanea (Somerset Rec. Soc. 56), ed. A. Watkin, 1941.

Depositions and other ecclesiastical proceedings from the courts of Durham extending from 1311 to the reign of Elizabeth (Surtees Soc. 21), ed. J. Raine, 1845.

'Fragment of Folio Manuscript of the Archdeaconry Courts of Buckinghamshire, 1491–95' (*Records of Bucks.*, xi, 1920–6, pp. 27–47, 59–76, 145–56, 199–207, 315–42), ed. F. W. Ragg.

Norwich Consistory Court Depositions, 1499–1512, 1518–30 (Norfolk Rec. Soc. 10), ed. E. D. Stone and B. Cozens-Hardy, 1938.

'Proceedings of the Ecclesiastical Courts in the Archdeaconry of Leicester, 1516–35' (*Associated Architectural Societies Reports,* xxviii, 1905–6, pp. 117–220, 593–662), ed. A. P. Moore.

A Series of Precedents and Proceedings in Criminal Causes from 1475 to 1640; extracted from the Act Books of Ecclesiastical Courts in the Diocese of London, ed. W. H. Hale, London 1847.

(iv)   *Parish Records*

Churchwardens' accounts of Betrysden, 1515–73 (Kent Archaeological Soc., Records Branch, 5), ed. F. R. Mercer, 1928.

Churchwardens' accounts of Croscombe, Pilton, Yatton, Tintinhull, Morebath, and St. Michael's Bath, from 1349–1560 (Somerset Rec. Soc. 4), ed. E. Hobhouse, 1890.

Churchwardens' accounts of Prescot, Lancs., 1523–1607 (Lancs. & Ches. Rec. Soc. 104), ed. F. H. Bailey, 1952.

Churchwardens' accounts of St. Edmund and St. Thomas, Sarum, 1443–1702, with other documents (Wiltshire Rec. Soc.), ed. H. J. Fowler-Swayne, 1896.

Churchwardens' accounts of All Saints, Walsall, 1462–1521 (Wm. Salt Soc. 3rd Series), ed. G. P. Mander, 1930.

The First Churchwardens' Book of Louth, 1500–24, ed. R. C. Dudding, Oxford 1941.

Lambeth Churchwardens' Accounts, 1504–1645 (Surrey Rec. Soc.), ed. C. Drew, 1941–50.

Peterborough local administration. Parochial government before the Reformation. Churchwardens' accounts, 1467–1573, with supplementary documents, 1107–1488 (Northants. Rec. Soc. 9), ed. W. T. Mellows, 1939.

Parochial collections made by Antony à Wood and Richard Rawlinson (Oxford Rec. Soc. 2, 4, 11), 3 vols. ed. F. N. Davis, 1920–9.

Ecclesiastical Terriers of Warwickshire Parishes (Dugdale Soc. Publns. 22), ed. D. M. Baratt, 1955.

The Medieval Records of a London City Church (E.E.T.S. o.s. 128), ed. H. Littlehales, 1904–5.

BIBLIOGRAPHY

(v)   *Visitations*

Visitations in the diocese of Lincoln, 1517–31 (Lincoln Rec. Soc. 33, 35, 37), 3 vols. ed. A. H. Thompson, 1940–7.

Lincoln Diocesan Documents, 1450–1544 (E.E.T.S. o.s. 149), ed. A. Clark, 1914.

The Customs of London otherwise called Arnold's Chronicle, London 1811, pp. 273–8.

Visitations of the diocese of Norwich, 1492–1532 (Camden Soc. n.s. 43), ed. A. Jessop, 1888.

Visitations of churches belonging to St. Paul's cathedral in 1297 and 1458 (Camden Soc. n.s. 55), ed. W. S. Simpson, 1895.

Visitations and Memorials of Southwell Minster (Camden Soc. n.s. 48), ed. A. F. Leach, 1891.

Documents relating to diocesan and provincial visitations from the registers of Henry Bowet, archbishop of York 1407–25, and John Kempe, archbishop, etc. 1425–52 (Surtees Soc. 127), ed. A. H. Thompson, 1916.

(vi)   *Collegiate and Monastic Records*

Cartulary and Terrier of the Priory of Bilsington, Kent, ed. N. Neilson, London 1928.

Register and Chronicle of Butley Priory, Suffolk, 1510–35, ed. A. G. Dickens, Winchester 1951.

Acts of the dean and chapter of the cathedral church of Chichester, 1472–1544, the 'White Book' (Sussex Rec. Soc. 52), ed. W. D. Peckham, 1952.

The Book of William Morton, almoner of Peterborough monastery, 1448–67 (Northants. Rec. Soc. 16), ed. W. T. Mellows, P. I. King, C. N. L. Brooke, 1954.

Acts of the Chapter of the Collegiate Church of Ripon, 1452–1506 (Surtees Soc. 64), ed. J. T. Fowler, 1875.

Registra quorundam abbatum monsterii S. Albani qui saeculo XVmo floruere (Rolls Series 28), 2 vols. ed. H. T. Riley, 1872–3.

(vii)   *Wills and Inventories*

Bedfordshire wills and administrations proved at Lambeth Palace in the archdeaconry of Huntingdon, 1379–1627 (Beds. Hist. Rec. Soc. 2), ed. F. A. P. Turner, 1914.

Some Bedfordshire wills at Lambeth and Lincoln, 1379–1570 (Beds. Hist. Rec. Soc. 14), ed. H. Jenkinson and G. H. Fowler, 1931.

Wills and inventories from the registers of the commissary of Bury St. Edmund's and the archdeaconry of Sudbury (Camden Soc. o.s. 49), ed. S. Tymms, 1850.

BIBLIOGRAPHY

Lancashire and Cheshire wills and inventories from the ecclesiastical court, Chester (Chetham Soc. o.s. 33, 51), 2 vols. ed. G. J. Piccope, 1857–60.

Lancashire and Cheshire wills and inventories at Chester, with an appendix of abstracts of wills now lost or destroyed (Chetham Soc. n.s. 3), ed. G. J. Piccope abd. J. P. Earwaker, 1884.

A collection of Lancashire and Cheshire wills not to be found in any probate registers, 1301–1752 (Lancs. & Ches. Rec. Soc. 30), ed. W. F. Irvine, 1896.

Lincoln wills registered in the district probate registry at Lincoln, 1271–1532 (Lincoln. Rec. Soc. 5, 10, 24), 3 vols. ed. C. W. Foster, 1914–30.

Some Oxfordshire wills proved in the Prerogative Court of Canterbury, 1393–1510 (Oxford. Rec. Soc. 39), ed. J. R. H. Weaver and A. Beardwood, 1958.

Somerset Medieval Wills, 1383–1500 (Somerset Rec. Soc. 16), ed. F. W. Weaver, 1901.

Somerset Medieval Wills, 1501–1530, (Somerset Rec. Soc. 19), ed. F. W. Weaver, 1903.

Somerset Medieval Wills, 1531–58 (Somerset Rec. Soc. 21), ed. F. W. Weaver, 1905.

Medieval Wills from Wells (Somerset Rec. Soc. 40), ed. D. O. Shilton and R. Holworthy, 1925.

Surrey wills, proved in the archdeaconry court: Spage register, 1484–90 (Surrey Rec. Soc. 5), 1921.

Wills and inventories from the registry of the archdeaconry of Richmond (Surtees Soc. 26), ed. J. Raine, jnr., 1853.

Wills and administrations from the Knaresborough court rolls, 1506–1666 (Surtees Soc. 104), ed. F. Collins, 1902.

Wills and inventories illustrative of the history, manners, language and statistics, etc., of the northern counties of England, from the 11th century downwards (Surtees Soc. 2), ed. J. Raine, 1835.

North country wills at Somerset House and Lambeth Palace, 1383–1558 (Surtees Soc. 116), ed. J. W. Clay, 1908.

Testamenta Eboracensia (Surtees Soc. 4, 30, 45, 53, 79, 106), 6 vols. ed. J. Raine and others, 1836–1902.

(viii) *Accounts*

A Small Household of the Fifteenth Century, by K. L. Wood-Legh, Manchester 1956.

Medieval Clerical Accounts (St. Anthony's Hall Publications No. 26), by P. Heath, York 1964.

(ix)   *University Records*

The Ancient Kalendar of the University of Oxford (Oxford Hist. Soc. 45), ed. C. Wordsworth, 1904.

The Daily Ledger of John Dorne, 1520 (in Oxford Hist. Soc. 5 and 16), ed. F. Malden, 1885, 1890.

Epistolae Academicae Oxoniensis (Oxford Hist. Soc. 35, 36), 2 vols. ed. H. Anstey, 1898.

Formularies which bear on the history of Oxford, c. 1204–1420 (Oxford Hist. Soc. n.s. 4, 5), 2 vols. ed. H. E. Salter, W. A. Pantin, H. G. Richardson, 1942.

Medieval archives of the University of Oxford (Oxford Hist. Soc. 70, 73), 2 vols. ed. H. E. Salter, 1920–1.

Munimenta Academica, or documents illustrative of academical life and studies at Oxford (Rolls Series 50), 2 vols. ed. H. Anstey, 1868.

Register of the University of Oxford (Oxford Hist. Soc. 1), ed. C. W. Boase, 1885.

Registrum cancellarii Oxoniensis, 1434–69 (Oxford Hist. Soc. 93, 94), 2 vols. ed. H. E. Salter, 1932.

(Cambridge) *Grace Book 'B', 1488–1544*, 2 vols. ed. M. Bateson, Cambridge 1903–5.

(Cambridge) *Grace Book 'Γ', 1501–42*, ed. M. Bateson, Cambridge 1908.

(x)   *Letters*

Clifford Letters of the Sixteenth Century (Surtees Soc. 172), ed. A. G. Dickens, 1962.

Christ Church Letters (Camden Soc. n.s. 19), ed. J. B. Sheppard, 1877.

Literae Cantuarienses, the letter books of the monastery of Christ Church, Canterbury (Rolls Series 85), 3 vols. ed. J. B. Sheppard, 1887–9.

Letters of the 15th and 16th Centuries (Southampton Rec. Soc.), ed. R. C. Anderson, 1921.

The Letter Book of Robert Joseph (Oxford Hist. Soc. n.s. 19), ed. H. Aveling and W. A. Pantin, 1967.

Paston Letters, 1422–1509 (Library edn.), 6 vols. ed. J. Gairdner, London 1904.

Plumpton Correspondence (Camden Soc. o.s. 4), ed. T. Stapleton, 1839.

The Stonor Letters and Papers, 1290–1483 (Camden Soc. 3rd series 29, 30), 2 vols. ed. C. L. Kingsford, 1923.

Supplementary Stonor Letters and Papers, 1314–1482 (Camden Soc. 3rd series 34), ed. C. L. Kingsford, 1923.

Letters and Papers of the Verney Family (Camden Soc. o.s. 56), ed. J. Bruce, 1853.

(xi) *Chronicles, Histories, Descriptions, etc.*
The Anglia Historia of Polydore Vergil, 1485–1537 (Camden Soc. 3rd series 74), ed. D. Hay, 1950.
A Relation or rather a True Account of the Island of England c. 1500 (Camden Soc. o.s. 37), ed. C. A. Sneyd, 1847.
The Great Chronicle of London, ed. A. H. Thomas and I. D. Thornley, 1938.

(xii) *Secular Court Records*
Select cases before the king's council, 1243–1482 (Selden Soc. 35), ed. I. S. Leadam and J. F. Baldwin, 1918.
Select cases in the exchequer chamber before all the justices of England (Selden Soc. 51), 2 vols. ed. M. Hemmant, 1933–48.
Year Books of Edward IV, 10 Edward IV and 49 Henry VI, 1470 (Selden Soc. 47), ed. N. Neilson, 1931.
Pleadings and depositions in the duchy court of Lancaster, temp. Henry VII and Henry VIII, (Lancs. & Ches. Rec. Soc. 32), ed. H. Fishwick, 1896.
A selection from the Prescot court leet and other records, 1447–1600 (Lancs. & Ches. Rec. Soc. 89), ed. F. A. Bailey, 1937.
Early Chancery Proceedings, Richard II to Henry VII (Wm. Salt Soc. n.s. 7), ed. G. Wrottesley, 1904.
Select cases in chancery, 1364–1471 (Selden Soc. 10), ed. W. P. Baildon, 1896.
'Clerical Life in the 15th Century, as illustrated by Proceedings of the Court of Chancery', (*Archaeologia*, 2nd series, lx, 1907, pp. 353–78), by C. T. Martin.
Select cases before the king's council of the star chamber (Selden Soc. 16), 2 vols. ed. I. S. Leadam, 1903–11.
Lancashire and Cheshire cases in the court of the star chamber (Lancs. & Ches. Rec. Soc. 71), ed. R. Stewart-Brown, 1916.
Staffordshire suits in the court of star chamber, temp. Henry VII and Henry VIII (Wm. Salt Soc. n.s. 10(i)), ed. W. K. Boyd, 1907.
Proceedings in the court of star chamber in the reigns of Henry VII and Henry VIII (Somerset Rec. Soc. 27), ed. C. G. Bradford, 1911.
Abstracts of star chamber proceedings relating to the county of Sussex, Henry VII to Philip & Mary (Sussex Rec. Soc. 16), ed. P. D. Mundy, 1913.
Yorkshire star chamber proceedings (Yorkshire Archaeological Soc. 41, 45, 51, 70), 4 vols. ed. W. Brown and others, 1909–27.

(xiii) *Urban Records*
Borough Customs (Selden Soc. 18), 2 vols. ed. M. Bateson, 1904–6.

Bridgewater Borough Archives, vol. iv, 1441–68 (Somerset Rec. Soc. 60), 1948.

Calendar of Records of the Corporation of Gloucester, ed. W. H. Stevenson, Gloucester 1893.

Records of the Borough of Leicester, vols. ii and iii, ed. M. Bateson, Cambridge 1901 and 1905.

Calendar of Letter Books of the City of London: Letter Book 'K', ed. R. R. Sharpe, London 1911.

Calendar of Letter Books of the City of London: Letter Book 'L', ed. R. R. Sharpe, London 1912.

Calendar of Plea and Memoranda Rolls of London, 1437–57, ed. P. E. Jones, Cambridge 1954.

Register of freemen of Newcastle upon Tyne, 1407–1710 (Newcastle upon Tyne Records Committee Publn.), ed. M. H. Dodds, 1923.

Records of the Borough of Nottingham, 4 vols. ed. W. H. Stevenson, London 1882–9.

Records of the City of Norwich, 2 vols. ed. W. Hudson and J. C. Tingey, Norwich 1906–10.

The rolls of burgesses and the guilds merchant of the borough of Preston Lancashire, 1397–1682 (Lancs. & Ches. Rec. Soc. 9), ed. W. A. Abram, 1884.

York Civic Records (Yorkshire Archaeological Soc. 98, 103, 106), 3 vols. ed. A. Raine, 1939–42.

(xiv)   *Taxation*

Valor Ecclesiasticus temp. Henry VIII, auctoritate regia institutus, 6 vols. ed. J. Caley and J. Hunter, London 1810–34.

Suffolk in 1524, being the return for a subsidy granted in 1523 (Suffolk Green Books x), Woodbridge 1910.

'The East Riding Clergy', (*Y.A.J.*, xxiv, 1917, pp. 62–80).

A subsidy collected in the diocese of Lincoln in 1526 (Oxford Hist. Soc. 63), ed. H. E. Salter, 1909.

(xv)   *Sermons, Polemics and Treatises, etc.*

The repressor of over much blaming of the clergy, by Reginald Pecock, sometime bishop of Chichester (Rolls Series 19), 2 vols. ed. C. Babington, 1860.

Instructions for Parish Priests by John Myrc (E.E.T.S. o.s. 31), ed. E. Peacock, 1902.

A Supplicacyon for the Beggars, by Simon Fish (E.E.T.S. extra series 13), ed. J. M. Cowper, 1871.

Loci e Libro Veritatum, by Thomas Gascoigne, ed. J. E. T. Rogers, London 1881.

The English Works of Sir Thomas More, 2 vols. ed. W. E. Campbell and A. W. Reed, London 1927–31.

The Apologye of Syr Thomas More, knyght (E.E.T.S. o.s. 180), ed. A. I. Taft, 1930.

Speculum Sacerdotale (E.E.T.S. o.s. 200), ed. H. E. Weatherley, 1936.

Middle English Sermons (E.E.T.S. o.s. 209), ed. W. O. Ross, 1940.

Mirk's Festial (E.E.T.S. e.s. 96), ed. T. Erbe, 1905.

Quatuor Sermones (Roxburghe Club 111), 1883.

Sermo Exhortatorius cancellarii Eboracensis hiis qui ad sacros ordines petunt promoveri, by William de Melton (London *c.* 1510).

Sermons by Hugh Latimer (Parker Soc.), ed. G. E. Corrie, 1844.

Sermons and Remains of Hugh Latimer (Parker Soc.), ed. G. E. Corrie, 1845.

Tudor Treatises (Yorkshire Archaeological Soc. 125), ed. A. G. Dickens, 1959.

Doctrinal Treatises etc., . . . by William Tyndale (Parker Soc.), ed. H. Walter, 1848.

The Book of Margery Kempe (E.E.T.S. o.s. 212), ed. S. B. Meech and H. E. Allen, 1940.

Ye Oldest Diarie of Englysshe Travell, ed. W. J. Loftie, London 1884.

The Pilgrimage of Robert Langton, ed. E. M. Mackie, Cambridge (Mass.) 1924.

(xvi) *General*

Letters and Papers illustrative of the reigns of Richard III and Henry VII (Rolls Series 24), 2 vols. ed. J. Gairdner, 1861–3.

Materials for a history of the reign of Henry VII from original documents preserved in the Public Record Office (Rolls Series 60), 2 vols. ed. W. Campbell, 1873–7.

Rotuli parliamentorum: ut et petitiones, et placita in parliamento, 6 vols. London 1832.

Calendar of Close Rolls, 1447–1509, 7 vols. London.

Calendar of Patent Rolls, 1446–1509, 7 vols. London.

Letters & Papers, Foreign and Domestic, of the reign of Henry VIII, 1509–47, 21 vols. London 1862–1920.

Calendar of Papal Letters, 1447–92, 5 vols. London.

Faculty Office Registers 1534–39, ed. D. S. Chambers, Oxford 1966.

Domesday of Inclosures, 2 vols. ed. I. S. Leadam, London.

III : *Secondary Authorities*

N. A. Adams, 'The Judicial Conflict over Tithes' (*E.H.R.*, lii, 1937, pp. 1–22).

J. W. Adamson, 'The Extent of Literacy in England in the Fifteenth and Sixteenth Centuries' (*Library*, 4th series, x, 1930, pp. 163–93).

G. W. O. Addleshaw, *The Beginnings of the Parochial System* (St. Anthony's Hall Publications No. 3) York 1959; *The Development of the Parochial System from Charlemagne to Urban II* (St. Anthony's Hall Publications No. 6), York 1954.

K. J. Allison and others, *The Deserted Villages of Oxfordshire*, Leicester 1965; *The Deserted Villages of Northamptonshire*, Leicester 1966.

J. Bale, *Index Britanniae Scriptorum*, ed. R. L. Poole and M. Bateson, Oxford 1902.

G. Barraclough, *Papal Provisions*, Oxford 1935.

H. S. Bennett, 'The Author and his Public in the Fourteenth and Fifteenth Centuries' (*Essays and Studies*, xxiii, 1938, pp. 7–24); *English Books and Readers, 1475–1557*, Cambridge 1952; 'The Production and Dissemination of Vernacular Manuscripts in the Fifteenth Century' (*Library*, 5th series, i, 1947, pp. 167–78); 'Medieval Ordination Lists in English Episcopal Registers' (*Essays presented to Sir Hilary Jenkinson*, ed. J. Conway Davies, London 1957, pp. 20–34); *Chaucer and the Fifteenth Century*, Oxford 1947.

M. W. Beresford, *The Lost Villages of Medieval England*, London 1954.

Bernard, *Catalogi Librorum Manuscriptorum Angliae et Hiberniae*, Oxford 1697.

J. W. Blench, *Preaching in England in the Late Fifteenth and Sixteenth Centuries*, Oxford 1964.

F. Blomefield and C. Parkin, *An Essay towards a Topographical History of the County of Norfolk*, 11 vols, London 1805–10.

D. S. Boutflower, *Fasti Dunelmenses. A record of the beneficed clergy of the diocese of Durham down to the dissolution of the monastic and collegiate churches* (Surtees Soc. 139), 1926.

M. Bowker, *The Secular Clergy in Lincoln Diocese 1495–1520*, Cambridge 1968; 'Non-Residence in the Lincoln Diocese in the Early Sixteenth Century' (*J.E.H.*, xv, 1964, pp. 40–50).

L. E. Boyle, 'The "Oculus Sacerdotis" and Some Other Works of William of Pagula' (*T.R.H.S.*, 5th series, v, 1955, pp. 81–110).

Y. S. Brenner, 'The Inflation of Prices in Early Sixteenth Century England' (*Econ. H.R.*, 2nd series, xiv, 1961–62, pp. 225–39).

G. T. O. Bridgeman, *The History of the Church and Manor of Wigan* (Chetham Soc. n.s. 15–18), 1880–90.

C. N. L. Brooke, 'Gregorian Reform in Action: Clerical Marriage in England, 1050–1200' (*Cambridge Historical Journal*, xii, 1956, pp. 1–21).

F. W. Brooks, 'The Social Position of the Parson in the Sixteenth

Century' (*Journal British Archaeological Soc.*, 3rd series, x, 1945–7, pp. 23–37).

W. W. Capes, *The English Church in the XIVth and XVth Centuries*, London 1900.

K. Charlton, *Education in Renaissance England*, London 1965.

G. G. Coulton, *Medieval Panorama*, Cambridge 1949; *Europe's Apprenticeship*, London 1940; *Ten Medieval Studies*, Cambridge 1930.

J. C. Cox, *Churchwardens' Accounts*, London 1913.

J. C. Cox and A. Harvey, *English Church Furniture*, London 1907.

E. L. Cutts, *Parish Priests and their People in the Middle Ages in England*, London 1898.

M. Deanesly, *The Lollard Bible*, Cambridge 1966; *The Significance of the Lollard Bible*, London 1951.

H. De Vocht, 'Excerpts from the Registers of Louvain University from 1485 to 1527' (*E.H.R.*, xxxvii, 1922, pp. 89–105).

A. G. Dickens, *Lollards and Protestants in the Diocese of York, 1509–1558*, Oxford 1959; *The English Reformation*, London 1964; 'Aspects of Intellectual Transition among the English Parish Clergy of the Reformation Period' (*Archiv für Reformationsgeschichte*, xliii, 1952, pp. 51–70); 'The Writers of Tudor Yorkshire' (*T.R.H.S.*, 5th series, xiii, 1963, pp. 49–76).

G. Donaldson, *The Scottish Reformation*, Cambridge 1960.

R. Donaldson, 'Sponsors, patrons and presentations to benefices in the gift of the Priors of Durham in the late Middle Ages' (*Archaeologia Aeliana*, 4th series, xxxviii, 1960, pp. 169–77).

C. Drew, *Early Parochial Organisation in England: The Origins of the Office of Churchwarden* (St. Anthony's Hall Publications No. 7), York 1954.

F. R. H. Du Boulay, 'The Quarrel between the Carmelite Friars and the Secular Clergy of London, 1464–68' (*J.E.H.*, vi, 1955, pp. 156–74).

H. L. R. Edwards, *Skelton*, London 1949.

G. R. Elton, *England under the Tudors*, London 1955; 'Informing for Profit' (*Cambridge Historical Journal*, xi, 1954, pp. 149–67); *Star Chamber Stories*, London 1958.

A. B. Emden, *A Biographical Register of the University of Oxford to A.D. 1500*, 3 vols. Oxford 1957–9; *A Biographical Register of the University of Cambridge to 1500*, Cambridge 1963.

G. F. Farnham and A. Herbert, 'Fenny Drayton and the Purefey Monuments' (*Trans. Leics. Archaeological Soc.*, xiv, 1925–6, pp. 88–112).

C. B. Firth, 'Benefit of Clergy in the Time of Edward IV' (*E.H.R.*, xxxii, 1917, pp. 175–91).

J. Foxe, *The Acts and Monuments of John Foxe*, 8 vols. ed. G. Townsend, London 1843–9.

T. S. Frampton, 'List of Forty Five Vicars of Tilmanstone' (*Archaeologia Cantiana*, xx, 1893, pp. 104–18).

E. Freshfield, 'Some Remarks upon the Book of Records and History of the Parish of St. Stephen Coleman Street in the City of London' (*Archaeologia*, 1, 1887, pp. 17–57).

J. A. Froude, *History of England from the Fall of Wolsey to the Death of Elizabeth*, vol. i, London 1862.

L. C. Gabel, *Benefit of Clergy in England in the Later Middle Ages*, Northampton (U.S.A.) 1929.

J. Gairdner, *Lollardy and the Reformation in England*, 4 vols. London 1908–13; *The English church in the sixteenth century, from the accession of Henry VIII to the death of Mary*, London 1902; 'Bishop Hooper's Visitation of Gloucester in 1551' (*E.H.R.*, xix, 1904, pp. 98–121).

V. F. M. Garlick, 'The Provision of Vicars in the Early Fourteenth Century' (*History*, xxxiv, 1949, pp. 15–27).

F. A. Gasquet, *Parish Life in Medieval England*, London 1906; *The Old English Bible and other studies*, London 1908; *The Eve of the Reformation*, London 1919.

F. F. Giraud, 'On the Parish Clerks and Sexton of Faversham, 1506–1593' (*Archaeologia Cantiana*, xx, 1893, pp. 203–10).

R. A. R. Hartridge, *A History of Vicarages in the Later Middle Ages*, Cambridge 1930.

E. Hasted, *The History and Topographical Survey of the County of Kent*, 12 vols. Canterbury 1797–1801.

G. Hennessy, *Novum repertorium ecclesiasticum parochiale londoniense*, London 1898.

R. Hill, 'Public Penance: Some Problems of a thirteenth century Bishop' (*History*, xxxvi, 1951, pp. 213–26); 'The Theory and Practice of Excommunication in England' (*History*, xlii, 1957, pp. 1–11).

W. G. Hoskins, 'The Leicestershire Country Parson in the 16th Century' (*Trans. Leics. Archaeological Soc.*, xxi, 1940–1, pp. 89–114).

P. Hughes, *The Reformation in England*, 3 vols. London 1950–5.

E. F. Jacob, *Essays in the Conciliar Epoch*, Manchester 1953; 'On the Promotion of English University Clerks in the Later Middle Ages' (*J.E.H.*, i, 1950, pp. 172–86); 'Reynold Pecock, Bishop of Chichester' (*Proc. British Academy*, xxxvii, 1951, pp. 121–54); 'Thomas Brouns, Bishop of Norwich 1436–45' (*Essays in British History*, ed. H. R. Trevor-Roper, London 1964, pp. 61–83).

P. Janelle, *L'Angleterre Catholique à la Veille du Schisme*, Paris 1935.

C. Jenkins, 'Cardinal Morton's Register' (*Tudor Studies*, ed. R. W. Seton-Watson, London 1924, pp. 26–74).

F. R. Johnston, 'Richard Burton, Vicar of Lancaster 1466–84' (*Trans. Hist. Soc. of Lancs. and Cheshire*, civ, 1952, pp. 163–7).

D. Jones, *The Church in Chester, 1300–1540* (Chetham Soc. 3rd series, 7), 1957.

C. L. Kingsford, *Prejudice and Promise in Fifteenth Century England*, Oxford 1925.

D. Knowles, *The Religious Orders in England*, ii, iii, Cambridge 1955, 1959.

J. Lawson, *A Town Grammar School through Six Centuries*, Oxford 1963; *Medieval Education and the Reformation*, London 1967.

A. F. Leach, *The Schools of Medieval England*, London 1915.

J. Le Neve, *Fasti Ecclesiae Anglicanae 1300–1541*, 11 vols. various editors, London 1962–5.

A. G. Little, 'Personal Tithes' (*E.H.R.*, lx, 1945, pp. 67–88).

W. E. Lunt, *Financial Relations of England with the Papacy 1327–1534*, Cambridge (Mass.) 1962.

J. H. Lupton, *A Life of John Colet*, London 1887.

K. Major, 'Resignation Deeds of the Diocese of Lincoln' (*B.I.H.R.*, xix, 1942–3, pp. 57–65); 'Fifteenth Century Presentation Deeds in Lincoln Diocesan Record Office' (*Essays presented to F. M. Powicke*, ed. R. W. Hunt and others, Oxford 1948, pp. 455–64).

O. Manning and W. Bray, *History and Antiquities of the County of Surrey*, 3 vols. London 1804–14.

J. K. McConica, *English Humanists and Reformation Politics*, Oxford 1965.

R. J. Mitchell, 'English Law Students at Bologna in the Fifteenth Century' (*E.H.R.*, li, 1936, pp. 270–87); 'English Students at Padua, 1460–75' (*T.R.H.S.*, 4th series, xix, 1936, pp. 101–18); 'English Students at Ferrara in the Fifteenth Century' (*Italian Studies*, i, 1937–8, pp. 75–82).

S. Moore, 'Patrons of Letters in Norfolk and Suffolk c. 1450' (*Proc. Modern Language Association*, xxvii, 1912, pp. 188–207).

J. R. H. Moorman, *Church Life in England in the Thirteenth Century*, Cambridge 1955; 'The Medieval Parsonage and its Occupants' (*Bull. John Rylands Library*, xxviii, 1944, pp. 137–53).

J. F. Mozley, *William Tyndale*, London 1937.

R. Newcourt, *Repertorium Ecclesiasticum Parochiale Londinense*, 2 vols. London 1708–10.

Northumberland, a History of, 15 vols. various editors, Newcastle upon Tyne 1893–1940.

E. M. Nugent (editor), *The Thought and Culture of the English Renaissance*, Cambridge 1956.

G. R. Owst, *Preaching in Medieval England 1350–1450*, Cambridge 1926; *Literature and the Pulpit in the Middle Ages*, Oxford 1961; 'Some Books and Book Owners of the Fifteenth Century St. Albans' (*Trans. St. Albans & Herts. Architectural & Archaeological Soc.*, 1929, pp. 175–94); *The Destructorium Viciorum of Alexander Carpenter*, London 1952.

J. E. Oxley, *The Reformation in Essex*, Manchester 1965.

W. A. Pantin, *The English Church in the Fourteenth Century*, Cambridge 1955; 'Medieval Priests' Houses in South West England' (*Medieval Archaeology*, i, 1957, pp. 118–46); 'Before Wolsey' (*Essays in British History*, ed. H. R. Trevor-Roper, London 1964, pp. 29–59).

E. H. Phelps Brown and S. V. Hopkins, 'Seven Centuries of the Prices of Consumables, compared with Builders' Wage Rates' (*Essays in Economic History*, ed. E. M. Carus-Wilson, London 1962, ii, pp. 179–96).

R. Phillimore, *The Ecclesiastical Law of the Church of England*, 2 vols. London 1895.

A. F. Pollard, *Henry VIII*, London 1951; *Wolsey*, London 1965.

G. Pollard, 'Medieval Loan Chests' (*B.I.H.R.*, xvii, 1939–40, pp. 113–19).

H. C. Porter, *Reformation and Reaction in Tudor Cambridge*, Cambridge 1958.

F. D. Price, 'Gloucester Diocese under Bishop Hooper' (*Trans. Bristol & Gloucestershire Archaeological Soc.*, lx, 1939, pp. 51–151).

J. S. Purvis, *A Medieval Act Book*, York n.d.; 'Dilapidations in Parsonage Property' (*Y.A.J.* xxxvi, 1944–47, pp. 316–37); 'A Note on Sixteenth Century Farming in Yorkshire' (*ibid.*, pp. 435–54).

F. R. Raines, *A close catalogue of rectors of Prestwich, from 1316 to 1632* (Chetham Soc. o.s. 103), 1878; *The vicars of Rochdale* (Chetham Soc. n.s. 1, 2), 2 vols. 1883.

H. Rashdall, *The Universities of Europe in the Middle Ages*, 3 vols. ed. F. M. Powicke and A. B. Emden, Oxford 1936.

H. G. Richardson, 'The Parish Clergy of the Thirteenth and Fourteenth Centuries' (*T.R.H.S.*, 3rd series, vi, 1912, pp. 89–128); 'An Oxford Teacher of the Fifteenth Century' (*Bull. John Rylands Library*, xxiii, 1939, pp. 436–57); 'Business Training in Medieval Oxford' (*A.H.R.*, xlvi, 1941, pp. 259–80).

R. H. Robbins, 'The Poems of Humphrey Newton esquire, 1466–1536' (*Proc. Modern Language Association*, lxv, 1950, pp. 249–81).

S. Robertson, 'The Rectors of Cliffe at Hoo' (*Archaeologia Cantiana*, xxxi, 1915, pp. 217–54).

E. G. Rupp, *Studies in the Making of the English Protestant Tradition*, Cambridge 1947.

H. E. Salter, 'An Oxford Hall in 1424' (*Essays in History presented to R. L. Poole*, ed. H. W. C. Davis, Oxford 1927, pp. 421–35).

F. Seebohm, *The Oxford Reformers*, London 1867.

J. Selden, *The historie of tithes*, London 1618.

J. Simon, *Education and Society in Tudor England*, Cambridge 1966; 'A. F. Leach on the Reformation' (*British Journal of Educational Studies*, iii, 1954–5, pp. 128–43, and iv, 1955–6, pp. 32–48).

H. M. Smith, *Pre-Reformation England*, London 1938; *Henry VIII and the Reformation*, London 1948.

R. S. Stanier, *Magdalen School* (Oxford Historical Soc. n.s. 3), 1940.

R. L. Storey, *Diocesan Administration in the 15th Century* (St. Anthony's Hall Publications No. 16), York 1959.

J. Strype, *Ecclesiastical Memorials, relating chiefly to religion, and the reformation of it, and the emergencies of the Church of England under King Henry VIII, Edward VI, and Queen Mary I*, 6 vols. Oxford 1822.

A. H. Thompson, *The English Clergy and their Organisation in the Later Middle Ages*, Oxford 1947; 'Ecclesiastical Benefices and their Incumbents' (*Trans. Leics. Archaeological Soc.*, xxii, 1944–5, pp. 1–32); 'Pluralism in the Medieval Church' (*Associated Architectural Societies Reports*, xxxiii, 1915–16, pp. 35–73); 'Notes on the Ecclesiastical History of the Parish of Henbury' (*Trans. Bristol & Gloucestershire Archaeological Soc.*, xxxviii, 1915, pp. 99–186).

A. H. Thompson and C. T. Clay, *Fasti Parochiales* (Yorkshire Archaeological Soc. 85, 107), 2 vols, 1933, 1943.

J. A. F. Thomson, *The Later Lollards*, Oxford 1965; 'Tithe Disputes in Late Medieval London' (*E.H.R.*, lxxviii, 1963, pp. 1–17).

S. L. Thrupp, *The Merchant Class of Medieval London*, Michigan, 1962.

K.S.S. Train, *Lists of the Clergy of Central Nottinghamshire* (Thoroton Record Series, xv (1–3), 1952–4).

R. Weiss, *Humanism in England in the Fifteenth Century*, Oxford 1957.

Glanmor Williams, *The Welsh Church from Conquest to Reformation*, Cardiff 1962.

J. F. Williams, 'Ordination in the Norwich Diocese during the Fifteenth Century' (*Norfolk Archaeology*, xxxi, 1957, pp. 347–58).

B. L. Woodcock, *Medieval Ecclesiastical Courts in the Diocese of Canterbury*, Oxford 1952.

K. L. Wood-Legh, *Perpetual Chantries in Britain*, Cambridge 1965.

C. E. Woodruff, 'The Records of the Courts of the Archdeaconry and Consistory of Canterbury' (*Archaeologia Cantiana*, xli, 1929, pp. 89–105).

General Index

Abraham, John, 205, 207
Absence, *see* Non-Residence
Acaster, W. Yorks., 83
Acolyte, 14
Acre, South, Norfolk, 87
Admission, *see* Benefices
Age, 33, 41, 59, 78, 185, 200–1
Agriculture, by clerics, 160–1
Alanus de Insulis, *De Planctu Naturae*, 89
Albertus Magnus, sermons of, 88
Albury, Herts., 136
Alcester, Warwicks., 175
Alcock, John, bishop of Rochester, Worcester and Ely, 83, 108
Alcock, Thomas, rector, 80–1
Aldington, Kent, 55, 146
Aldwinkle, Northants., 85, 160–1
Alen, Thomas, 60n
Aleyn, John, rector, 201
Aleyn, Thomas, rector, 31
Aleyn, Thomas, 11–12; wife of, 11
Aliens, *see* Foreigners
Allensmore, Herefords., 151n
Alresford, Hants, 137
Ammonius, Andrew, 35
Angmering, Sussex, 166n
Anti-Clericalism, 10, 192–6
Ap Howell, Geoffrey, vicar, 184
Apostasy, 177
Appleby, Westmorland, 136
Appropriation: scale of, 147;
    costs of, 180n
  see also Religious
Ap Rise, Edward, incumbent, 60n
Aquebaiulus, 19; *see also* Parish clerks
Archdeacons: and dilapidations, 140

examination of ordinands, 16
induction of presentees, 43, 201
officials of, 43, 54
procurations, 143–4
visitations, 113, 140, 143–4
see also Goldwell, Magnus, Cornwall, Durham, Norwich, Salisbury, and Wiltshire
Arches, court of, 54, 110n
Aristotle, works of, 89
Arnold, E. Yorks., 167
Ash, Kent, 185
Ashridge, Herts., 176
Aston Tirrold, Berks., 158
Atkynns, William, rector, 159
Atley, Athelstan, vicar, 38
Atwater, William, rector of Ditcheat, bishop of Lincoln, 35, 112
Augmentation of vicarages, 165–6, 179–80
    at Hornsea, 166–73
Austin Canons, *see* Canons
Autobiography, of an incumbent, 204–5
  (cf. 200–1)
Avarice, of clergy, 135
Aveley, Essex, 65
Averroes, commentary on Aristotle, 89
Aylesbury, Bucks., 138
Ayleston, Leics., 46
Aylsham, Norfolk, 9

Baginton, Warwicks., 137
Baildon, Thomas, clerk, 132
Bainbridge, Christopher, archbishop of York, 128, 210
Baker, John, rector, 10–12
Balinghem, Calais, 51

231

Bourgchier, Thomas, archbishop of
  Canterbury, 31, 33, 44–45, 58
Bourne, Lincs., 53
Bowers Gifford, Essex, 10–12
Boxley, Kent, 158
Bradshagh, Christopher, clerk, 132
Bransby, Thomas, 170, 171
Brant, Sebastian, *Narrenschiff*, 193
Braughing, Herts., 57, 64–65, 69, 84,
  106, 200, 207–9
Bread, purchase of for Mass, 145
Brent, Thomas, pluralist and courtier,
  29, 52
Briçonnet, Guillaume, bishop of Meaux,
  190
Bridgnorth, Salop, 30
Bridgwater, Somerset, 159
Bridlington, E. Yorks., 153 163
Bridport, Dorset, 22–23, 37, 172n
Bringhurst, Leics., 34, 106, 138
Brixton Deverill, Wilts, 27
Broke, John, 207
Bromyard, Herefords, 53
Broun, William, chaplain, 28
Brownhill, George, priest, 107
Brudenell, George, rector, 137
Bruern, Oxon., 28
Buckingham, Duke of, 33
Buckingham, Edward, Duke of, 52
Bugthorpe, E. Yorks., 19
Bukster, Aleyn, (clerk?), 111
Bulfynch, Nicholas, chaplain, 31
Bulgen, Master, vicar, 208–9
Buntingford, Herts., 106
Burgh, John de, *Pupilla Oculi*, 1
Burgh, Mariane, 105
Burton on Trent, Staffs., 113
Burton Pidsea, E. Yorks., 19
Burton, Henry, rector, 55
Burton, William, abbot of Alcester, 175
Byngham, William, rector, co-founder
  of God's House, 83
Bynne, Henry, 205
Bynne, Maurice, 205

Cady, Alan, 11, 12
Cady, Margery, 11
Caldbeck, Cumb., 143n

Caldey, Henry, vicar, 86, 159
Cambridge: God's House, 83
  Jesus College, 81
  King's College, 139
  St. John's College, 79
  Stourbridge fair, 39
  see also Graduate Clergy, Universities
Cammell, John, rector, 163
Campden, Glos., 84
Campeggio, Cardinal, 27
Candlesby, Lincs., 110
Canons: Austin, 175, 178, 180
  Premonstratensian, 177–8
  see also Religious
Canterbury: archbishop, charitable sub-
  sidies, 23–24, 145–6;
  consistory court, 152
  court of audience, 179
  patronage, 31
  simony 37, 38
  Christ Church, and royal patron-
  age, 29
  diocese, clerical ignorance, 77
  criminous clerks, 212
  exchanges, 44–45
  graduate clergy, 81
  non-residence, 56
  tithe suits, 152
  monk of, 177
  province, 23–24, 145, 146
  St. Gregory, priory of, 179
  see also Arches, Prerogative Court
Cape, Thomas, 46, 47
Carleton, N. Yorks., 5
Carlton, W. Yorks., 52
Carmelianus, 52, 57n
Carmelites, *see* Friars
Carpenter, Alexander, *Destructorium
  Viciorum*, 48, 88, 94–95
Carpenter, John, bishop of Worcester,
  112
Carpenter, John, rector of Compton
  Bassett, 185
Carr, Nicholas, vicar-general of Bishop
  Nikke, 198
Carshalton, Surrey, 136
Carter, John, Cluniac monk of Wenlock,
  177

INDEX

Castle Combe, Wilts., 52
Castor, Northants., 53, 158
Catcher, William, 46
Caterall, Richard, clerk, 130
Catholicon, 88
Cawood, W. Yorks., 131, 132
Caxton, William, printer, 93
Caynham, Salop, 184
Chafford, Essex, deanery, 201
Chalcedon, *see* Councils
Chaldon, Surrey, 45
Chancellor, the Lord, patronage of, 28
Chancery, court of, 37, 43, 161, 185
Chantries: and absentees, 56; and education, 84
  see also Chaplains, Exchanges
Chaplains: chantry, 22–23, 56, 61, 83–84, 89, 107, 141, 185
  household, 185
  parochial, accommodation, 141–2
    book owners, 87–88
    education, 19, 20, 81–82
    employment terms, 25–26
    farming benefices, 66–67
    numbers, 21–22
    poverty, 25
    preaching, 94
    services, 5
    stipends, 22–25, 64, 168–70
    taxation of, 23–24
    wealth, 80
Chapters, general, 144
Chardstock, Devon, 54
Charitable subsidies, *see* Subsidies
Chart, Great, Kent, 52
Charterhouse, *see* London
Chaucer, Geoffrey, works of, 89; on cursing for tithes, 150
Cheddar, Somerset, 147
'Chekemaisters', 65, 68
Cheshunt, Herts., 94, 152
Chester, Cheshire, 22
Chests, loan, 80
Chichele, Henry, archbishop of Canterbury, 82
Chilcombe, Dorset, 52
Children, of clergy: 106–7, 107n, 116
  see also Promiscuity, Women

Chilton, Somerset, 159
Chipping Norton, Oxon, 67
Chishall Magna, Essex, 61
Chislet, Kent, 111
Cholderton, Wilts., 160
Chrism, purchase of, 145
Christopher, Sir, parish priest, 149
Christopher, William, 9
Churches, *see* Parish churches
Churching, of women, 8
Churchwardens, 65n, 68, 69
Cilium Oculi, 1
Civi, Master Benedict, 205
Civi, Dominic, rector, 40, 66–67, 200–7
Civi, John Andrew, 202, 205, 206
Clandon, East, Surrey, 33
Clapham, Surrey, 45, 53
Clarke, Richard, 168
Clavering, Essex, 162
Clement VII, 125
Clergy: terms for, xi–xii
  endowing students, 79–80, 85
  relations with laity, 64–65, 84, 152, 155–6, 158, 160, 162, 191–2
Clerici Attincti, 121, 125, 128
Clerk, John, Ll.D., rector of Ditcheat, 35
Clerk, John, simoniac, 37
Clerks, *see* Parish clerks
Cleobury, North, Salop, 62
Clifford, Lord, 41, 52
Clifton Campville, Staffs., 139, 140, 141
Clun, Salop, 157–8
Clyfton, John, rector, 163
Co-adjutors, 185
Cobdow, John, 201, 203
Cobham, Kent, college of, 30
Coker, East, Somerset, 64n
Cokeson, John, 155–6
Colchester, Essex, 80n
Colet, Sir Henry, knight, 33
Colet, John, dean of St. Paul's: benefices of, 33
  sermon, xi, 15, 72, 76, 77, 92, 187, 189
Collations, *see* Benefices
Common Pleas, court of, 119
Commons, House of, *see* Parliament

Quinton, Northants., 137

Radley, William, wife of, 105
Radwinter, Essex, 61
Rand, John, incumbent, 43
Rayleigh, Essex, 161–2
Rede, Lord, judge, 60n
Rede, Thomas, rector, 138
Rede, William, 138
Regimen Animarum, 1
Religious: among beneficed clergy,
    175, 176n, 177–8, 209
    corrupt canons, 106
    educational endowment, and in-
        struction of clergy, 79, 82–83
    exploitation of clergy, 179–80
    nuns promiscuous with clergy, 105
    see also Appropriation, Friars
Reyner, Stephen, 131; Thomas, 131
Reynold, John, stipendiary, 67
Ribbesford, Worcs., 184
Riccal, E. Yorks., 141
Richard III, previously Duke of Glouc-
    ester, 29, 120
Richmond, N. Yorks., rector of, 38
Richmond, archdeaconry: graduates, 82
    non-residence, 62
Rickard, Richard, 9–10
Rickmansworth, Herts., 55, 177
Ridlington, Norfolk, 109
Rimpton, Somerset, 31
Ringmore, Dorset, 27
Ripon, N. Yorks.: 132
    hospital, 53
    minster, 51, 116
Riston, E. Yorks., 22, 141, 153, 154,
    159, 166–73
Robert, Sir, chaplain, 64
Robynson, James, vicar, 55
Robynson, Nicholas, rector, 87
Rochdale, Lancs., 136
Roche, John, vicar, 111
Rodger, John, priest, 84
Rolle, Richard, works of, 86
Romford, Essex, 162
Romney, Old, Kent, 51
Roo, John, curate, 107
Rothbury, Northumb., 143n, 158

Rotherham, W. Yorks., 83
Rotherham, Thomas, archbishop of
    York, 24n, 83, 129, 210
Rouen, book printed at, 1
Russell, John, vicar, 160
Ruthyn, Richard, vicar, 159
Ryder, Christopher, clerk, attainted,
    121n, 128
Rye, Sussex, 52, 156–7

St. Albans, Herts., 113
St. Augustine, of Hippo, 3, 6–7, 88
St. Bridget, 86
St. German, Christopher, lawyer and
    author, 70
St. Logan, Cornwall, 43
St. Osyth, Essex, 177
St. Wendron, Cornwall, 80
Saintbury, Glos., 81
Salisbury, Wilts., archdeacon of, 54
Same, Nicholas, incumbent, 61
Sanctions: degrading, 114, 134
    deprivation, 62, 114n, 134, 201
    excommunication, 114
    fines, 114, 116–7
    imprisonment, 121
    penance, 114, 116–8
    pilgrimage, 116–7
    suspension, 114
Sandwell, Staffs., 180
Sandwich, Kent, 138
Sapey, Upper, Herefords., 62
Sarratt, Herts., 111
Saull, John, priest, 111
Savage, Thomas, archbishop of York,
    59, 128, 129, 210
Sawbridgeworth, Herts., 34
Sawge, Agnes, 106
Sawge, William, vicar, 106, 208
Scarborough, N. Yorks., 148n, 149,
    153, 154, 156, 157, 163–4
Schools: chantry, 83–84
    collegiate, 83
    episcopal endowment, 83
    grammar, 83
    lay endowment, 83
    monastic, 82–83
    see also Teachers